The Spell Of Aberrant

by

Cynthia Perkins

Table of Contents

Dedication

This book is dedicated to my mother, who has gone to reside in heaven with Jesus. Also, to my family and to my Aunt Debbie, who faithfully read every chapter as fast as I could roll it out. I love you all very much.

Chapter 1
The Attic Discovery

The screeching was louder than it had been before. It made the hair on the girl's neck stand up. Her blood ran cold, and she was terrified. The horse ran as fast as it could go, and the human on its back allowed it. Holding on for dear life, Breanne prayed that they were running fast enough even as she watched the ground fly by in a blur. The lather on the horse's neck concerned her; she knew they could only run for so long before the horse could not take it anymore, and then the worst would happen. That thing would get them. With its long claws and pointed fangs, it would tear them to pieces. She didn't want to cry again; she couldn't afford to cry again. If she lost it now, they would be doomed for sure. She called out to the horse, encouraging him to run faster toward safety. As if the horse could read her mind, and against all odds, their speed picked up.

The thing flying overhead, a little behind the horse and rider, screeched again, louder this time. It was getting closer; she could feel its presence. Subconsciously, she slumped lower in the saddle, although she was about as low as she could possibly get, she felt a little safer. She had seen the red eyes gleaming in the night sky when she turned around before; she did not want to turn around again. This had to be the creature of the Dark Mage. Only he could conjure up a creature so terrifying and evil. She had heard of these creatures before and only half believed the stories told by Marcus and Emiril. How could something so evil truly exist? Where she came from, these types of creatures were found only in fairy tales and never in real life. She wished she were home right now, safe in her bed with the warm covers pulled up snug around her. She could almost feel the softness of her sheets and smell the familiar scent of home.

SCREECH!! She cringed, and all good memories left her. Once again, she was on the back of a horse in the middle of the night, and they were running for their lives from a terrifying creature, dead set on ripping them to pieces. "God, please let us make it to the glen, please. I want to see my family again, I really do!" she prayed.

The glen was a safe place. A place she knew the creature could not go because it was protected by Elven magic. Nothing bad could get her there, at least not yet. If the Dark Mage had his way, that would change all too soon. She peered into the darkness, hoping to see something, anything. She knew they were getting close. They had been traveling for so long before that thing found them, and now, they had been running for miles, and she was sure they must be close. She stared deep into the night, the sound of the horse's hooves rhythmically beating on the ground, his labored breath boring into her heart, reminding her that he was only flesh and blood and was only capable of so much. She begged God again to let them get there safely. Just when she was about to lose all hope, she thought she saw a glimmer in the distance. She looked harder, searching the darkness, and then saw it again, the faint glimmer of the shield. Her heart leapt with joy, and the horse picked up on her newfound enthusiasm, lunging forward in one more small burst of speed. She was surprised there was anything left in him at all, but was very thankful when the dreadful creature, also realizing where they were, screeched the most hateful screech yet and flew faster, trying to close the gap between them before it was too late. She could sense it getting closer and tried to focus on the glimmering shield, now only a few hundred yards ahead of them.

The shield was the boundary line between the elves' territory and the outside world. Elves were magical beings that lived in solitude from the rest of the inhabitants of the realm. Nothing evil could penetrate the shield; it had a way of reading one's heart to determine their intentions. If a person was evil, they could not pass through the shield, but if they were pure of heart, they could come and go at will. Because this shield was in place, the elves were free to live in peace. Their race, after all, was naturally peaceful, but they would not back down from a fight when one was brought to their door. So, in a sense, the shield kept away the need to go to war, as no one could enter their realm who intended to upset the peace and harmony there.

Suddenly, the horse started to tremble, and his hoof beats became irregular. Breanne sat up a little. They were but twenty yards from the shield, only a few more strides for the horse. "Oh, don't give up now," she cried, "we're nearly there!" Tears sprang to her eyes. She reached up and stroked the horse's neck; his ears turned back to her as she called encouragement to him. Their speed had greatly diminished, and she could sense the creature catching up. She could hear a triumphant mewling sound coming from deep within it as it sensed their predicament. She felt rather than saw it right behind them. Any moment now, she would feel its claws ripping through her. She would feel its teeth as they sank into her exposed shoulders. She could feel the warmth of the creature's breath on her neck; she could smell its breath, the acidic, rancid odor of death. All hope was lost; they would die after all, despite their heroic run through the deepest night, they would die. She closed her eyes and thought once more of home as hot tears flowed freely down her cheeks.

Chapter 2
Whispers of the Spellbook

Breanne sat reading her book in the near-dark attic. The only light came from one bare bulb hanging from a frayed electrical cord over a table in the middle of the room, a table that was laden with stacks of papers.

She liked coming to the attic at night to read while everyone else in the house slept. It was peaceful and quiet; no one was hovering over her, telling her what to do. It wasn't that she didn't like it at her grandfather's house; it just wasn't home. She wished her parents hadn't gone away on their second honeymoon. She wanted to be home, in her own bed, not two thousand miles away in a dark attic in Boston.

It was winter here, and the storms were constantly rolling in off the ocean, which was right outside, so close in fact that she could have thrown a stone into it when the tide was up. They were having a storm right now, a bad one at that, and it made her uneasy. The wind was howling outside, and the rain beat down on the roof, making it sound as if the whole thing would collapse at any moment.

Just then, the shutters came loose, banging loudly against the side of the house. Breanne jumped up quickly and ran to the window. She opened it, reaching out to resecure the wildly flapping shutters. As soon as the window opened, the rain came flooding in, getting everything wet so quickly that Breanne was afraid she would not have enough time to get the shutters latched and the window shut again before the entire contents of the attic were ruined. She grabbed for the shutters once, twice, and again a third time before she could wrest them away from the wind and reunite them. She latched the hook firmly. She also pushed up the slide locks that would ensure they did not come loose again. She pushed the window down with a bang and latched it as well. By the time she got all of this done, her hair was dripping wet, and water was coursing down her face. She winced in pain as a drop slipped into her eye, burning slightly due to the addition of her salty sweat, which had traveled with it. She rubbed the pain away and surveyed the mess the wind and rain had left behind. Papers were strewn all over the attic, half of them wet.

Her grandfather was going to be upset when he saw this mess. She felt bad, although it had not been her fault really, the shutter had come unlatched due to the wind, and she had only tried to correct the situation before anyone was awakened by the loud banging on the house. But if she had been in bed asleep, she thought, like everyone else, this would not have happened. Oh well, nothing left to do but clean it up.

She started to gather up the dry papers first in hopes of keeping them that way. She was amazed at how far some of them had flown throughout the attic; they were in every corner of the room. She casually glanced at them as she put them back on the table where they had originated from. She wasn't really snooping, she thought, after all, they looked to be just ordinary papers one would have lying around an attic, old telephone and electric bills, some bank statements, warranty papers from an electric blanket, the toaster and vacuum, nothing too important. Then she noticed a paper that looked much older in the corner.

She had to crawl on her hands and knees to reach it. It was yellowed with age and almost brittle to hold. She was very careful with it as she crawled back out of the corner to see better in the light. The writing was in cursive, very weird cursive to be exact. She was having a very hard time making out the words. It seemed to be written to someone named Lucas Mailstorm. She tried to make out the words but could only decipher a few.

To Lucas Mailstorm

something something HIDDEN something something something ATTIC.

CAN'T LET something FIND IT FOR FEAR HE WILL something something.

IF THAT HAPPENS, something something, AND ALL WILL BE LOST

BEST REGARDS someone

She could not believe what she had read. It sounded like a mystery right out of a Sherlock Holmes book. She, of course, would be the loveable Watson. She surely would not be Holmes, as she had never been one of too much importance. She was the third born in a family of four kids. Not popular at school and surely not as smart as most people who solve these types of mysteries, she was, however, very curious. She wondered if the note had been written to her grandfather's relatives. She did not want to ask him, though, because she was afraid he would take it away, and just as fast as her mystery appeared, it would disappear. She wondered if the attic in the note was this attic, the one she was sitting in now. How exciting, she thought. She decided to look around a little to see if she could find any secret hiding places where something important could be lying in wait for her to find.

She started by looking at each wall. She had read many books where there were secret compartments in the walls, and all one had to do was push a secret lever and wa-la, a secret door would open to reveal vast treasures. She poked and pushed at everything that looked odd on every wall, but did not find a secret lever. Well, she thought, there are sometimes trap doors in floors that you pull up, and things can be hidden there. So, she crawled over every inch of the floor and only managed to find two pennies and one old baseball card, which, on further review in better light, did not appear so old. Well, where else could I look, she thought. She looked up at the sound of a new wave of heavy rain on the roof and smiled. That's got to be it, she thought, there is nowhere else to look. It must be hidden in the roof. She got the chair she had been sitting in and started to comb the roof for secrets. After half an hour, she gave up. She was getting tired, and she was disappointed that she had searched everywhere and found nothing. She sat down in the chair and began to read the letter again.

To Lucas Mailstorm

Something something HIDDEN something something something ATTIC.

CAN'T LET something FIND IT FOR FEAR HE WILL something something.

IF THAT HAPPENS, something something, AND ALL WILL BE LOST

BEST REGARDS someone

That word after hidden, two letters in it, could that be "in"? And after that three letters, could that be "the"? So "something something HIDDEN IN THE something something something ATTIC." And then before ATTIC, again two letters and three letters, "something something HIDDEN IN THE something IN THE ATTIC.

Ok, she thought, now we are getting somewhere. So, something is hidden in the attic. Now, in what is the question? She looked around the attic. She knew it wasn't the walls, the floor, or the roof; she had searched those in depth. Well, what else is up here, she thought, growing impatient. Just then, there was a flash of lightning and a clap of thunder so loud she nearly fell out of the chair from fright. She rubbed her eyes from the bright light that had filled the attic, and when she opened them again, all she could see was the lightest colored thing in the room, the gray chimney sitting close to the table in the middle of the room. As her eyes began to dilate again, due to the low light conditions, and her vision returned, she once again looked at the chimney. Of course, she thought, people have been known to make secret compartments in chimneys, especially in the old days. She jumped out of the chair so fast she nearly tipped it over. She grabbed it quickly to keep it from banging on the floor and potentially waking anyone who was sleeping down below. She walked as quickly as she could to the chimney and began to search it in earnest.

She poked, pried and pushed on every inch of the thing. And she found, nothing. She was now very depressed. How could this turn out so badly? She was sure she had found the most excellent of mysteries but now she was sure the letter must have been referring to another house and a different chimney. She laid her forehead on the chimney and sighed, then jumped back a good foot when she heard brick scraping on brick directly in front of her face. She looked at the spot she had been resting on and could see one of the bricks slightly out of place. She walked back to it and pushed on it with her hand. It did not budge. She pushed harder, still nothing. Well, something had made it move, she thought, but what? Ok, let's try again. She put her forehead back on the chimney and stood perfectly still, waiting. Nothing happened. Oh, what the heck, she said, and sighed again. The now familiar sound of brick on brick filled her ears. She leaned back and looked. The brick had moved again, now sitting further into the chimney. And this time, she could see that there was some kind of an opening just under the bottom of the brick that was sliding. She pushed on the brick harder this time, then stopped. Not because the brick did not move but because she realized how futile the action was. If it had not moved before when she had pushed it, why did she think it would move this time? So what did move it? Not her forehead, it had been leaning on the brick above the sliding one. The only thing in front of the sliding brick had been her mouth and she certainly did not push it with her lips. Then what? Wait! She had it. She leaned closer to the brick and blew on it. She saw just the tiniest movement. Then she opened her mouth and breathed her hot breath on it as if she were fogging up a mirror. The brick slid another inch. She squealed with delight in spite of the noise, and then she began breathing on the brick over and over until she was light headed and the brick had moved back far enough to reveal — a hidden compartment.

Chapter 3
Through the Dark Portal

The tears burned her cheeks as they coursed down her very cold face. She thought about her parents. What would they think if they never saw her again? They would never know what had happened to her. There would be no grave for them to visit, and she would be buried in a faraway place all alone. She cried in earnest now, hanging on ever so tightly to the great horse who had tried to save her life. He had run so fast for so long, but he was too tired and spent to make it the rest of the way. She wished he would survive at least. She heard the beast screech again, and this time it was so close it made her ears hurt. She heard the horse whinny in rage and fright. She felt him tremble over and over, but she knew it was mainly from exhaustion; he was so brave. Then, through her tightly clenched eyes, a bright light appeared that burned her eyes, causing more tears to well up. She was reminded of the flash of lightning in her grandfather's attic that had temporarily blinded her all that time ago. What was this light? Was it the light people talked about when they died? But the beast had not reached her yet, at least she didn't think it had. Maybe it had, and this was death. Then she heard the beast screech again. The screech that came from the monster this time was by far the loudest one yet. She could hear the hatred and rage in it as well as pain. Pain, she thought. Why would it be feeling pain, and what was that light if it was not death? She opened her eyes slowly and saw the glimmering shield just as she and the horse passed through it. How could this be, she wondered, how did we make it to the shield? Then all was black, and she saw nothing more.

The light wounded the beast, and it pulled back in pain just before its claws gripped the rider on the horse's back. The creature screeched a terrifying noise so loud that people were woken from sleep five miles away, wondering what it was that had disturbed them. The pain that coursed through its body was unbearable. It was magical and ran deep within it, burning and searing its way through muscle and tissue.

The Dark Mage could feel it as well. He cringed and writhed in his chair. His aides tried to calm him, but he pushed them aside and threatened to kill each one if they should touch him again. He could not break his connection with the creature, or he would lose the horse and rider. He tried to focus, but again the flash of light and the searing pain. He cried out loud this time and began to sweat, blood seeping from his pores. The intense pain was almost too much. He strained to see anything through the creature's eyes, anything at all. Then he caught a glimpse of something that shimmered in the dark, barely discernible, but he did see it for only a moment. Pain, oh so much pain; he had to break the connection with the beast, or he feared he might suffer the same fate. He turned away from the creature's mind and crawled back towards his own just as the light came again. The swiftly fading, agonizing cries of the beast were all that was left of the connection they once had. Then all was silent, and the Dark Mage was once again in his own mind, in his own body. He opened his eyes and tried to remember what it was he had seen.

Emiril stood resolute as she once again cast the light spell. She knew it was the only weapon she had that would kill the creature. She also knew that the creature was not alone. The Dark Mage rode with it, not on its back, but in its mind. She knew the light spell would break the connection he had with the creature and turn him back to where he had come from. She could feel the life leaving the creature as it rolled in the air, trying to escape the pain from the spell as it seeped through flesh and muscles. She could feel the Dark Mage's presence as well and knew he, too, was in pain. He was in pain yet reluctant to leave. He was searching for something, and she was not going to let him find it if she could help it. Again, she cast the spell and again. Each time, she knew the creature was moving closer to death and the Dark Mage was being forced to leave. One last time, she cast the spell, and the creature plummeted to the ground with a loud thud, and a gush of air escaped its dying body. Then it was over. The creature was dead, and the Dark Mage was gone. She wasn't sure what he was looking for, and she wasn't sure if she had prevented him from finding it, but she had tried, and now at least Breanne and the horse were safely in the glen.

Chapter 4
The Chase in the Woods

Breanne peered into the hole just below where the brick had been. It was very dark and there were many cobwebs. She didn't know if she should just stick her bare hand in there; there could be spiders, or, like in the movies, there could be a booby trap, and she could be poisoned or have her hand cut off. At this last thought, Breanne decided there was no way she was sticking her hand in that black hole. She started looking around the attic to see if there was anything that would work as an extra hand. She rummaged through a few boxes and found a pair of her grandfather's old leather work gloves — not exactly what she was looking for, but they did make her feel better about spider bites. She kept looking, and in a box of old kitchenware, she found exactly what she had envisioned: a pair of tongs. They were old-fashioned but perfect for what she had in mind. The two long metal pieces crisscrossed in the middle and were held together by a screw, just like scissors. Unlike scissors, though, they had grippers on the end of them, which a cook could grab a piece of food with without risk of being burned. The end you held onto had holes for your fingers, and you worked them like a pair of scissors; they were perfect.

She ran back to the hole. It was so black in there, but she did not have a flashlight, and she didn't dare go downstairs to look for one for fear of waking someone up, so she was going to have to make do with searching blindly. She put on the thick, leather, spider bite protection gear and tried to put her heavily gloved fingers through the small holes of the tongs. She knew right away that was not going to happen. She weighed the risk of being bitten by a spider against not being able to use the extra-long tongs, not to mention the safety of not getting her real hand cut off, should there actually be a hand-cutting-off device in the hole, and decided that the tongs outweighed the gloves in usefulness, so off they came. Now she could slip her tiny fingers into the holes of the tongs, and she slowly stuck the gripper end into the hole. She felt around for anything, anything at all, and was not disappointed to discover there was indeed something in there. She heard metal on metal as the tongs, guided by her probing hand, found something about six inches deep into the hole. She opened the end of them and tried to grab the mystery metal; she did not get a good hold of it, and it slid two inches to the right. Again, she opened the tongs, and this time she felt them close on the metal object. She held her end tightly together so the object would not slip out of her grasp, and began to pull it out slowly, trying not to bump the walls of this little hiding place. The object came into view as she brought it the rest of the way out in one swift movement, fearing at the last second she would drop it back into the blackness from where it had just emerged. She dropped the object into one of the gloves she picked up off the floor; she still did not think she should touch it with her bare hands. There it was, she couldn't believe it, a real hidden treasure, and she had found it. She had to refrain from jumping up and down and squealing in delight; she had to be quiet, especially now.

She hurried to the table to get a better look at it under the only light there was. She saw that it was a pendant in the shape of a black dragon with its wings held open in a circle around its body. The eyes were a red stone of some kind which shone very brightly in the light. The detail in the carving was incredible; you could see each scale and each tooth as well as all the muscles and claws. Whoever created this was an incredible jewelry maker. She could not tell what kind of metal it was made of. It was black and very heavy for its size, about four inches tall and four inches wide. The metal shone like polished gold, but she had never seen black gold before. There was only one mark on the pendant, on the back; it looked like a crown with the letters KB under it.

She looked at the pendant a minute longer, then she thought, I wonder if there is anything else in there? She grabbed the tongs and went back to the hole. She poked them down again and felt around. She didn't feel anything at first, but then, as the tongs got to the edges of the compartment, she noticed that there was space around each edge. She tapped the tongs on what she thought to be the bottom of the compartment but did not hear the sound of metal on brick; instead she heard a dull thump. There was something else in there all right, but she was not going to be able to pick it up with the tongs like she had the pendant. She withdrew the tongs and looked into the hole but it was just as black as before. She was growing frustrated. There was definitely something else in there and she wanted it. But what about booby traps, having your hand cut off? She thought about how she had retrieved the pendant. She had the tongs in there and nothing had happened. She decided that if there had been something in there that would cut off a hand, surely it would have been triggered when she was poking around in there with the tongs. She was going to have to put on a glove and try to retrieve whatever else was in that black hole. If she lost a hand in the process, she decided, it was worth it, after all, they didn't live that far from a hospital, maybe they could put it back on. Of course, she really didn't believe she was going to lose a hand or she would not have been able to stick hers in there, at least that's what she told herself.

With the giant glove on, her hand could barely work the fingers as she reached slowly into the blackness. She closed her eyes and waited for the pain which would indicate a severed limb. No pain came. She moved her hand around and waited, still no pain. Breathing a sigh of relief, in fact, she realized that she had been holding her breath, she slowly opened her eyes. Apparently, there really wasn't a hand cutting off device in the hole after all. She smiled at herself for being so scared. "Ah, get a hold of yourself, Breanne," she muttered. She took another deep breath then got to work trying to pry out whatever was in the hole.

She could tell it was rectangle shaped and it felt very much like a book. The problem was she could not get the thick fingers of the gloves between the thing and the walls of the compartment. She needed something smaller to use as a pry bar. She thought about the tongs but they were too thick together and spread apart they would not fit in the hole.

She didn't want to think about what popped into her mind next, but there it was anyway; she could take the gloves off and risk being bitten by a spider, the one thing that truly did frighten her. She withdrew her hand from the hole and looked at the glove. Why did it have to be so big? Why couldn't she have found a pair of Grandma's gardening gloves instead? She didn't want to go rummaging around again; it would take too long and make more noise than she wanted to, now that she really did have a secret to protect. She sighed and slowly took the glove off. She looked at her tiny hand and then looked into the blackness. She was sure there were spiders in there; she could feel it in her soul. She wasn't sure why she was so afraid of spiders, but she always had been. As a child, she would not enter a room if she thought there was a spider in it; it had been a nightmare for her poor mother. Well, spiders or not, if I want that book, this is the only way to get it, she thought. She started to reach into the hole while tears welled up in her eyes. Just before she lost sight of her fingers, she froze.

Oh my gosh, she screamed in her mind, why didn't I think of it before? She quickly withdrew her hand and plopped down on the floor, tearing off one of her shoes. Then she took her sock off and replaced the shoe, smiling the whole time. She stood up and deftly pulled the sock up over her hand and halfway up her arm as well. When she was little, and it would snow, she and her brothers and sisters would play outside. When they had exhausted their supply of warm, dry gloves, they would move on to socks. Their mom would get frustrated having to wash a whole load of socks at the end of the day, but she never stopped them.

She would just smile and wave out the window, and when they came in at the end of the day, exhausted and half frozen, there she would be, standing next to the kitchen table with four steaming mugs of hot chocolate and a plate of freshly baked chocolate chip cookies. Breanne sniffed and realized that a tear was running silently down her cheek. She quickly wiped it away and wiped her nose with the back of her sock-covered hand. She missed her parents; they had been gone two weeks already and would be gone still another two. They deserved this vacation, she knew that, but it did not make it any easier to be away from them. She loved them so very much.

She had to focus; she could not get caught up in missing her parents, or she would do nothing but sit up here and cry the rest of the night, all mysteries forgotten. She looked into the hole again, this time with newfound courage gleaned from the cotton and spandex shield she now wielded on her arm. She reached slowly into the hole, the thought of hand cutting off devices still in the farthest corner of her mind, whether she wanted it there or not. She felt for the edge of the object and easily slipped her now slim fingers between it and the wall of the compartment. She pulled, and the object began to move. It was kind of hard to get out, though. She had to reposition it so it would come out of the hole lengthwise, not sideways, but she managed to do this, and in a minute, she was standing there holding a big, leather-bound book that looked like it had come right out of a fantasy story.

Chapter 5
Shadows Over Fayhall

"Mom, is that you?" Breanne asked in a groggy voice. She could hear someone in the room, and she called again. "Who's in here?"

"Hush now or you'll wake up the whole house," a voice said quietly.

Breanne thought she recognized the voice and tried to see who was talking, but the room was barely lit and the person was in the shadows. She was confused and not quite sure where she was. The events of last night eluded her memory. All she knew was that her head hurt and she felt terrible. She started to move as if to get up, and a wave of dizziness overtook her. She decided that was not a good idea and lay her aching head back down on the bed and began looking around the room.

It was decorated in greens and browns, with borders of ivy along the trim and paintings of woodland scenes adorning the walls, which were made of hand-hewn planks. A fire burned on the side of the room where the voice had come from, and she could see a big wooden door opposite that. The bed she was in was big and comfortable; in fact, it was *very* comfortable and warm. She thought the mattress must be stuffed with down because she seemed to sink comfortably into it, no matter which way she turned. She let herself linger for a moment in the softness of the sheets she was lying on and pulled the fur blanket up to her chin, the softness of it brushing her cheek. Then memories started to flood back to her. She had been running through the night on the back of a horse, being chased by an evil creature! Her heart started to pound as her memories filled her mind.

They had been running so long, and they were so close to the glen, but they had not made it; the horse had faltered; he could not go on! But

19

if they hadn't made it, where was she now? And there was the light, yes, the light, she remembered it now. It had blinded her and stung her eyes even through closed lids. It was such a white, pure light and yet so powerful. And when she had opened her eyes, she remembered that she had seen the shield as she and the horse passed through it. They had made it after all! They must be alive! At least she must be, she did not know about the horse. She felt a great sorrow rush over her at the thought that he might not have made it. Then she thought about Marcus. Was he alive? She was panicked with the thought of her friend's safety. With her memories of recent events returning, she surmised that she must be in Daedhrog, the elfin glen. She was safe; the evil monster could not get her here. The elves were more powerful than any other creature in the land, and she was safely in their care now; she was sure of it. She was so relieved she sat straight up, causing her head to throb again as dizziness overtook her, but she didn't care; she was alive! "But what about Marcus and the horse, are they ok?" She hadn't meant to say it aloud, but she couldn't help it. Marcus was such a dear friend, and JC was such a brave horse, more of a friend now, too, you might say, and they had saved her life. She had tears in her eyes from worry.

"They are fine, stop worrying," she heard the voice say.

She was startled to hear the voice again; she had been so caught up in her thoughts that she had forgotten anyone else was here. Again, she thought she recognized that voice, but she couldn't quite place it. Her memories were back, but she was still so groggy and light-headed that she could not recognize who it was. But no matter, her friends, kind Marcus, and her strong, brave horse were all right.

Then the person who had been talking to her stepped out of the shadows, walked over to the bed holding a cup with steam rising from it, and held it out to her. "Drink this and you will feel better," she said. Breanne's eyes flew open, and her mouth dropped. She made no attempt to grab the offered cup; there was now a face to the voice. She was both startled and surprised, but mostly happy to see her friend, Emiril.

"Oh Emiril!" she cried. "It's you." The sight of her friend drove all of her fears away. The fear of the evil creature, the fear of not knowing where she was, but mostly the fear of being alone. Although Breanne had only known the elf for a very short period of time, Emiril was one of the few people in this world whom she could call a friend, and that meant more to her than anything, anything except going home, of course. "How did you get here, and how did I get here? I mean, I know I rode here, but how did I get in this house, and how long have I been here?" The questions came in one big rush, with no ending, and Emiril had to put her hand up and stop Breanne from continuing.

"Slow down, child. First, drink this." She offered her the steaming cup again, and this time Breanne took it, sipping the warm, sweet liquid. Immediately, she could taste blackberry and honey, but there was another flavor as well, one she couldn't quite put her finger on. She knew Emiril was a medicine maker and figured there must be something in here to make her head stop hurting, so she drank it all while she listened to Emiril answer her questions one at a time.

"Firstly, after I left you back in Ethuanova, I had to go to Malarcis to talk to the sorceress Mindoneth about your arrival here. Only she would know exactly how you got here and why you came, but most importantly, how to get you back." She smiled at Breanne in that warm, understanding, sympathetic way a mother does when you have a problem and don't know what to do. Moms always make you feel like they can solve any problem with that one look, and Emiril, although she wasn't Breanne's mom, made her feel as if she could fix anything right then and there. She was very grateful to her, and she was beginning to love the elf like she loved her own mother, who she missed so desperately right now. Maybe Emiril can get me home, she thought; at least I know she's trying.

"Does she know how I can get back?" Breanne asked hopefully.

Emiril looked at her intensely, her lavender eyes gleaming in the dim light of the room. In spite of everything going on, this fascinated Breanne. Were they actually glowing in the dark? She had to will herself back to their conversation. "Yes," Emiril said flatly. Breanne waited a moment when Emiril did not go on. She looked at Emiril with raised eyebrows, not wanting to break the silence that had suddenly filled the room; she was beginning to feel uneasy again. Emiril closed her eyes, sighed, then opened them, and what she said next made Breanne's blood run cold and dashed all her hopes of ever making it home.

Chapter 6
Emiril's Light

The book was very old; she knew this the minute she saw it. The cover had to be leather, and the pages were a material she had never really seen before, but she thought maybe it was papyrus. She had learned about papyrus in school, a type of plant the ancient Egyptians used to make paper. It was a very big book, about twelve inches tall and eight inches wide. There were about eight hundred pages, she guessed. She sat down at the table and opened it to the title page.

The words were written in the same weird cursive as the letter she had found. She was surprised to see, below the title, a hand-drawn picture of the dragon pendant. The artwork was exquisite, just like the real thing. As old as the book was, the colors were still vibrant and looked as if they had only been drawn yesterday. There was so much detail in the drawing, it was as if she were looking at the real thing. Even the blood red eyes appeared to be real, staring at her with a look of malevolence which gave her the creeps, and so she turned her focus back to the title. She studied it for a while and finally decided it read: *The Book of Ogolel*. She wasn't sure if Ogolel was a person or a place. That was all that was written on the title page; there was no reference to a publisher and no date, like you would find in today's books. She turned the page. There was a map, but the names were nothing that she had ever heard of before. She recognized the shapes of mountain ranges which had names like: Spires of the Sarr Birds. What was a Sarr bird, she thought? And another mountain range was named: Living Mountains of the Unknown Dragon. Unknown dragon, that almost sounds Chinese. Didn't they have celebrations where they dressed as dragons and paraded down the street? Or was that the Japanese? No matter, this book was definitely not written in Chinese or Japanese, so she put that thought out of her head and looked at the map once more. She saw in the middle of the map a place with squiggly lines with a title that read: *Swamp of Confusion.* These places were very strangely named, and she was starting to think she had found a very old fantasy novel, perhaps the oldest fantasy novel ever written.

She turned the page. The words on the next page were set up like a recipe in a cookbook. There was a title and what looked to be a list of ingredients, and then what appeared to be directions on how to make something. She looked at the title, and it read: *Spell of Calm.* The ingredients needed for this spell appeared to include, "One vial of babbling brook water, one leaf from a willow tree, one blade of grass from an open field," and lastly, she caught her breath for a moment, then laughed to herself as she read the last ingredient, "One hair from a unicorn's mane." She was sure now this was a fantasy book of some sort. There was no such thing as a unicorn. She had simply found an old book, but it was a book of fiction and not the real mystery she had hoped for. Although the book would be really interesting to read, she loved fantasy books, especially those with dragons and unicorns in them.

She flipped through the pages and saw many other spells with many other strange and absurd ingredients, such as: *The Spell of Stoutness,* which included as one of the ingredients, "the toenail of a red bearded dwarf." She laughed out loud at that one. Another spell for courage needed as an ingredient, "One fifth of the heart of a lion bold and true." Wow, she thought, poor lion. It didn't pay to be brave in this land.

She was starting to get tired now and looked at her watch; it was nearly four a.m. She was surprised at how late it had gotten, or was the correct term, how early it had gotten; regardless, she had lost track of the time with all that had happened, and it was no wonder she was tired. Her grandparents got up early, around six a.m., and she knew she had better be in bed by the time they got up. She would find it difficult to convince them she had gotten up earlier than they; she *never* got up early, and even more difficult to explain why she had stayed up so late, especially now that she had something to hide, at least for now.

She was about to stand up and put the book somewhere for safekeeping until tomorrow, or was it tonight? She shrugged, then looked at the book in her hands; she was only halfway through it, and the thought of what could be at the end would eat at her until she could sneak back up here, and that wouldn't be for hours. She had to at least flip through the book to see what might be different and or exciting. She grabbed a handful of pages and started flipping through them. Spell after spell after spell. Well, at least it's consistent, she thought. She dropped the pages she had been looking through and turned to the last page of the book. There once again was the dragon from the pendant staring at her. She grimaced when again she looked into its eyes, still feeling the malevolence they portrayed. This drawing was *exactly* like the first one, and for being drawn by hand, she was surprised as she looked back at the title page, that she could not see one difference between the two. She kept looking from one to the other, and still she could not see anything different between them. Then she grabbed the pendant and compared it as well, absolutely the same, down to every minute detail. Each dragon appeared to have the same number of scales, the same number of toes, and the same lines around its mouth and eyes. Whoever this artist was, she had new respect for his or her work. This page also contained a spell, but unlike the other pages, which had been plain, containing only words, this page contained the drawing of the dragon with an innately drawn border around the edges. She looked closer at the latter, and it appeared to be birds in flight, one after the other, making a complete rectangle around the page with no openings. The birds themselves were foreign to her; they had long tails similar to a peacock but short necks, and in the true style of a fantasy book, four feet. They were a brown color, and their legs and beaks were green. Odd, she thought, even for a fantasy book, and unbidden the thought of "green eggs and ham" popped into her mind. She laughed. I wonder if this is where you get the green eggs from? She thought. Well, Dr. Seuss, now I know your secret. Wait until I tell the world. She laughed again.

Serious again, she looked more intently at the spell. Why was this one singled out in the book to have such adornment when the others had not? She looked at the title: *The Spell of Aberrant*. She looked at the rest of the spell; there was no list of ingredients with this one, only the picture of the dragon pendant. She subconsciously tightened her grip on it and then saw a paragraph underneath it. And what did Aberrant mean? She had never heard the word before. She hated it when she came across words she didn't know the meaning of; it made her feel stupid. She knew that she wasn't really stupid, that she just hadn't learned everything in the world yet, but she still hated it. Well, what does the paragraph say? Maybe that will help. Sometimes, when you hear a word in a sentence, it helps you to understand what it means; they do that a lot in spelling bees.

She began to read, but with the cursive being so unusual, she was having a hard time. She decided to read it aloud; she learned to do this when she was having problems reading in elementary school, which had really helped back then. She began, stumbling over the words which were so unfamiliar to her.

> *Dark portal yee arth commanded by Ogolel then mighty sorceress to open they mouth and allow access to then realm of then otherworld.*

Outside, a loud clap of thunder startled her, followed by a flash of lightning. She gripped the dragon pendant harder and continued on.

> *Allow then bearer to cross through your hidden defenses un maimed and whole.*

She was too caught up reading the spell to notice the pendant growing warm in her hand and to see that the dragon's eyes had become redder and glowed ominously.

Bring them hence to then place of then Fire Dragon of old to stand afore then mighty sorceress go.

Another clap of thunder and flash of lightning, louder and more intense than the first, went unnoticed as Breanne tried to make out the last word of the spell, which had been smudged at some point in time. She fidgeted with the pendant but did not really pay attention to the reason why, it had grown uncomfortably warm in her hand. She should have paid attention however; she should not have been so intent on making out that last word, and then… "I have it!" she said triumphantly.

'Ogolel'

Thunder so loud it threatened to deafen her, lightning so bright the whole of the attic was illuminated!

Breanne felt strange, her body seemed to feel weightless. She felt queasy like she would throw up. The walls of the attic seemed to waver and she could see glimpses of the trees outside. She looked up and saw attic roof then stars then roof again. What was happening? It was then she noticed the heat radiating from the pendant. She looked down at her hand and saw red glowing eyes staring back at her. The eyes looked so real, so evil. She could hear a whooshing sound, getting louder. She tried to put the pendant on the table but she could not let go of it. It was as if it had a hold of *her*. She tried to stand but her body refused to obey. She looked at/through the wall again and this time she could see fields when the walls disappeared, and it was no longer dark. She looked up and saw the sun shining through the disappearing and reappearing attic roof. What was going on? She wanted to scream for help; she tried, no sound came out of her mouth, and if it had, no one would have heard her over

27

that whooshing sound. What was that? It was so loud now she put her hands to her ears and tried to block it out, which was not easy with the pendant clasped tightly in one fist. She closed her eyes and prayed that this nightmare would end. "Please God, let this be a dream, let me be asleep and let me wake up in my bed."

Suddenly the whooshing sound stopped and Breanne started to feel normal again. The dizziness passed and she no longer felt the urge to vomit. She didn't want to open her eyes yet. Then she heard birds chirping. She felt the sun on her head and wind rustled her hair. She knew she wasn't in the attic anymore but she was afraid to see where she was.

Chapter 7
Marcus the Protector

She slowly opened her first eye and then the other. This can't be real, she thought. She closed her eyes tightly again, waited until she counted to twenty, then opened them again. The scene had not changed. She was sitting on the ground in the middle of a big green field surrounded by enormous trees, mostly oak with some fir mixed in. The sky overhead was a deep blue, and the breeze on her skin felt wonderfully warm.

The attic was completely gone. There wasn't even a trace that it had existed; no table, no chair, no papers, nothing. She had to be dreaming; this couldn't be happening. Could it? Of course not, her mind screamed! You fell asleep and you are dreaming, that's all. She knew it was very cliché, but she did it anyway; she pinched her arm as hard as she could. She winced at the pain and then felt stupid. Everyone who does that already knows they aren't dreaming, and it always hurts; this time was no exception. She rubbed her arm to ease the pain.

She suddenly became aware that she was still holding the dragon pendant in her hand. She was relieved to see it because it was a connection to her world, and it made her feel less alone. Even if it was only an inanimate object, it was still something, and from the looks of things, the only thing that had come with her to this place, so she clutched it more tightly. She finally decided that this had to be real, and the first thing she needed to do was figure out how it had happened. She retraced the events that had led up to this moment. She was in the attic as usual, reading, when the shutters blew open. She closed them and made a mess doing so. She cleaned it up, and while doing that, she found the letter. After reading the letter, she found the secret hiding place in the chimney and the pendant. She also found the book of spells. She was

29

reading the last spell in the book right before she felt funny and, "Oh my Gosh!" she screamed out loud. Somewhere in one of the trees, a bird took flight. "The spell, I read that spell out loud, and when I finished reading it, things started to happen, and I felt weird, and now here I am." But that was just a fantasy book, she thought, not a real spell book. There was no such thing as real magic; everyone knew that. But regardless of what she told herself, the facts were still the same. She was sitting in a completely different place than she had been before, where that was, she didn't have a clue, but here she was just the same, and that book had to be the reason she was here. Then once again she cried out loud, "Where is it?" Frantically, she stood up, looking around her, confirming what she had noted before: there was nothing here from the attic except her and the pendant she held in her hand. Tears started to well up in her eyes, and she felt utterly helpless.

She didn't know how long she stood there silently crying, but when she came back to her senses, she decided she had to do something, anything but just stand here and cry. After all, she had no idea where she was and if it was a safe place to be, and what she would do when it got dark out here. She shuddered to think of what kinds of wild animals might roam this field at night. That last thought got her moving. She took a step to the left, stopped, turned, and took a step to the right, and stopped again. "Oh, what's the use?" she said. "I don't even know which way to go."

She surveyed the area around her, and far off on the other side of the field, she thought she saw what may be a path of some kind. Where there's a path, there must be people, she thought; unless of course it's an animal path, in which case I don't want to go that way, but I can't just stand here either. She was starting to get frustrated again, and she finally decided to at least go check it out, cautiously though.

Slowly, while constantly looking around her, she headed in the direction she hoped would be a people path and not an animal path. Paying more attention to watching for wild animals and not enough to where she was walking, she stepped on a rock that poked her foot painfully. She suddenly realized she was still in her pajamas and slippers. Oh great, she thought, I don't even have clothes on. I *really* need to find a town before it gets dark, or I could freeze to death out here, never mind be eaten by a lion or a tiger. Well, if there are lions and tigers here, they don't live just anywhere after all. That last thought made her feel better, well, a little better. She still worried about what other kinds of animals lived here.

She had been walking with her head down, watching for more rocks, and when she looked up, she was startled to see the path directly in front of her. Well, actually, now that she was here, it was quite a bit bigger than a path, more like a road. It reminded her of a wagon road she had seen in old western shows on TV. It was dirt and had ruts in it where, over time, the wheels had dug into the ground. She looked closer and could see footprints as well as horses' hoof marks on the road. She felt elated; this meant that she was not alone here in this place, and that she might be able to find someone who could tell her how to get home. But which way to go? To the left, the road seemed to lead straight into the trees; it was dark in there… enough said, to the right it is! Without hesitation, she turned and headed away from the dark, scary trees toward what she hoped was civilization.

Her pace, which had started out at a fast walk, was now down to a slow plod. Her feet hurt and her legs ached. She didn't know how long she had been walking this lonely, desolate road, which had at first seemed her salvation and was now the bane of her existence, but it felt like forever. She was sweating and her throat was very dry; her tongue was sticking to the roof of her mouth, and she just knew this must be what it felt like to be lost in the desert. No wonder people go mad out there in the desert, she thought. This is horrible. She walked some more and then some more. She was daydreaming about home; her mom and dad returning from their honeymoon and taking the children home. She smiled at this thought, then immediately snapped back to reality, her smile lost, replaced by a look of horror. What if they did come back to get them, and she wasn't there? What would they think? Would they think she ran away? Would they think she had been kidnapped? She hated to think of her parents worrying for her safety, her mother crying, her father doing his best to comfort her and be strong while worrying himself. Oh, if only she could let them know that she was alright. But she couldn't, she couldn't for many reasons, not the least of which was because SHE HAD NO IDEA WHERE SHE WAS! She stopped. What was that sound? She strained to hear better. It was coming from her left. She noticed a line of small willow trees had been running parallel to the road, and looking back, had been for a while now. Wow, she thought, how did I miss that? The noise was coming from inside the thicket. Suddenly, she realized what that noise was and leapt off the road, running for the trees with no thought of wild animals in her head at all. The only thing she cared about right now, and which she almost fell into before she managed to stop herself, was water... cool, clear water, and there it was right in front of her. She had never felt so happy, at least she said that now. She had said it many times before and would say it many times after, but suffice it to say, she was *very* happy at that moment in time. She knelt down beside the stream and began to scoop water up in her hand and drink it. The coolness felt so good on her tongue, and it fell away from the roof of her mouth. She eagerly drank and drank, and then a thought popped into her head: Should I have boiled this first? The thought came, but she didn't stop drinking, even though she kinda thought maybe she should have boiled the water first. Oh well, one thing at a time, she thought, dehydration today, worms tomorrow. How *do* you get rid of worms, though? she wondered.

Chapter 8
The Pendant Awakens

When her stomach was near bursting, she stopped drinking. Another thought popped into her head. I don't think you're supposed to drink a lot of cold water when you're dehydrated; I think it can make you sick. She just stared at the stream, a little late now, she thought nervously. She wished she had something to carry water in so she could take some with her, in case the stream left the road, but she didn't, go figure. With one last look at the cool, refreshing water that she felt had saved her life (kinda dramatic, she told herself), she turned to go.

Her nose was suddenly buried deep in the fur of a horse's neck. She blinked, and horse hair met eyelashes. She looked up and could see nothing but the underside of the horse's jaw. She took two steps back; the second one landed her three inches deep in the stream, and she felt her slippers start to take on water. That didn't matter at this point in time; what mattered was the giant horse with the blonde-haired creature on it. How in the world did I not hear *that? she thought.* How long had they been there? Why am I not dead, was her next thought. This whole time, she and the blonde creature had been staring at each other; she, with a look of awe, terror, surprise, and self-loathing (for not hearing them come up); the creature… nothing, no sign of emotion whatsoever. This was very disconcerting to her. At least frown or smile or something, she thought, then I might at least have an idea if I am about to die. Her feet were starting to get cold; her slippers had soaked up as much water as they could and were now more like sponges than footwear.

Breanne couldn't take the tension anymore. "Hello," she stammered, half choking on the words, her teeth beginning to chatter from the cold water and fear. She waved one small hand, not too dramatically for fear the creature would think she was going to attack and strike first. She waited… nothing. Well, she thought, maybe "Hola." She smiled when she said this, a smile that was almost scary to look at, because it was very hard to smile when you are so scared. It looks sort of like a jack-o-lantern that has sat out in the weather too long, its carefully carved face no longer resembling what it started out as. Still no response from the creature. Breanne was starting to replace fear with irritation. How long was she supposed to stand here freezing to death (again, a little dramatic, she reminded herself), before she found out what was to become of her at the hands of this creature? She put her hands on her hips now, forgetting that she was supposed to be afraid and flatly stated, "I'm freezing, my slippers are wet, and my feet are cold. I am going to walk out of this stream now and go over there." She pointed a few feet forward and to her left. "I am not going to hurt you," she added as a precautionary statement, after which she took first one step and then another, all the while watching the creature on the horse out of the corner of her eye.

When she made it alive to her intended destination, she let out a silent sigh of relief, turned, and again stared at the creature. And the creature, although it had moved its head to follow her progress, once again sat just as motionless as before, staring right back at her. The eyes are what got Breanne's attention, and she began to really study the creature; they were not any color she had ever seen on a person or creature before. They were a lavender color. Not dark purple, but a light hue, and they almost seemed to be glowing. She looked more closely at the creature and noted the pointed ears, almost like a bat, she thought. They didn't have fur on them, but they were definitely shaped like bat ears, long, slender, and pointed at the top (she chased away a thought of vampires). The creature had long blonde hair that was the color of the sun when it was highest in the sky; it was actually very beautiful. It wore some sort of armor from the looks of it. She had seen pictures in books

34

of this type of stuff before; she thought they called it chainmail because it was not solid metal but literally woven from links of chain. The robe under the armor was a beautiful blue color, and it wore breaches that were black. Its boots came to just below the knee and were made of black leather. The more she looked at the creature, the more she started thinking how much it resembled a fantasy creature called an elf. The horse the creature rode was huge, much like the draft horses that pull the wagons at a parade her family attended annually in her hometown. It too had armor on. A plate was made to cover the vulnerable areas of his face, and a large breastplate protected his massive chest. He was a deep black color and had those hairy feet Breanne liked. His mane and tail were long and flowing. Together, they were an awesome sight. Suddenly, Breanne realized she was not afraid of them anymore.

At *exactly* the same moment Breanne stopped being afraid of the creature/elf, it spoke. "Child, where do you hail from?" it asked.

Breanne knew instantly that it was a female; the voice was melodious and soft, not at all unpleasant to listen to. In fact, it was almost hypnotizing, and she had never heard that accent before; it was so different. Breanne stared at her blankly for a moment, still mesmerized, and then, realizing she had not answered the question, she stated very matter-of-factly, "Boston." The creature/elf looked puzzled. It was the first sign of emotion from the creature/elf since their encounter, and she was glad to see it. It proved she was, well, not exactly, but kind of human.

"Where is this 'Boston'?" she asked. "I do not believe I have heard of a village with that name. And I know all the villages in this realm." This last statement was spoken with authority and pride. Her look was back to its usual blankness.

Breanne was beginning to feel weak and helpless before the creature/elf. What were her intentions? Was she friendly like Breanne thought, or should she be afraid after all? Maybe her diminishing fear was a spell, like the ones in the book, like the way aliens could master your mind and make you feel and do things. Her thoughts were turning more alarming by the second. Maybe this creature was not an elf, maybe she was an alien, and Breanne was on some weird planet in the middle of the universe. That would explain the way she felt just before she left the attic and found herself here in this place. Oh no, if she were on an alien planet, she thought, that would mean she just drank alien water, uhgh, and worse yet, if she did get worms, they would be alien worms. She almost threw up at this last thought. How do you get rid of *alien* worms?

Even though she was starting to become afraid again, she was sure of two things. She was not going to let aliens or any other manner of creature make her do anything she didn't want to do, and she was going to find a way home. These thoughts gave her back her courage, and with that and this newfound determination, she looked at the creature/elf/alien and, in a tone more courageous and demanding than she really felt, she asked, "What village are *you* from?"

Again, the creature/elf/alien looked puzzled. But then, Breanne thought, maybe she looked annoyed too. Courage failing, fear mounting. Maybe that wasn't such a good idea to turn the tables on her after all, she thought. If she is an alien, she could melt my brain, or an elf could put a spell on me and turn me into a toad. She involuntarily took one step back, her slippers making a squishing noise, and decided she would hop into the stream if she became a toad and swim away as fast as she could, although she really didn't want to become a toad, and it made her feel ill to think about living the rest of her life as an amphibian. The look on the creature/elf/alien's face was still mostly puzzlement, but now there was another emotion forming there as well, one Breanne could not quite make out yet.

The creature/elf/alien spoke in a voice a bit more ominous than before, the melodious tone less pronounced and now seeming to have a hint of anger in it. "How is it that you do not know where I dwell?" Her lavender eyes bore into Breanne's brown ones, where once they had appeared to glow, now they appeared to smolder. Breanne tensed, getting ready to hop into the stream on what she thought would soon be her new toad legs, and swim away. "Are you not from this realm?" Then Breanne could see her face change just a little into that emotion she had not been able to put her finger on before; yep, definitely anger, Breanne thought. She looks like Mom when I make her mad. The creature/elf/alien continued, even more ominous looking and sounding than before, Breanne's fear definitely returning now. "Maybe you are a spy for the Dark Mage." As she finished this last statement and before Breanne had even realized she had moved, the creature/elf/alien had drawn her bow that had previously been hidden, slung across her back, and nocked an arrow in it; and the arrow was pointed directly at Breanne.

Well, Breanne thought, a toad would have been better than death; she didn't see this coming. She instinctively raised her hands up in a submissive manner. "I'm sorry," the words flowed out of her mouth as fast as they could, "I'm very sorry. I am from Boston, Massachusetts, or at least I am staying there with my grandma and grandpa until my parents return from their honeymoon. I did not mean to insult you or make you mad. I really don't want to die right now, and I am incredibly sorry. Is there anything else you want to know?" She looked at the creature/elf/alien and smiled her best smile, hoping her apology had been good enough to keep her from becoming a pincushion.

Chapter 9
The Forest Trial

"My name is Emiril, daughter of King Badhor and Queen Norin. I live in Daedhrog, land of the elves, and you child, are not from here," the creature/elf/alien said, unknocking the arrow; at which point, Breanne sighed in relief and her knees trembled less noticeably. I guess I am not going to die today, she thought. Well, that just leaves worms to worry about now, and she thought she could maybe feel something wriggling in her stomach. Knock it off, dummy, she said to herself firmly. They wouldn't be there this soon anyway. She lowered her hands and looked at this figure, who was no longer a creature/elf/alien, but a self-proclaimed elf (not alien worms) and apparently a princess as well. Emiril looked at the girl. She was short, about five feet four inches; she might weigh one hundred twenty pounds, her hair and eyes were brown. She resembled the people who lived in Ethuanova, but there was something different about her. "How did you get here?" Emiril asked her.

Breanne thought about the question for a moment; she didn't even know where *here* was. "I am not sure where this is," she started. "But I think I came here because I read a spell in a book I found."

Emiril's eyes flew open. She leapt off the horse in one fluid movement and in two steps was standing in front of Breanne. "A book of spells?" she almost yelled. "Where is it? Did you bring it with you?" Her excitement was evident, and Breanne was almost scared to tell her the book had not come through with her, but she did. Emiril stepped back, a look of sheer disappointment on her face. She appeared to have an idea of what the book was, and Breanne asked her if she knew it. "What?" the elf asked, distracted by her thoughts. Breanne again asked her about the book. "Oh, the book, yes, I know it. But before I tell you about it, why don't you tell me what *you* know about it and how you found it and where you found it." She paused, sighed, and then said, "Why don't you just start from the beginning and tell me everything. I am going to need to hear it all anyhow."

Breanne wasn't exactly sure who Emiril was, but she did know about the book and that was one step closer to getting home, so she told Emiril about finding the book and reading the spell only to find herself here in this place, wherever that was, and when she got to the part where they met, Breanne said rather sheepishly, "Well, you know the rest."

Emiril walked over to an area where the grass was thick and soft and sat down, motioning Breanne to follow. She had a look of tenderness about her now that Breanne was startled to see; before, she had seemed so opposing and downright scary, actually. As Breanne sat down, Emiril looked her over from head to toe. "Are you a sorceress in your world?" she asked.

"What's a sorceress?" Breanne asked.

Emiril asked the question differently, "Do you perform magic?"

Breanne laughed softly, "Oh, a magician, no, why?"

"Well, your clothes, if you are not a sorceress, then why do your clothes have stellar symbols on them? Only magicians have clothes with these types of symbols."

Breanne looked at her pajamas. They were a blue flannel top and bottom, and they were covered in moons and stars. "Oh!" she said. "In our world, these symbols are on many things. They don't represent magic, well, not all the time anyway. But there are no *real* magicians, or as you call them, sorcerers, in our world anyway; we don't *really* do magic. We pretend." She remembered a time when her dad had taken her and her brothers and sister to a magic show. They had been very little and they had joined other kids their age who were seated on the floor in a semi-circle around a magician. He had proceeded to pull a cute white rabbit out of a hat and pour milk into a paper and have it disappear; but the trick that Breanne had liked the most was when he had pulled a coin from behind her father's ear. She had been so amazed; back then, she thought it had been real. She knew better now. Remembering all this made her sad again, and she had to fight back tears. She looked at Emiril. "It's fun, but it's not real," she said sadly.

"I see," Emiril said softly, noting the melancholy mood this inquiry had caused.

There was a moment of silence between the two. Emiril was waiting for Breanne to feel better, and Breanne was trying very hard to make that happen. She shivered and decided she had better take off her slippers as they were still very wet and her mother had always cautioned her that "having wet feet makes one sick." When she removed them, she saw that her feet had become white looking and wrinkled on the bottom, a condition that can occur when one spends too much time in the bathtub. But the worst part was the fact that they were freezing, and she rubbed them briskly, trying in vain, it seemed, to warm them up.

Emiril, who had been watching all of this, asked her, "Do you not have any other shoes?"

Breanne looked up. "No," she said sadly, "I only have what I'm wearing. Nothing else came here with me."

Upon hearing this, Emiril got up and walked over to her horse, reached into a bag on the saddle, and rummaged around for a minute, finally pulling out some things which she then took to Breanne. "Try these," she said. "They are going to be big on you, but they will keep you warmer than your, well… I am not sure just what to call the clothes you have on now."

Breanne smiled. "They're called pajamas," she said. "We wear them to bed where I come from." She took the things Emiril offered her, holding them up one at a time, her eyes widening each time she held up something new. There was a tunic made of some kind of soft leather that was a beautiful red color, some pants like the kind Emiril was wearing, also made of leather, but this pair, instead of being black, was a soft brown color, and lastly, a pair of boots, again like the ones Emiril wore, they too were black. She smiled gratefully at Emiril, thanking her over and over, and went behind a thick shrub to change. After she got the new clothes on, she didn't know whether to keep her pajamas or not. She decided she would probably not need them anymore and decided to leave them. When she started to walk back to where Emiril waited, she suddenly remembered she had left the pendant in the pocket of the pajama pants. She ran back and got it, grateful she had remembered it. She didn't want to lose the one thing she had that represented home to her. She felt around on the new pants, and although they were not anything like the kind of pants she was used to, she managed to find a pocket on the inside, which she put the pendant into. There was a little drawstring to tie it shut, and when it was safely put away, she felt better.

Emiril smiled and nodded in satisfaction when Breanne emerged from behind the shrub. "You look great," she said. "And the clothes are not *that* big on you, they will be ok for now." Breanne wanted to hug her, but instead she thanked her again and told her how much she appreciated the clothes and how warm she was now. "You are welcome," Emiril said, smiling, and patted the grass across from her. "Come sit now, we have a lot to talk about, you and I."

After Breanne got comfortable, Emiril started. "First, let me tell you, you are in Ibacion. Daedhrog, where I am from, is south of here. We are close to Ethuanova, about a day's ride north. That is where I was going when I met you. I have a friend there that I am meeting. But before I tell you more, I need to know everything you can tell me about that book. Can you describe what it looked like and the name of it?" she asked.

Breanne had never heard of any of these places. She was sure she was no longer on Earth, although she was not yet truly convinced she was on another planet. But if she was not on Earth or another planet, where exactly was she? She decided she would ask Emiril these questions later, because regardless of where she was, she wasn't going anywhere anytime soon, and that book sure seemed to be important to her. "Well," Breanne started, "the book was named after someone. The name was O-something, Ogle, Ogel, something like that; it's hard to remember exactly."

"Was it Ogolel?" Emiril asked, her voice tense.

"Yes, yes, that was it, do you know that person?"

"I'm afraid I do," Emiril said with a look of great concern.

"Who is it?" Breanne asked.

"Someone not so nice, who hundreds of years ago tried to overthrow the Elven kingdom," Emiril said, and the emotion in her voice was a mix of anger and sadness.

"What happened?" Breanne asked. She wanted to hear more about this person who had written that awful spell which had brought her here.

Emiril looked at her thoughtfully. "I guess you *should* know this," she said. "This *is* why you are here. Ogolel," Emiril began, "was once a very beautiful elf. She was one of the king's trusted advisers. She knew powerful magic, more magic than any elf except the king and one other." There was a sound of awe in her voice. "She lived in the palace with the royal family, and they loved her as one of their own. She had many suitors due to her great beauty, but she never took a life mate. She only

42

cared about her magic, and she became more and more powerful every day."

"What did she look like?" Breanne asked.

Emiril looked at her, and her face softened. "She was second in beauty only to the queen." Her voice was filled with admiration. "She had long flowing black hair which hung below her waist. Her eyes were the color of snow when the sun shines on it; the most beautiful blue nature has to offer, and her skin was like beautiful ivory. And she seemed to glow from within. Everyone loved her, especially the queen. Can you guess why?" she asked. Breanne shook her head, not wanting to speak and ruin the moment. "They were sisters," Emiril said, smiling, but Breanne saw a hint of sadness in her eyes.

Then Breanne realized something. "She's your aunt!" she said, smiling, proud of the connection she had made.

Emiril smiled back. "You are right," she said, "she is my aunt." Her eyes looked misty.

"If she were a magician," Breanne said, musing, "then the book must have belonged to her."

"Sorceress," Emiril corrected, "and yes, the book is hers, in fact, she wrote it; those spells are hers." Her face darkened again.

Breanne saw this and was a little concerned but mostly excited. "Then she can help me get home. Where does she live? Can we go there now?"

"Slow down, child," Emiril said quickly. "There's more to this story, and I am afraid you are not going to like it." Her facial expression made Breanne think that she was right; she wasn't going to like what came next. She had been hoping this Ogolel would be able to send her home;

43

now she wasn't so sure. She settled back down to hear the rest of the story.

"Ogolel was very powerful," Emiril continued. "She started to feel that she was being taken for granted by the king and queen. She felt that no one appreciated the greatness of her powers. She watched the Elven kingdom revere the royal family while she stood in the shadows, and she grew angry. She was, after all, the *sister* of the queen. She felt that because of her great powers, she should be the queen. So one day, she made an alliance with the Dark Mage, telling him that if he helped her overthrow the throne, he would sit on it with her, as her king. Of course, she had no intention of letting that happen, but he did not know this and agreed to help her."

"Wait," Breanne said quickly, "who is the Dark Mage?"

Emiril stopped, realizing she was forgetting Breanne was not from this world, and did not know about the Dark Mage and what he had done. "The Dark Mage is not an elf," she said, "he is a man, and he is from the village of Malarcis. He got his powers from the dark forces by promising them that when he died, they could have his soul." Breanne saw Emiril shiver. "There are rumors, though, that Ogolel passed some of her powers on to him, through some kind of spell she wrote and the mixing of her blood with his. No one is really sure what type of magic he can do. Some say he can only perform spells, and some say he has magic in his blood now and can cast spells without incantations. I personally do not know." She looked at Breanne with a look of concern. "They are only rumors though, as of yet, no one has been able to prove any of it." Breanne felt a chill pass over her, and she too shivered.

"Ok, now that you know who the Dark Mage is, let us move on," Emiril said louder than she had intended. It was perhaps a subconscious way of shrugging off the ominous feeling that had settled over the two of them. "Ogolel and the Dark Mage convinced some of the army to join in with them, and together they tried to take over the kingdom. What Ogolel did not know was that the king knew of this plan because he had become suspicious of Ogolel and had spies watching her every minute of the day. He waited until they made their move and sprung his trap.

"On that day, they came marching right up to the castle gates, and with their small number of followers demanded that the king step down from the throne. The king warned them that they were committing the greatest crime there was, treason against the throne, and that the punishment for their crime was death. He gave them every opportunity to back down and stop their assault. They did not back down however, even though they were outnumbered and stood no chance against the king's army. No one could understand what gave Ogolel her courage to stand against the king that day. Then, she withdrew the book of spells. The king and queen were two of the handful of people who knew what it was. Most people did not know what an evil it was that Ogolel now held."

Emiril said this last statement while looking at Breanne intently. Then suddenly, Breanne gasped, comprehending the look Emiril was giving her. "Do you mean the book that I read, that was the book of spells, the one she had with her?" She said this in awe, eyes and mouth wide open.

"Yes, it was," Emiril said, smiling at Breanne's reaction to this realization. "And inside the book was one of the greatest spells ever written. It had the power to take a living creature and send them from one world to a whole different world, never to be seen again."

"Oh my gosh!" Breanne jumped up once again. "That's the spell that brought me here, isn't it?" her excitement overflowing. "She was going to use it on the king, wasn't she?" Breanne's face was lit up and she could not stand still. She could not believe that she had used the same spell from the story on herself, albeit accidently. But she was not a magician, how could she have worked the spell? She stopped pacing, forced herself to sit down and asked Emiril.

"I am not sure how you were able to work the spell," Emiril said. "I intend to find out, though. But, do you want to hear the end of the story?" she asked.

"Oh, yes, sorry," Breanne said apologetically. "Please finish."

Emiril continued, "Well, there she was, standing in front of the king, book in hand, about to read the spell. But thanks to the spies, the king knew about the book and the spell it contained. He had enlisted the help of another great sorceress to help him defeat Ogolel when the time came. Her name was Mindoneth, and can you guess who she was?"

Breanne thought for a minute. "Was she related to the king?" she asked. Emiril nodded, eyebrows raised in question. Breanne thought some more. "I know," she said, smiling. "I bet it was *his* sister."

Emiril smiled. "Close," she said, "she was his mother." Still smiling, Breanne thought to herself, Wow, mama's here, now Ogolel's going to get it. "You should have seen the look on Ogolel's face when Mindoneth walked out on the steps to join the king," Emiril said with humor in her eyes. "She looked as if she were going to faint."

"Wait a minute," Breanne said, holding up a hand, "wait just a minute, are you trying to tell me you were there?" she asked in disbelief.

Emiril looked at her, puzzled. "Why wouldn't I be?" she said matter-of-factly, "I am the king's daughter, do not forget."

Breanne looked at her skeptically. "Well, wasn't this a long time ago? In fact, didn't you say hundreds of years ago?" she said.

"Yes," Emiril said. "It was, let me think, two hundred and forty-three years, I think. I could be off a few years; I would need to check for sure. Why?"

"Emiril," Breanne said, her eyes wide and mouth gaping. "How old *are* you?"

Emiril looked at her quizzically. "I am four hundred and twenty-eight she said. Why are you looking at me like that?"

Breanne's eyes could not have gotten any wider if she had reached up and pulled them open with her fingers. She looked as if she had just seen Elvis walk by, when everyone knew he was dead. "Four hundred and twenty-eight years old," Breanne said this as a half-statement, half-question. She was in shock and was trying to pull herself together. "Emiril, do you know how long people live where I come from?" she asked. Emiril shook her head. "The oldest person I have ever heard of only lived one hundred and fourteen years, and they were so old they couldn't do anything anymore. In fact, most people don't live past eighty if they are lucky. No one, and I mean no one, lives as long as you are right now. Are you a child? Or are you an adult? How long do elves live for?"

Emiril looked at Breanne with humor. "I am not a child." She said, "I am not exactly sure what you mean by an adult, as you called it, but I am not an elder yet. I will be an elder when I turn five hundred. My father, the king, is an elder; he is eight hundred and twenty years old."

Breanne could not believe this; no way did beings live this long. Of course, these were elves we were talking about, not humans. And she didn't know any elves with which to make a comparison. Maybe they *did* live hundreds of years after all. Although the more she thought about it, didn't the bible talk about people living for hundreds of years, but that was a long time ago; that didn't happen anymore. "How old is the oldest elf then?" she asked.

"Let me think," Emiril said. She looked down and put her finger on her chin. Breanne chuckled inside. She looked sort of like that famous statue, didn't they call it the Thinker or something like that?

"I think the oldest elf I know of lived one thousand and eight years. He was the wisest elf ever. But most elves don't live past nine hundred; some live to be nine hundred forty or so, but not too many." Then she looked at Breanne with pity in her eyes. "I feel sorry for beings who live such short lives. I cannot imagine dying so soon. It must be difficult to bear."

Breanne sat silently now, thinking about her *own* short life. Wow, I had never looked at it this way before, she thought, but really, I guess we do live for a short while. But then again, no one had really felt cheated, because they didn't know elves existed and that they had these wondrously long lives. The way humans aged, though, Breanne thought, how terrible it would be to live for such a long time with wrinkles, false teeth, and gray hair. On the other hand, if they lived longer, maybe they would age better, and the wrinkles would stay away until they were several hundred years old. And maybe they would not have two sets of teeth, but four or six — that way, when the old ones fell out, there would be new ones to take their place, like sharks; this would cut down on the cost of false teeth. Then she thought, think how many kids you could have if you lived to be eight hundred, think how full the earth would be, there wouldn't be any room for anyone to live. Maybe it was a good thing people didn't live so long. She looked at Emiril, who still looked sad.

"Thank you for feeling sorry for us, Emiril," she said, "But honestly, no one knows anything different. We don't realize our life span is so short. I didn't know anything lived as long as you do, so I felt that if I lived to be eighty, that would be a good thing." Even as she said this, though, and now that she knew how long elves lived, she felt a little disappointed in her short life span, even though she knew the earth would not be able to support all those people. "Although," she continued, "the bible talks about people who did live that long once, but that was a very long time ago, and no one has seen anything like it lately."

"What is the bible?" Emiril asked.

"Oh, well, the bible is a written record of our God. It tells us about him and his son, Jesus, and the people who lived thousands of years before us."

"We too have a God," Emiril said reverently. "He is a great being and lives in the vastness of the sky; he created our realm and breathed life into the first elf. He is a great strength to our people. Some believe that is where we elves get our powers from."

Thinking again about the spell that had brought her here, Breanne wondered how she could have made the spell work that night in the attic when she was not a sorceress. There had to be more to it.

"Hey," Emiril said, interrupting her thoughts, "we have not finished the story."

"Yah," Breanne said, smiling. "Your grandma is about to kick Ogolel's butt."

Emiril laughed and began the story once more. "So, as I said, Ogolel almost fainted when she saw Mindoneth walk out and stand beside the king. You see, Ogolel was very powerful, and she would have been a close match for the king alone, but she was no match for both of them. Of course, as scared as she was, she knew that she could not back down either, and that is what scared her the most. If she backed down, she would be put to death immediately. She had to try something. She opened the book of spells, and when she did, the king and Mindoneth, in unison, put their hands together and cast a spell on her. The spell was one of disarming; it was intended to strip her of her powers. But when Ogolel opened the spell book, she wasn't looking for a spell to use against the king anymore; she was looking for a spell with which to escape. Just as the king and Mindoneth's spell hit her, she was reading the last word of *her* spell. She grabbed the Dark Mage's arm, and in a pillar of black smoke and lightning, they vanished. But before they disappeared, we could see that the spell the king and his mother had cast had partially worked. Ogolel had grown older, and her hair had turned partially white, signs that a sorceress is losing her powers.

"We are not sure to what extent her powers were lost, though, and most elves are still afraid she may return someday to try and claim the throne again. That will never happen as long as the king and his mother are alive, though. Now, the only indication of the amount of power she had lost was the fact that as she was fading away, Ogolel dropped the book of spells. But when one of the king's guards ran to retrieve it, it disappeared before he could grab it. We figured she had placed a spell on the book for just such an occasion. We never knew where the book had gone, until now. And no one has heard from her since. We do know where the Dark Mage is, though; he lives on the Island of the Ancestors, but as of yet, we have been unable to go and get him. There is some sort of power that protects the island, and all who try to sail there are never seen again. Until the king can figure out what sort of magic it is, no one is allowed to go there, and the Dark Mage, as far as anyone knows, never leaves the island. And now, unfortunately, you see why Ogolel cannot help you get home. But do not lose hope yet," she said quickly as Breanne's face filled with dread. "There are others who may know how to help you, and I will do everything I can to get you back to your world." Emiril looked at Breanne; Breanne looked back at Emiril, and they both knew that a deep friendship was starting between them.

50

Chapter 10
Edlin's Kindness

The mist swirled around the pond, first enveloping the trees on one side, then releasing its hold on those and enveloping the trees on the other. It gave the appearance that the pond was moving, gliding effortlessly through the forest, sliding onward to a destination unknown to its inhabitants. The snakes, frogs, and insects that lived there did not seem alarmed by this. Wherever they were going, it did not matter to them; they were content living in their pond, no matter where it took them. What did matter, however, and what they did not know, was the fact that their secret world was about to be invaded. Invaded by an evil so vile, none of them would survive.

Since the death of the creature, the Dark Mage had been working on a new spell. This new spell was very difficult to conjure, and it had taken all of his skill to perfect it. Now, after weeks of hard work, he was prepared to use it. He had gathered all the ingredients required; some were collected at the expense of others' lives. He had gotten the incantation just right. All that was left was to find the perfect birthing place, and he had found it.

The moon, shining on the pond, cast its reflection back into the dark meadow; the mist reflected the light back several times, allowing the faintest moonlight to illuminate more than it ordinarily would have. Illuminated in this moonlight was a dark figure cloaked in black, hood pulled over his head, black eyes probing the darkness. He was walking silently through the trees at the far end of the meadow, glancing around furtively for signs of other people. He needed complete solitude if he was going to complete this spell, but more importantly, solitude was needed for the subduing of the creature he was about to call up. One misstep and he would be killed. He saw no one.

The chosen spot was on the opposite end of the meadow from where he now emerged from the trees, and he crossed quickly, feeling vulnerable in the openness. Somewhere nearby, a screech owl alerted to his presence filled the night with a warning call; a doe with her fawn bounded silently deeper into the woods, seeking safety from the approaching evil. The frogs suddenly sensed the intruder and stopped calling to one another; a snake slithered across the pond and landed on the opposite shore, where it quickly disappeared into the forest. All had become deathly quiet. The Dark Mage stood on the bank of the pond and stared into the black, murky water.

For an hour, he stood motionless, eyes glazed over, looking for all intents and purposes as if he were dead, yet standing, kept somehow from falling lifeless beside the water; a stone statue in the dark meadow. He focused his attention on the far reaches of the spirit world, the world where all manner of dark creatures reside; its doorway just beyond the reach of his world, accessible by only the most powerful magic. Unassisted, the creatures could not cross the threshold into his world, but now they lurked by the doorway he had opened with his mind, waiting, as if knowing their chance to escape their dark world had come. Patiently, he searched the darkness, he searched the hoard of creatures gathered together, searched for the one creature that was more powerful than all the rest, the one he would bring to his world. His wait ended when the creature suddenly and viciously forced its way into his mind, ripping and clawing at his sanity, trying to overpower him and pass through the doorway.

His eyes flew open as he stumbled and nearly fell into the pond. His mind fought the creature, keeping it at bay. If it overpowered him, he would die, and the beast would be unable to cross over. But the beast did not know this; it saw the open door, the Dark Mage barring the way, and it wanted in. So, it ripped and tore at his mind, trying to rip a hole in the mental lining that formed the barrier between his world and freedom.

As quickly as he could, the Dark Mage removed the items from the bag he had been holding. He held them up in the misty moonlight one at a time, reciting parts of the spell over certain objects, after which he threw each one into the pond. The pond itself started to churn and boil, steam rising from its surface; the inhabitants of the pond, now turned into a caldron, began to cook. The pond became a graveyard for its many residents; other creatures, more fortunate, ran or flew away into the darkness of the woods as fast as they could. The air was turning hot, and the Dark Mage began to sweat. Great droplets of blood fell from his forehead. The blood was a side effect of using his magic, a magic given to him by the dark forces themselves, to be repaid upon his death with his very soul.

He was fortunate; the creature he fought was indeed strong, the strongest he had ever encountered in the spirit world. After acquiring his magical abilities, he had journeyed there many times to train with his new powers, where no one would see, and to learn the secrets that that world had to offer. It was during one of these training exercises that he had learned how to bring the creatures into his world. The first time he had tried it, before he could unlock the door, the creature had nearly killed him, and he had needed to break the connection or die. The second time, he managed to bring the creature over, but had not been able to subdue it, and he had had to kill it. The third time, however, everything had gone perfectly; he had brought the creature over, subdued it, and it was his. He had been one with the creature; this connection allowed him to navigate through his world without leaving his island refuge. He could read the creature's thoughts, see what it saw; it was an invaluable weapon, would do as commanded, even kill on command. Then someone had killed it, nearly killing him in the process. He wasn't sure who the killer was, but he was going to find out, and when he did, he was going to make them pay. Now he needed a new creature; he needed help finding them, the horse and rider whom he had been searching for all this time. He almost had them; he had seen them through the creature's eyes. One more minute and they would have been in his grasp, and she would have been pleased. She would have given him praise and honor, but that was stolen from him by the killer. The killer had made her angry with him, and she had threatened to kill him.

He tensed, his anger growing, and for a second, he lost his concentration in his fight with the creature. It took the opportunity to intensify its attack, nearly overcoming him, and he had to use all his willpower to keep the creature at bay. His anger was now replaced by a growing fear, fear that when the time came, he would not be able to subdue the creature; and fear that if he could not subdue it, he would not be able to kill it, before it killed him.

Gaining control once again, he focused on completing the spell. He concluded the incantation with a broad sweep of his arms, then stuck them straight out in front of him, palms up, and the door began to open. The creature burst through, before the last of the mental restraint had been removed, before the door was completely opened, tearing it to pieces, the Dark Mage felt as if he would go mad. Water exploded from the pond in the form of a boiling geyser forty feet tall, the inside of which was black. Inside its watery womb, the creature waited, waited to enter this new world, waited to be reborn. Then the geyser began to take on a new form, growing wings and a tail, black as the night sky. Even without their body, the wings began to beat and the powerful wind they generated threatened to knock the Dark Mage off his feet. If the spell was broken now, while the creature was between worlds, they would both be lost in the in-between, a world of total blackness, void of all noise. A person's mind was lost in that abyss, their body and all their senses rendered useless. There was no escape from the in-between, a fate worse than death itself; it was a living death. He had to stand firm and not lose control. The water began to recede into the pond, and slowly a shape took form. There was now a body to accommodate the wings and tail. There were large, tree-stump-sized legs, ending in feet with long, razor-sharp claws. All but a small portion of the water had re-entered the pond; the creature, writhing and struggling, was now almost entirely free of the spirit world. The Dark Mage watched in awe as a long neck began to grow out of the body, snaking upwards; the deeper black of the creature silhouetted against the night sky. The neck continued to grow, then it began to widen and twist around until it formed the shape of a head. The eyes started as a red glow floating in midair, and then, as if suddenly catching up, the bone and skin formed around them. The mouth was the last part of the creature to appear, the teeth gleaming white in the moonlight, each one twelve inches of death. The Dark Mage had only minutes now in which to subdue the creature while it was still in a state of confusion upon being reborn into his world, or it would be a fight to the death, and he wasn't convinced he would win.

Chapter 11
The First Battle

"Now that I have told you about the book, I want to know more about you," Emiril said. "What is your world like? What about your family, do they know where you are?"

Upon hearing her last question, Breanne once again found herself fighting back tears, a never-ending battle lately. "My world is very different from yours," she started. "We live on what we call a planet, and there are many land masses called continents, which are surrounded by vast oceans. Each continent has different races of people on it."

"You mean like here, we have Orcs, Dwarves, Elves and so on?" Emiril asked.

"Well, sort of. But we are all people, just different in color or language. It's hard to explain," she said. "In your world, an elf is different from a man, but in our world, all people are the same thing, a person, but…Oh this is useless, I'm not explaining it right."

"Yes, actually you are," Emiril said quickly. "I understand. Here, there are men, but the men who live in the North speak a different language than the men who live in the South. And their hair is dark; the men in the South have light hair. But like you said about your people, they are not different species, they are all men."

"Yes!" Breanne said, "the same species, I should have used that term. We are all the same species and yet we live like we are not." She thought about that for a minute. Why did people live this way? Why did they choose to separate and pretend they were not the same as each other? If people lived as one species, wouldn't they get along better? She looked at Emiril, "Do the men who live here get along?" she asked.

"Yes they do, especially if they need to go to war, they fight together; but never against each other. Do your people fight against each other?" Emiril asked, her eyes betraying her astonishment at the thought.

Breanne was ashamed to admit it, but she told her they did, and when Emiril asked why, she did not have an answer for her; there was no good one to give, only greed. People were greedy she thought, they only wanted more for themselves and were willing to fight someone else to get it. Well, maybe not all people were like that, but most of them were.

"Tell me about your family," Emiril said, quickly changing the topic. Breanne looked up at her, and when Emiril saw the look that had replaced the last one in Breanne's eyes, she thought to herself that the topic change had only gotten worse. She looked like she was going to cry. Emiril was sorry she had asked the question but it was too late.

"I live with my mom and dad," Breanne said in a wavering voice, her lip trembling visibly. "I have two brothers and a sister. No, my family doesn't know where I am. My brothers and sister and I were staying with my grandparents when…." she paused, wiped her eyes with the back of her hand, took a deep breath and continued, "when I came here. I don't even know how long I have been gone or if my parents are back from their honeymoon yet. They might not even know I'm missing," she finished quietly.

Emiril looked at Breanne with tears in her own eyes now and thought to herself, the poor thing, I don't care what it takes, I am going to get her home to her family. She stood up; Breanne watched as she walked to her horse and in one graceful leap, she was sitting in the saddle. Wow, that was impressive, Breanne thought, her mood lightning. Emiril was cool.

"Well, are you coming?" Emiril asked.

"You're going to take me with you?" Breanne yelled, jumping up excitedly.

"Of course I am, silly. Did you really think I was going to leave you out here; you'd be dead in no time, you can't even hear a giant horse walk up behind you," she said and laughed heartedly.

Breanne laughed too, her face red with embarrassment, and walked over to the horse. She looked up to where Emiril was seated—it seemed like she was on top of a mountain—and thought, this is not going to be easy, the horse must be fifteen feet tall (dramatic she thought, he is definitely not that tall, but close). "How do I get up there?" she finally asked Emiril.

"Jump," came the reply.

"Yah right," she said with a notable sound of condemnation in her voice. "You expect way too much from me, you know. I saw you jump up there, I can't do that. You're joking, right?"

"No, really," Emiril said encouragingly, "jump."

"Then how, do you mean, jump up straight, or a running jump?" Breanne asked, confused and thinking to herself that Emiril was crazy.

"Just jump straight up," Emiril said with conviction.

"All right," Breanne muttered. But it isn't going to work, she thought to herself. I'm just going to batter myself against the horse until he, or was it she, gets mad and stomps me to death. Then Emiril will see that I was right, that I can't jump up there like she did. She stopped thinking about getting stomped to death and did as Emiril asked, she jumped straight up beside the horse. Although she jumped as high as she could, she only managed to get about a foot off the ground, not even high enough to get a good hold of the saddle. Should have paid more attention in PE, she thought, this is going to hurt. She squeezed her eyes shut tight and waited, then suddenly realized she was not falling back down as she had expected she would, but she was in fact, falling up. What the… wait a minute, people don't fall up, they fall down. What was going on? In a few seconds, she was high enough that she could swing her leg over the back of the horse and she did so quickly, grabbing Emiril's waist as well. She wobbled some, and almost slipped off the other side, then finally, got herself situated in the middle of the horse's enormous back. Only then did she notice Emiril laughing and thought to herself, so much for first impressions. "How did you do that?" she asked.

"Do what?" Emiril asked, still laughing.

"You know what, and keep laughing, you wise elf," Breanne said. Wise elf, she thought, where did that come from?

"I'm an elf, or should I say a wise elf," Emiril said still laughing "I can do magic, remember. I thought you were going to go over the other side there for a minute though." She laughed harder. "Are you ready?"

"Yeah, I'm ready," Breanne said, chuckling with her now. "I must have looked funny," she added.

"Yes, you did," Emiril said, laughing harder still, her lavender eyes gleaming brightly.

They turned away from the stream and started down the road in the direction Breanne had been heading before. Well, she thought to herself, at least I was going the right way.

They hadn't gone far when Breanne suddenly thought of something, and she no longer felt embarrassed about not hearing Emiril approach at the stream. She had a feeling she knew why she hadn't heard them and she asked Emiril, "When you came to the stream, did you use your magic to make it so I wouldn't hear you?"

"I wondered how long it would take you to figure that out," Emiril said teasingly. "I have all kinds of tricks up my sleeve. The ones you've seen so far are just small ones. Wait until you see something big," she said proudly.

Breanne smiled and thought, she is going to make that magician from home look like an amateur.

"Where are we going?" she asked, looking around at the scenery. It was much nicer traveling this road on horseback than it had been trudging along on foot, under the searing sun like before. (Almost dramatic she told herself, remembering all too well how thirsty she had been and therefore giving herself some leeway.)

"We are going to Ethuanova to see that friend of mine I told you about, remember?"

"Oh yes, I remember," Breanne said.

"If I don't go, he will wonder what happened to me and he will get worried. Besides, we have some important things to talk about, now more than ever." Breanne heard a slight foreboding in her voice.

Breanne thought how great it would be to have a phone right about now. Then they could just call her friend and tell him they couldn't make it. Of course, she didn't really see how it mattered; she had nowhere else to go anyway.

She once again looked at her surroundings. There was a forest on their right, and she assumed it must be large because it had been there since she had started traveling this road. To the left, there was open grassland but off in the distance, it looked as if there could be more trees of some sort, and it looked like a haze hung in the sky over them. She thought about the map in the book. "Hey Emiril, do you know anything about the map in the book?"

"I have not seen inside the book. What sort of map was it?"

"Well, it was a map of a world. I can't remember any of the names. Oh, wait I do remember the mountains were named after a bird, but I can't remember the name of the bird," she said with frustration.

"Was it a Sarr bird?" Emiril asked.

"Yes! That was it," Breanne said happily. "Do you have mountains here with that name in them?"

"Yes we do, the Spires of the Sarr Birds," Emiril said, pointing off to the left and slightly ahead of where they were. "If you look over there, you can make out some of the higher peaks. Can you see them?"

Breanne looked intently across the field and into the horizon. She squinted her eyes against the glare of the sun. She could just make out the tops of the mountains Emiril was pointing to. "Emiril, that book had a map of your world in it," Breanne said excitedly. "I can't remember the names of most of the places, but I remember what the world looked like, and I remember the place where you live because you said it was south of where we are. It must be the place on the bottom of the map. And Emiril, what is a Sarr bird?" She had remembered the question from the attic, when she had first looked at the map; she hoped the answer would be as exciting as she thought it would be.

"A long time ago, this time before me," Emiril said playfully. "A young elf fell in love with a beautiful young girl. His father did not approve because she was not an elf, but he loved her and courted her anyway. On one of their upcoming outings, he wanted to prove to her how much he loved her, by giving her something unique, something no one else had or could have. He thought long and hard and finally decided to create a bird for her. One that was as beautiful as it was unique. The bird was a brown color and its beak and feet were green, the tail feathers were very long and majestic, but the most unique thing about the bird

61

upon first observation, was the fact that it had four feet; other than that, it wasn't that much different than some of the other birds around here. He gave a mated pair to the girl that evening, but to his dismay, the girl thought the bird was ugly and turned it away. Broken hearted, the young elf took the birds and left, never to see her again. He went up into the mountains that night and let the birds go free. It was only then, by the light of the moon that the real beauty of the birds was revealed. When they flew into the sky, they shone brightly the color of gold and their beaks and legs glowed an emerald green. The reason for this was that the birds were created using real gold and emeralds. And when a Sarr bird loses a feather and it falls to the ground, it turns into pure gold, and if you find a Sarr bird that has died, you find a pile of golden feathers and emeralds; the emeralds were its beak and feet. When the girl found this out, she realized what she had turned down. How could that elf make such a fool of her? She was livid and she tried to rekindle her relationship with the young elf so that he would give her the birds back. But the birds had not only been a token of his love for her, but a test of her love for him, and she had failed the test. He turned her away just as she had turned the birds away. Everyone spoke of what a fool she had been and to this day people remember the story. These days, when you are close enough to the mountains at night, you can see the Sarr birds flying around the spires, glowing golden in the moonlight, and that is how the mountains got their name."

"Wow," Breanne said. "Is that a fake story or a real story?" she asked.

"Oh, it's true, all right," Emiril said. "I found a golden feather once. Most of the time the birds stay so high up in the mountains it is almost impossible to find any, let alone the body of a dead one. But once, when I was traveling to the Tomb of Father Forr for the funeral of a friend of mine, I found one. The tomb is only about halfway up the mountain, so it was relatively unusual to find one there. I still have it, and when people say they don't believe me, I show it to them."

"Do you have it with you now?" Breanne asked, wanting very badly to see it.

"No, sorry," Emiril said, chuckling. "It was one of the tail feathers so it is very long and heavy, hard to pack that on a horse. But when we get home, I will show it to you."

Home, Breanne thought, "Are we going to go to your home, Emiril? Is that what you mean?"

"Yes, after we meet my friend, we will go to my home and you can meet my father. He will be very interested to hear how you came here."

Breanne thought how wonderful it would be to meet a king. Then she got nervous, she had never met a king before.

Chapter 12
Wings in the Night

The pain was intense. Grabbing his head, he stumbled backward, tripping on an exposed tree root. He almost fell, then recovered his balance at the last minute. He screamed out loud, animals roaming the woods, ran in terror. The creature was so powerful, too powerful. He had locked minds with it, had tried to subdue it quickly, but the creature had been waiting, waiting for just that moment. It had grabbed hold of his mind before he had even realized the connection was made. And now, they were locked in a battle, a battle the Dark Mage knew, was to the death. He cried out again as the creature clawed at the fabric of his mind; his body was trembling and great droplets of blood coursed down his face. He was losing, the realization was sickening. He was going to die beside this pond in the middle of the woods, at the hands of the creature *he* had summoned. He tried one last time to wrest his mind from the creature's grasp. For a second, he thought he could feel the creature's grip loosening. Hope welled in him, but then it was back in full force. He fell to the ground, hands gripping his head, body writhing in agony.

It was then, in the last few seconds before he gave up the fight and surrendered to the spirits, who had been standing nearby watching this struggle, that he felt the creature's grasp on his mind suddenly rip away. One minute, he was in the death grip of the creature, and then suddenly, he was free. He breathed in deeply, his mind clearing quickly.

"Get up, you fool!"

He heard the voice and immediately his blood ran cold. He almost wished he *were* dead.

"Get up!" the voice screamed again.

He got to his feet as quickly as he could and almost toppled over when dizziness overwhelmed him. He glanced around looking for her. She was standing on the opposite side of the pond from him. Her body old and frail looking; he could feel her anger from where he stood and had to stop himself from running away. It wouldn't do any good, he thought; she would stop me before I got ten feet.

"Focus your mind," she said harshly. "Concentrate."

He could see the creature, it was halfway through the doorway, staring at him with a look that had literally almost killed him, and if the creature had its way, *would* kill him. It suddenly lunged at the opening between the two worlds and he jumped back instinctively.

"Now!" she screamed in rage.

He closed his eyes and willed himself to search for the creature. The fear of her was greater than the fear of it, so he fought the urge to turn and run. Then, in the deepest darkness, he found it. The creature, sensing the man, once again rushed towards his mind, ready to finish what it had started. The Dark Mage braced for the impact, but unlike before, something held the creature back, mere inches from him. He relaxed a little, and wondered to himself what had happened. Then he felt a power so great it was hard to bear, realizing then that she was here. She was the one who had pulled the creature back the first time. She had saved his life. With her here, the creature could not kill him; he knew that her power was too great; she would not allow that to happen. There was a part of him who was elated and a part of him who resented it. He had wanted to subdue the creature on his own, but it had nearly killed him. He knew he would never be as powerful as she was, and he resented that too.

He felt her prod his mind and he focused on the creature. This time, he could feel something new emanating from it—fear—not of him, but fear of her. He almost felt sorry for the creature then, he knew that fear all too well.

He grabbed the creature's mind with his own and she helped hold it. He focused his will upon the creature who tried to struggle, but was held tight by the pair. You will do my bidding, his will commanded, you will obey me. The creature felt itself being consumed by the will of this man he had almost killed, and it grew angry. His kill had been stolen from him, his freedom too. Growing angrier, the anger overpowering the fear he now felt, he turned his attention to the woman who had taken that from him. He clawed at her mind; she did not flinch. He struggled violently; he could not shake her grip on his mind. Then he felt the other one taking advantage of his distraction, grab his mind tighter and his own will started to diminish. He fought for his life against the two sorcerers who had gripped his mind, but to no avail. Their thoughts entered his, overpowering them. They forced his mind to step back into the far reaches of his soul and they took up residence in the space left empty. He could only watch now as his essence slipped farther and farther away. And as they inhabited his mind, he could not help but respond to their every command. They were in charge of him now, mentally and physically. He surrendered in defeat and in the same moment, the Dark Mage collapsed by the side of the pond.

Chapter 13
The Hidden Glen

They travelled north all day. Breanne, who was not used to riding a horse, was beginning to wish she had walked instead; her bottom hurt something fierce. The trees on their right were a constant view for the pair. What a huge forest that must be, she thought, glad she had not gone the other way on the road and entered it instead. She was sure she would have gotten lost, or eaten by some kind of weird animal (A little dramatic, well, maybe considering where she found herself, it could happen, couldn't it?). The view on their left however, had changed as they progressed north. What first had been open grassland, had begun to fill in with trees; groves of oak and aspen, interspersed with maple and birch, were now turning steadily into a thick forest of firs similar to the one on the right. She wondered how much longer it would take to reach Ethuanova. She wasn't sure she'd be able to walk again if it took too much longer. She shifted from one side of her bottom to the other, trying to ease the pain.

Emiril, sensing Breanne's discomfort, turned over her shoulder and smiled. "It is only a little way farther," she said. "Should not take another half hour or so."

"Thank God," Breanne said. "I don't know how much longer my bottom can hold out." She smiled, a little embarrassed. "I am not used to riding a horse."

Emiril laughed. "Well, if it is any consolation, my bottom still hurts sometimes too."

Just as Emiril had predicted, after about a half hour, the smell of wood smoke filled Breanne's nostrils. She perked up, looking around for its origin. She didn't see anything until they rounded a corner in the road and entered a thicker cover of trees. At first, her eyes had trouble picking out the houses through the trees, then as she became accustomed to the lower light conditions, she saw first one, then two and finally several small wooden structures built under the cover of the tree canopies. She saw small children laughing, running from one house to another, a black and white dog yapping cheerily at their heels. Women sat in front of these houses, engaged in all sorts of different activities, such as peeling potatoes, hanging clothes out to dry and stoking fires, by which racks of meat hung drying. She smiled at the ones who looked up from their tasks to watch them pass; they did not smile back, but instead gave them a look of distrust, bordering on threatening, they looked as if they were planning to jump them, kill them and eat them (Way too dramatic, she scolded), but she started to feel afraid anyway.

"Emiril," she whispered in the elf's ear, "why are they looking at us like that?"

"Hang in there," Emiril whispered back, "almost there, will explain then."

Breanne did not realize at first, but she had tightened her grip on Emiril's waist so much that she now realized it must have been uncomfortable for the elf so she loosened it. She tried not to look at the women who were now intently watching them, but found it hard not to look at the children laughing and playing. They were every bit as human looking as she was. They were dark haired, most of them, but occasionally she did see red hair; however, she saw only one child with blonde hair, a young girl who smiled sweetly at her, making her feel less afraid, and less like she was about to get eaten. She was a beautiful child and Breanne could not help but notice the girl had bright blue eyes.

When the horse came to an unexpected stop, her head slammed into Emiril's back, the chainmail scraping her chin. She looked at Emiril who had turned her head back to say something.

"Time to get down," Emiril said. She reached across her stomach and then back with her right hand, offering it to Breanne. "Grab hold, swing your right leg over and slide down using my arm like a rope," she said. "It is easier to get off than on, no magic this time." She said this and smiled, still amused by Breanne's reaction when she had helped her mount the horse.

Breanne had not forgotten, and smiled back with a look that said, very funny. She did as instructed and was down safely in two seconds; getting down *was* much easier, she thought to herself.

Then Emiril gracefully leaped from the horse's back and was standing beside her, as if she had put no effort into it at all. Breanne was once again impressed, and jealous, by the gracefulness of the woman.

"Let's go," Emiril said and started walking towards a structure that was larger than the others. Smoke came out a chimney located on the roof and unlike the other houses she had seen, it was round. She saw no windows, which to her was quite odd. There was a large porch that circled the building; she wasn't sure if it went entirely around, as she could not see the other side of the structure. She could hear loud talking, followed by boisterous laughter emanating from within and she wondered if it was a house or some sort of community building. Her question was answered when Emiril crossed the porch and without knocking, opened the big door. Light spilled out of the opening, bathing them in a yellow glow. Even standing on her tip toes, Breanne could not see over Emiril's shoulder. The elf was at least six inches taller than she, but she could hear many different voices, indicating several people were inside. She could also smell smoke from a fire, and best of all, food. She realized now how empty her stomach was, and involuntarily placed both

69

hands over the spot that felt the emptiest. Emiril hesitated in the doorway for a moment and Breanne noticed she seemed to be looking for something, or someone. She must have found it or them, because she stepped inside, motioning for Breanne to follow; which she quickly did, letting the door close behind them.

Emiril led them across a room full of tables, where men sat talking and laughing. She noticed they had tall mugs of some kind of drink and some had big plates of food. Her stomach growled loudly upon seeing this bounty and she was not sure whether Emiril heard it or not.

On the far wall was a long counter which had a small man behind it. He was scurrying back and forth, filling mugs and handing them to a lovely woman, who in turn would take them to the tables where the men would give the lovely woman a pat on her bottom as well as money, in a currency Breanne did not recognize.

On her way back to the counter, the woman caught Breanne's eye and smiled at her. Breanne smiled back and decided she liked this woman. She was wearing a long red dress which looked like it was made from satin. The light shone on the material, and the dress seemed to shimmer when the woman walked. The bodice was cut low and Breanne tried not to look at the woman's protruding bosom. She had a very nice figure and the dress fit her snugly. She also noted that the woman's hair was red; it was one of her features that made her so beautiful, and the other was her blue eyes, much the same color as the girls outside, she thought.

Breanne stopped short, almost bumping into Emiril, who had stopped beside a table where a very large, blonde-haired man sat, slowly sipping at a mug filled with an amber liquid. He was wearing a coat made from some kind of animal fur, mostly white, with different hues of brown and some black mixed in; it looked soft. He had a brown shirt on under the coat, like the dress the woman wore, this shirt also looked

70

like it was made of satin, and soft leather pants much like what they were wearing. His boots too, seemed to be much the same fashion as theirs, only more masculine. His hair was long and drawn back in a ponytail, his beard close cut. He looked to be around thirty years old, Breanne thought. He was very tan and muscular. She thought if he stood up, he would be at least six feet tall, probably taller.

"I see you still live," he said to Emiril, a blank expression on his face.

"Yes," she said, also with a blank face, "as do you."

"I see you are not alone," he continued with a look of interest just barely noticeable in his eyes.

"No, I am not." She looked at Breanne, who immediately turned a vivid red from embarrassment. She hated being the center of attention. "This is Breanne."

The man looked at her. Breanne saw instantly that his remarkably blue eyes were full of intelligence. He stared straight into her eyes and what seemed deeper still, until she felt he would enter her soul. She began to feel a flutter in her head, feeling a little dizzy, she didn't know what was happening; when it appeared he would not enter her soul, she finally looked away. The fluttery feeling left her immediately. He smiled at Emiril, who nodded back.

"Sit, sit," he said jovially.

Breanne was not sure about this man, but Emiril seemed to know him and trust him. She relaxed a little, knowing Emiril would not let anything happen to her, or at least she thought she knew that. So, she sat with them, Emiril across from the man and Breanne beside her. "Do you want a drink of something?" Emiril asked Breanne.

71

Breanne's expression suddenly changed; Emiril saw on her face a combination of eagerness and discomfort. She was looking at Emiril, eyebrows raised, and then she looked at the man and then back at Emiril. She wanted to say something, that much was evident, but Emiril could see that it was for hears only. She smiled, held a finger up to the man, who was watching with both interest and amusement, and leaned over to Breanne. "What's the matter?" she whispered.

Breanne looked at her new friend. It was hard to say this, as she considered it to be rude but, she had no choice. "Emiril," she whispered back, "I am really sorry, I don't want to make you feel uncomfortable, but I don't have any money." She looked at Emiril embarrassed, and then she glanced furtively at the man, hoping he had not heard.

Emiril smiled at her, what a sweet child she really was. Before she even realized she was going to do it, she reached out and hugged Breanne. "Don't you worry about that," she whispered in her ear as caringly as she could. "I know your situation and I don't want you to worry about that while you are here. It is not your fault." As an afterthought, she said, "Besides that, I am a princess, I am rich." She straightened up and looked at Breanne, winking.

Breanne had tears of gratefulness in her eyes. She smiled at Emiril. "I really am thirsty," she said, "what do they have here?"

Emiril thought for a moment, and then said, "Mostly they serve different types of ale," at which point Breanne decided they must be in a tavern. "But I don't think that you drink ale," she said. Breanne wrinkled her nose and shook her head, Emiril smiled at her. "They did once serve a drink that was made from the fruit of the Erum plant; it was sweet and made your stomach warm when you drank it. Do they still have that here?" she asked looking at the man. He looked at Emiril, and she knew none of what had just transpired had gotten past him, he nodded and Emiril waved the lovely woman over to their table.

Breanne was a little surprised that when the woman approached, Emiril addressed her by name. "Iola, it is good to see you," she said affectionately. "We would like to order a couple of drinks. One yellow ale and one of those drinks made from the fruit of the Erum plant, please."

"It is good to see you as well," Iola said and once again smiled at Breanne. "Who is your friend?"

"Iola, this is Breanne. Breanne, meet Iola. I was going to introduce you to this big lug here in a minute," she said to Breanne as she gestured to the blond-haired man, "but now's as good a time as any. This is Marcus, my friend I told you about. Iola is his wife."

"It is nice to meet you, Breanne," Iola said nodding.

"And you too," Breanne said and she got that feeling again, that she was going to like this woman.

"Well, two drinks coming up," Iola said, turned and walked back to the counter.

"I am glad to meet you as well, Breanne," Marcus said from across the table. His blue eyes sparkled in the light from the oil lamp sitting on the table. Breanne couldn't help but notice again how beautiful they were. She suddenly realized she was staring and she looked away blushing. Marcus smiled to himself. He was used to people looking at him this way, his looks made him stick out in a crowd. He looked at Emiril. "Is this the reason you are late?" he said, indicating Breanne. "I was beginning to think the worst, and twice Iola asked me to go look for you. She can be quite determined. I think in another hour I would have met you on the road," he laughed.

"Yes, she can be, but that is what makes you love her, don't forget." Emiril smiled and then said, "Yes, the reason I am late is because I got held up." She looked at Breanne out of the corner of her eye and then gave him a look that said, she would explain it all later. He nodded and drank some more of his ale.

Breanne sat there trying not to be irritated. She didn't know if they thought they were being clandestine, thinking she did not understand what they were talking about, or if they were worried about the other people in the room. She decided to give them the benefit of the doubt and assume it was other people they were concerned about. She looked around the room, surveying the crowd, they were ordinary looking enough. Dark hair, average build, no one really stood out. She realized then just how different Marcus really was compared to the rest of the people here. His blond hair and blue eyes… she remembered then that Emiril had said the Northern people were darker haired than the Southerners. So, Marcus must be from the South, but why was he up here? It was probably because of Iola, she thought, she had red hair, she was probably a Northerner.

Her thoughts were interrupted when she noticed a man across the room, sitting by himself. He wore the hood to his cloak over his head so she could not see any of his characteristics except that he was of slighter build than the others in the room. She realized then that she was staring at him. She couldn't help herself; she knew it was rude, but she couldn't help it. She could tell though that he was staring at her too. She couldn't see his face, but she could feel his eyes on her just the same. She willed herself to look away, alarmed by this man who felt wrong. She didn't know what exactly she meant by that, but she just knew she felt something when she looked at him that wasn't right. She waited a moment, acting casual, and then she leaned over closer to Emiril and quietly said, "Don't look right now, but do you see that man across the room with the hood on?"

Emiril looked at Breanne in astonishment. What keen instincts she has, she thought. "Don't look at him again, ok. Don't even think about him, because he can read your thoughts if they are unguarded. I have known about him since we came in. I will explain it all later." She smiled reassuringly at the girl. Inside however, she was beginning to worry. She knew the man could not read hers or Marcus' thoughts, but he could read Breanne's; she was like an open book, she knew, because Marcus had read some of it already. And if he could, so could the man across the room. She needed to get out of here without drawing attention to the two of them. If she got up and left now, after Breanne's comment, he would surely know, just as he already knew Breanne had discovered him, that they had something to hide. So, she sat there talking with Marcus as if nothing was wrong, and tried to shield the girl the best she could.

Iola showed up with their drinks just in time to diffuse the tension. "Here we are," she said pleasantly. She placed the drinks on the table and then looked back at the man behind the counter to see if he was watching. When she was sure he wasn't, she leaned over and stole a kiss from Marcus. Emiril laughed and told her she was going to report her.

"Don't you dare, Emiril," she said jokingly, "if you do, I won't cook supper for you this evening." She looked at Breanne and winked. "I'll still cook for you though, Breanne."

Breanne smiled back, partly because of the joking and partly because the thought of food and eating thrilled her; she was starving. She forgot about the little man, for now.

Marcus patted Iola's bottom when she turned to go. Breanne saw tenderness and love in his eyes. She thought to herself, he must be a good husband. She looked at the drink that had been placed in front of her. It was steaming, she smelled it, it smelled delicious. She could smell cinnamon and cloves. It smelled similar to apple cider. She stuck the tip of her tongue in the liquid; it tastes like apples, she thought. She picked up the mug and took a sip. This is exactly what apple cider tasted like she concluded. She realized she had drunk half the mug in seconds and then made herself slow down and savor it. Emiril noticed that the drink was a hit with Breanne; she would remember that in the future.

Her stomach half full of, what she was going to call apple cider, Breanne sat watching as Emiril sipped her ale slowly, and chatted idly with Marcus about hunting, and weather and all manner of things that adults seemed to talk about in order to bore their children. She was still young enough that their conversation had this same effect on her. She turned her attention elsewhere and began to study the room, it was round, and tables were positioned on the walls and in the center of the room. The counter ran in a half circle along one wall matching the curvature of the wall. Behind the counter there were shelves with mugs and plates and bowls lining them. There were two doors, the one they came in and one behind the counter. The latter seemed only to be for the workers. She wondered where it went, then saw Iola come through it with a plate of food and figured it must go to a kitchen. Along the wall opposite the counter there was a large fireplace, she watched as flames engulfed a log that had to be three feet long. The flames, orange, yellow and blue in spots, seemed to dance in a rhythmic motion as they gingerly coerced, then eagerly consumed their prey. Her eyes glazed and she could not look away from the spectacle of life and death being played out in the fireplace. She felt her head start to swirl. Who are you? her mind echoed. Strange, she thought, the flames grew more vicious in their eagerness to satiate their hunger. Who are you? the thought was strong in her mind, almost forceful. Who am I, she thought in a trance, who am I? Thoughts started to form in her mind, she could see the attic, she could hear her grandfather's voice calling to her, "Breanne!" His voice turning more urgent, she could see the table in the attic, covered with papers. "Breanne!" "Who are you?" She felt confused, as if she were being pulled in two directions. "Who are you?" forcefully, commanding. "Breanne! Breanne!" her grandfather calling, the attic shaking. "Who are you?" Violent shaking, the table in the attic began to bounce up and down on the floor, the book slid from one end to the other. "Breanne!" The voice was no longer that of her grandfather's, her vision started to return, the trance was fading. "Breanne!" Through the haze, she saw Emiril looking at her, her face distorted in concern. Emiril shook her gently once more. She blinked her eyes and looked quizzically at the elf. "What's wrong?" she said groggily.

"Breanne, look at me!" Emiril said urgently.

Breanne, now more awake, looked at her friend. "I feel funny," she said.

"I know," Emiril said gently, "don't take your eyes off of me." She looked deeply into Breanne's eyes and Breanne could feel her friend reach into her mind. She started to get scared, but the look on Emiril's face was one of concern. Breanne realized something must be wrong and she sat still, staring into Emiril's face, while Emiril searched her mind. She sat for what seemed like hours to her, but was actually only a few seconds, when she felt a small flutter inside her head and an oppressive force she had not realized was there leave her. Emiril blinked and then looked at Breanne. She smiled, but Breanne knew it was a forced smile. She started to say something and Emiril shook her head no to quiet her. Breanne felt as if she were half in a trance. She noticed that Marcus was no longer seated with them. She was going to ask Emiril where he had gone, but remembered she was supposed to be quiet. Emiril just sat there, silently beside her, looking into her eyes, watching, but for what she didn't know.

"He is gone now, I could not catch him," Marcus said, suddenly appearing behind Emiril. "Is she safe now?" he asked Emiril, concern in his voice.

"I believe so," Emiril said. It was only then that she took her eyes off Breanne and turned to Marcus. "You know what this means, do you not?" she asked him, fear etched into her face.

"Yes," he said, Emiril's fears showing in his face as well. "She will know about her now." He looked at Breanne as he said this; it made Breanne's blood run cold.

Chapter 14
Secrets of Mindoneth

Eassa ran as fast as his short legs could go, but the blond man was much taller and was gaining on him. He dodged around trees and scurried under bushes. Branches and thorns left welts on his exposed skin, blood seeped out of the deepest wounds; he did not feel the pain. He ran for his life. If the blond man caught him, he would surely kill him; he did not have to read his mind to know that, so he ran.

Two miles into the chase, he started to slow. He chanced looking behind him and saw the blond man still running strong behind him. He was losing his head start, and the small amount of time he gained by being shorter and able to scramble under things faster than the blond man, was beginning to be less of an advantage. He could not continue at this pace. He started to panic. He was trying to figure out where he was; he had not paid attention when he bolted from the tavern. He had just run, trying to distance himself from this relentless blond man. He began to realize there was no hope of escape. He thought about simply stopping and begging for mercy, and he almost did, when he felt a presence above him. He looked up, the tree canopy so thick he almost couldn't see, but then through a small opening he saw black. He was elated; he searched with his mind, sending out a mental distress call.

The Dark Mage saw the messenger running through the woods; he could feel his mental plea for help; he could feel the desperation in that call. But mostly, he could sense the urgency of the message the man was carrying. Looking through the creature's eyes, he saw where the portal needed to be. He performed the incantation and it opened up in front of the fleeing man; the man ran right through it, then it was gone. All of this happened in less than a second. He told the creature to return to the island and unlocked their minds in time to see the man almost run into the wall.

Marcus ran behind the man as fast as he could. He had to catch him. He couldn't let him tell anyone about Breanne. If the Dark Mage found out about her, then she would too. Breanne was in terrible danger. He ran faster, cursing the low hanging shrubs he had to crawl under which allowed the man to get further ahead. He ran for what seemed like hours, when the distance started to close between them. He could feel the man's fear. He knew he would catch him and poured out his last reserve of energy, the distance between them closing fast. A few more minutes and he would have him.

Suddenly, the man vanished. Marcus stumbled, recovered his stride and looked ahead in disbelief. The man was no longer there. This couldn't happen, could it? He stopped running, what was the use, there was no one to chase. Panting, he looked around once more to be sure the man hadn't simply lain down and hid in the shrubs. But he knew he hadn't, he had seen him vanish with his own eyes. He cursed, then turned around and starting running back. He had to let Emiril know as fast as possible. They had to get Breanne to Daedhrog where she would be safe.

One moment he was running through the woods and the next, he was running across a room where he stopped short of hitting the wall. He stood there gasping for air, trying to catch his breath; the pain in his side was noticeable now, as was the pain from the welts. He looked behind him and dropped to his knees. He was in the throne room of the Dark Mage who was sitting there staring at him.

"Sire," he stuttered between gasps for air.

The mage held up one hand, "In a moment," he said, "catch your breath." It wasn't that he was so kind; he simply did not want to lose patience with the man while he was trying to tell him what had happened and kill him before he could hear what he had to say. He had a feeling the information would be useful to her and she would favor him because of it. So, he waited. But his patience would wear out soon.

The man shook violently as a chill ran down his back. He tried to steady his nerves, knowing if he did not, the mage would probably kill him. He had heard of him killing other messengers like himself, and he had never wanted to come here, but here he was. His breathing was beginning to slow; he could feel his heart rate returning to normal.

"Sire," he began again. This time the Dark Mage did not stop him. "I have found an outsider and have come to report it as required." He stopped, looking at the Dark Mage. With the wave of his hand, the Dark Mage beckoned him foreword.

As he approached the throne, he grew even more nervous. He had locked minds with others before, but that was nothing, they were not powerful sorcerers. He had heard of people who had locked minds with the Dark Mage and came away imbeciles, their minds destroyed by the one encounter. He stopped, sunk slowly to the floor and bowed his head. He forced himself to open his mind, and forced himself to keep it open, even though fear and self-preservation demanded that he close it as fast as he could. He knew if he did that though, it would not stop the Dark Mage from entering. He would simply tear his way in, and that would mean death for sure. He waited. Then he felt the presence of the Dark Mage enter his thoughts. A chill ran down his spine. He grimaced at the malevolence he felt emanating from him. He felt pain as the Dark Mage began to pick through the layers of his subconscious, looking for the images of the tavern and his brief interlude inside the girl's head. The pain was growing; no longer able to stay in a kneeling position, Eassa curled into a ball on the floor. He started to tremble violently from the strain the Dark Mage was placing on his mind.

The Dark Mage tore through thought after thought, flinging them carelessly aside with no regard for the damage he might be doing to the man's mind. He only cared about finding the information that was stored in there for him. He stopped, having found what he had been looking for, tucked safely away in the back of the man's mind and he slowly pulled it out. Images began to stream through his subconscious; he watched them play out before him. The inside of a tavern, two people walk in but the sunlight is so bright, can't tell who they are. They cross the room and sit down at a table. Suddenly he recognizes one of them, the elf princess Emiril; she is sitting with a blond man and a dark-haired girl. There is something different about the girl, suddenly she notices the mind reader, and he becomes interested in her; they lock minds. The Dark Mage's heart rate skyrocketed, his breathing came faster, and he looked at the images before him in disbelief. This girl was not from here, he saw an image of a room in a different world, a room filled with darkness except for one small light above a table. The light was unlike any he had seen before, it burned without flame. There was an older man. A table… suddenly, the vision started to become hazy and he could no longer see it clearly; things were blurry and hard to make out. He detected another presence. Someone else was there now, shielding the girl's mind. He strained to make out what he was seeing, the table shaking, something sliding across it that looked like a book, and then the vision was gone. The other presence had severed the connection. The Dark Mage left the messenger's mind, Eassa felt him leave and the pain left with him. But the Dark Mage left behind a feeling of evil that would haunt Eassa the rest of his life, which had thankfully been spared.

Chapter 15
Ogolel's Reach

Emiril helped Breanne stand; she was a little wobbly on her feet and felt like she might fall down at any moment.

"Can you walk?" Emiril asked.

"Yes, I think so, I'll try," Breanne said, and she took a few steps then started to topple over. Marcus caught her by the arm and supported her the rest of the way out of the tavern.

"Let's go to my place first," Marcus said, after they were out of hearing range of the people in the tavern. "Then we can get her to Daedhrog."

Emiril nodded and helped Marcus half lead, half carry Breanne towards a house set back in the trees a few hundred feet from where they were.

As they approached, a little girl came running up to them. "Hello, father," she said cheerfully. Through her haze, Breanne realized it was the same little girl who had waved at her when they had first arrived in Ethuanova. She saw the girl look at her quizzically and tried to smile; she hoped it looked all right because she felt as if her body was not responding to her the way it should. A flash of teeth from the girl smiling back reassured her it must have gone ok. And then she fainted.

"Quick, get her inside," Iola said. Turning to her daughter she said, "Go to your aunt's and stay there until I come get you. Tell no one about this." The girl nodded and left.

"I met her by the stream that runs along the old road," she heard Emiril saying.

She tried to open her eyes; blackness swirled behind her closed lids. Her mind swirled with it.

"I ran as fast as I could, but then he disappeared before my eyes," Marcus was saying.

She wanted to wake up. Why couldn't she open her eyes? She saw shadows dart in and out of her view, darker than the blackness that enveloped her. They played with her, first appearing on the right, then disappearing only to reappear on the left. Her head began to spin with the effort of trying to keep up with them. She thought she heard a fire, pans rattling, and Iola's voice. She drifted into the blackness, the black shadows forgotten. She heard her mother calling to her and she swam through the blackness, searching, calling to her.

She felt warmth on her forehead, and swam up, up into the light that was barely visible through the murky darkness. The light grew brighter as she went and she swam faster. She not only used her arms, but kicked her feet as well and she began to surface into that blessed light, the darkness melting away as she did.

Her eyes fluttered open. She saw a blurry image in front of her. "Mom?" she asked.

"Shhhh." The voice sounded familiar. "Don't try to speak, just try to wake up." It was Iola. She focused her strength on opening her eyes and keeping them open. They kept wanting to close and push her back into the terrible darkness she had just escaped from. She couldn't let that happen, she wanted to be awake. She smelled something good, was it was food? She focused on the smell of it, her stomach beginning to growl as she realized she was starving. She blinked her eyes several times, her vision beginning to clear. She saw Iola's face clearly now. She was smiling.

"You've given us all quite a scare, young lady," she said, sounding stern but the worried expression on her face gave her true feelings away.

Breanne smiled back. "Sorry," she said weakly.

Then suddenly Emiril was there, and Marcus. They looked as happy as she was starting to feel. They looked at each other, expressions of relief passing between them. "We were starting to wonder about you," Marcus said, patting her gently on the shoulder. Smiling, she looked up at him with growing feelings of warmth and friendship.

Then she looked at Emiril. Was that a tear she saw in the elf's eye? She reached a hand out to her and Emiril took it, holding it tightly. "We missed you," she said, her voice raspy. She looked away from the small group and wiped her eyes with the back of her hand. "Iola," she chastised, "your onions are burning my eyes." Marcus winked at Breanne; they all knew it was not the onions that had drawn tears to the eyes of the tough elf.

"In that case," Iola said laughing "we should eat them." She got up and headed across the room to where a cast iron pot simmered over the fire. She lifted the lid and immediately a delicious aroma permeated the air. Breanne's stomach turned cartwheels when her nose delivered the message that there was good smelling food close by. She involuntarily grabbed her stomach with both hands to settle it down. She didn't know what kinds of animals they ate here, maybe it was some kind of deer with two heads (kind of dramatic but not really, she thought, after all, they have four legged birds here), but whatever it was, Breanne was prepared to eat it. Emiril and Marcus helped her get up and then led her to the table.

Emiril, Marcus and Iola sat silently at the table, each one looking knowingly at the other. While Breanne had lain unconscious, Emiril had taken the opportunity to tell Marcus and Iola the story of meeting her and how Breanne had found the book and then inadvertently used the spell that had brought her to their world. They too knew about Ogolel and how dangerous she was. The elves were not the only ones to taste her wrath. She had once destroyed a whole village because they had refused to make her their queen. Other manner of beings had run-ins with her as well. She had captured mountain trolls and enslaved the poor diJCitted creatures, putting them to work building her castle, and under threat of death if they refused, she had made the dwarves mine gold and gems for her. All of Ibacion was terrified of the evil sorceress; no one dared stand against her. Now this girl shows up using a spell from the book Ogolel has been trying to find for the past few hundred years. She would stop at nothing to get that book; they all knew that; they were all at risk. Death came too easy to the ones who opposed Ogolel; they all realized the direness of the situation they found themselves in. Now that Breanne was all right, they needed to get her to safety. But first they needed to formulate a plan on how to do that.

Breanne was not paying attention to any of this silent conversation, she was busy eating Iola's dinner, and in fact she was on her third helping. She had figured it out; she had not eaten in the equivalency of two days, that is, if she worked the math out right. She had vanished from her world at nearly four a.m. and had been in this world for almost a day and a half. She hadn't eaten since six o clock the day she left, and she was starving. She did sadly notice however, she was starting to get full. She took two more big bites then sat back in her chair and breaking the silence, she hadn't realized was there, declared that she was full. The tension broken, the others laughed. "It's about time," Emiril said jokingly. "I thought you were going to burst at any moment."

Breanne looked at her friend and laughed with her. Then she thanked Iola for the food. "It was wonderful," she said.

"You're welcome," Iola told her. "I wish more people were as enthusiastic about my food as you are." She said this last comment while

86

looking straight at Marcus who pretended to look at the ceiling. She laughed and Marcus did too. He loved her food and she knew it.

When the laughter subsided, Emiril cleared her throat, an indication that it was time to get serious. They all looked at her, Breanne in expectant confusion, and waited for her to begin.

Chapter 16
The Dwarf's Warning

There was something about that girl. Yes, she was not from this world, but that wasn't it; he couldn't quite put his finger on it. He had *sensed* something about her, something hidden, even from her. No matter, he thought, straightening his tunic. He had to tell *her* the news. She would be pleased with him, he smiled at the thought. The only way the girl could have gotten here was by using the spell, and the only way she could have gotten the spell, was if she had found the book that probably was what he had seen in the vision. He was excited, his insides quivering from the excitement. He had to steady himself, his hands were shaking. He had been looking for it for so long; he could almost feel the soft leather in his hands, smell the crisp pages. She would reward him for this, he was sure of it. He needed to make contact with her; he needed to tell her the good news. He looked at the messenger lying in a fetal position on the floor. He was in such a good mood, he decided to let him live. He left the throne room, almost gliding across the floor his mood was so light. He turned down the hall and headed for the chamber of solitude.

Closing the big iron door, he shut himself into utter darkness. The chamber was a perfect square, twenty feet by twenty feet. The walls, floor and ceilings had been insulated to keep out the rest of the world; neither light nor sound from the outside entered this chamber. He stood just inside the doorway for a moment. This is what he imagined the in-between would be like, the only difference was, in here at least you could hear yourself talk. In the in-between you could hear nothing at all, or so he had been told. An involuntary shudder passed over him as he thought about the lost souls trapped in that living death. He hated coming in here, but he needed no distractions when he summoned her. Distractions could kill him, and he had no wish to die today.

Although he could not see, he walked directly to the chair sitting in the center of the room. He knew the way, he had been here many times before. He counted the steps off, one, two... twenty, he reached out blindly, felt the arm of the chair and seated himself. He stretched, took two big breaths, exhaling slowly and began to clear his mind. Contacting *her* was nothing like entering the mind of the messenger or even the creature. This was extremely dangerous; one false move and he could be killed. She was so powerful, the stress from that much power entering his mind alone could kill him; not to mention what could happen if she were to grow angry with him.

He felt his mind slowly leave him. He felt it float into the darkness, sailing on a current seen only by the spirits and some sorcerers. This had always been terrifying for him. Once, while using this dark spiritual highway, he had bumped into a creature from the spirit world and the creature had not been happy about it. It had nearly killed him before he could flee back to the safety of his mind and sever the connection. Even then, it had almost been too late, the creature had all but pushed his way through the mental doorway between his mind and the darkness. It had taken him weeks to recover from that experience, and several weeks more before he found the courage to use the current again. He was a lot more vigilant these days; he stayed clear of anyone or anything that might be traveling the dark highway.

He was getting close, he could feel her power, and his mind sought it out. The force of the power was oppressive; he found it difficult to concentrate. The ease at which he had been travelling the current was no longer, he struggled to make any forward progress. Her spirit spilled into the darkness as if she could not contain the whole of her essence inside the earthly boundary of her body. She seemed to exist in both realms at once. He figured that was how she knew so much about the comings and goings of both worlds; she was a part of both worlds. He could go no further and stopped struggling to make headway, and then she was there. Her presence in his head felt as if it was a part of him. She enveloped him, intentionally, stealthily, completely; his spirit trembled in her presence. Like a deadly snake, she slithered through his mind, searching for the message he carried, probing his memories until she found it. He did not need to tell her anything about the girl or the book, she simply knew. His mind was his, and then it was not. She took what she wanted and he could not have stopped her if he had wanted to. Her voice penetrated his mind like water penetrating parched soil. It sieved into the very tissue itself, and like a sponge sucking up this water, his brain was filled with her presence. Back in the chamber, his body convulsed, blood poured from his sweat glands. His eyes rolled back in his head and foamy spittle escaped his lips.

He could feel her pleasure in the news he brought. She was indeed happy with him. He was elated; things were good when she was happy with him. He did not want to think about the times when she was not; there were far too many of those times; again he shuddered. Then she gave him her instructions: Find the girl, and *kill* her, then bring her body and all her things to me. The book was not important, her thoughts interrupting his; it was where no one could get to it. She wanted the girl dead; she wanted her and her things. His thoughts revealed his loyalty to her, it would be done. Then, just as slowly and stealthily as she came, she left. His mind was once again his own. He was alone in the darkness.

He turned and let the current bring him back to his body, eyes scanning the darkness, ever vigilant, ever watchful. His eyes opened, he breathed deeply, and wiped the spittle off his mouth. His body ached, he was soaked in blood, but he was alive. It was always good to wake up in this world alive, after locking minds with Ogolel.

He left the chamber and returned to the throne room, half noticing the messenger was gone. He had his instructions; he must find the girl and kill her. He sat on his throne, closed his eyes and summoned the creature.

Their minds locked, sharing mental pictures between them. The creature could see the girl, and he knew the command… kill. It took to the air, wings beating fiercely, its long tail flowing behind it, and then its red piercing eyes started searching. It would continue to search until it found her, no matter how long it took. It would never give up, it would die searching unless it was called off. And when it did find her, it would kill her. God help anyone the relentless creature sought.

Far away in a small house in the woods, Emiril shuddered, an icy cold chill ran down her spine, and she knew they were now in more danger than any of the others could imagine.

Chapter 17
The Mountain Pass

"Breanne," Emiril began. "While you were ill, I took the liberty of telling Marcus and Iola about our meeting and how you got to our world." Breanne's eyes got big. "It's all right," Emiril continued, "they can be trusted, with our lives." She gave Marcus an intense look when she said the last, and Breanne figured that he must have proven that once already by the way they looked at each other. Now I need to tell *you* a few things.

"Ogolel has been looking for that book you found for a very long time and will stop at nothing to get it. Do you remember that man in the tavern, the one you asked me about?" Breanne nodded, she felt uneasy just thinking about him. "He is what you call a mind reader." Emiril continued, "I knew he was there, I was hoping he would not notice us, but when you noticed him, he felt it and that is why he read your mind. He was trying to find out why you were interested in him."

"He did what?" Breanne said needing confirmation of what she thought she had just heard. She was both fascinated and scared at the thought of having someone read her thoughts. She didn't even know that was actually possible, even here. It was so sci fi, now she really did feel like she was on another planet.

"He read your mind," Emiril repeated, "but it is more than that really," she said. "It is hard to explain. Let me put it this way, when you became interested in him, your mind opened a doorway from your mind to his. He passed through this doorway and was able to lock minds with you. It is not your fault." she said quickly, when Breanne suddenly looked guilty. She went on, "he was able to see your thoughts, your memories, he…"

Breanne cut her off, "You mean he knows about the book?"

"Well, I do not know," Emiril confessed. "Once I realized what was happening, I tried to shield you from him, but I don't know how long your minds were locked together. He might know everything, he might know nothing."

"So that is what happened to me at the tavern," Breanne half stated half asked. "That is why I felt funny. And that is why I got sick?" she asked.

Emiril looked at Marcus; he raised his eyebrows and shrugged. A lot of help you are, she thought. She thought about it a moment, she wasn't sure what to say about that. Then she looked back at Breanne. It is always best to tell the truth, she thought. "I am not sure why you had such a bad reaction to the mind lock," she told her. "I have never seen anyone react quite the way you did. It could be because you are not from here. I just do not know. I will have to consult someone about that, someone who knows a lot more about this stuff than I do." She thought Breanne looked even more scared, but all in all, she was taking it quite well. Now if she could just calm her own nerves, she would feel a lot better.

"Now," she said more grimly. "That man at the tavern... although Marcus chased him for miles, got away with whatever he was able to glean from your mind. And as I said, that could be nothing, a few things, or everything, we just do not know. What we do know though, is where he is going with that information. In fact, he is probably already there." Breanne looked at her friend questioningly. Reluctantly Emiril finished. "He is going to the Dark Mage," she said solemnly.

Breanne's eyes took on the look of a deer being hunted in the woods. The others could not help but feel sorry for the girl. Iola put a reassuring arm around her and Breanne melted into her, seeking all the comfort she could get.

"We are not trying to scare you unnecessarily, Breanne," Emiril said gently. "But you need to know what you are up against, what we are all up against." Breanne looked around the table, they were all shaking their heads in agreement. "We are not going to leave you on your own, we are in this together." She smiled at Breanne and that smile made Breanne feel better, if only a little better. Emiril continued, "The Dark Mage will pass on what he learns to Ogolel and she will stop at nothing to find you. You are the key to the book, if she finds you, she finds the book. And if she finds you, I can't protect you by myself." She tensed up, looked at Marcus again and then said, "She *will* find you, Breanne." Breanne's blood ran cold, she shivered involuntarily and Iola held her tighter, pulling the shawl she was wearing around them both. She only imagined how Breanne must be feeling; she herself was beginning to feel terrified.

Marcus spoke for the first time since the conversation started. They all looked at him. "The Dark Mage has a creature he uses to spy on people and look for things. He mind locks with it and he can see what it sees. When I was chasing that man today, I felt its presence above us. It was after it showed up, that he disappeared."

"Disappeared?" Breanne asked quietly in astonishment.

"Yes," Marcus said. "The Dark Mage is powerful and has many spells he can use to his advantage. Once the creature finds you, he can use one of those spells on you, and there is nothing we can do to stop him."

Breanne now felt as helpless as anyone could. The Dark Mage was going to come and take her away, take her to Ogolel and then God only knew what would happen.

"Breanne," Emiril asked again. Breanne looked up this time, she had been so wrapped up in her thoughts of impending doom she had not heard Emiril the first time. Emiril smiled. "We did not mean to make it sound so helpless. What we meant to convey to you was how serious a

94

situation this is. I think that we may have given you the idea that we cannot protect you *at all*. We can, we just need to get you to my father. He will know what to do better than I. He has dealt with Ogolel before. Remember the story I told you?" Breanne nodded. Emiril smiled again. "So you see, we do have someone to turn to." Breanne felt a little better; Emiril could see her relax. She did not want to scare her, but she needed to be scared; her life depended on it.

Emiril took a deep breath and let it out. "So, as I was saying, you need to go to Daedhrog, where you will be safe with the king." Breanne wondered why she said 'you need to go' instead of 'we need to go.' "And," Emiril continued delivering the news, "I need to go somewhere before I go to Daedhrog, so I am going to let Marcus escort you there."

Breanne quickly sat up, the shawl falling off her shoulders. "Emiril, why can't I go with you?" her voice almost at a yell. "How can I go to your home without you, no one knows me there?" She looked at Marcus apologetically; there was no need, he understood. It wasn't that she didn't trust him, she did, it was just that she didn't want to be apart from Emiril. She had grown very fond of the elf and although she did not yet realize it, she was leaning on her, and seeking comfort from her, as if she were her mother. Breanne could feel her eyes start to fill with tears and she quickly looked away from the others. She felt powerless.

Emiril was touched. She could feel the emotions emanating from the girl and she now realized she felt the same way about her. But Breanne was in real danger and the longer she stayed out here, unprotected, the more likely it would be that Ogolel would find her. "Breanne, I too feel the way you do," she began, "but you must seek the safety that Daedhrog offers, and I need to go see someone else before I go there. If it were not important that I do this, I would go with you."

Breanne sat in silence. The others did too, waiting for her to come to terms with everything she had just learned. The fire in the hearth snapped and popped as it began to burn a piece of wood rich in sap. She liked this house, it was peaceful. She thought about Emiril and how much the elf had come to mean to her in such a very short time. She knew it was because Emiril had found her and as far as she was concerned, saved her, but this was more than that, she genuinely cared for her as well. She was very kind and funny and the best thing was, she was sure Emiril cared about her as well. Well, she said to herself, you sure aren't showing her you care about her by not trusting her. She wanted to tell that part of herself to shut up, but she knew that that part of Breanne was right. If Emiril did care about her like she thought she did, then she needed to trust her to make the right decisions; after all, her life apparently depended on it. Now that she was done wrestling with herself, she looked at the others and smiled, indicating that she would accept what they were planning. She could visibly see the tension leave them, their shoulders dropped and their faces, once etched with worry, now looked relaxed; they were even smiling. She was glad she had such good friends to help her. She would probably be dead by now if it weren't for them. (Definitely not dramatic, she thought eerily.) She decided she would trust them from now on.

"Well," Marcus said breaking the silence. "We'll leave at first light."

Emiril got up, walked around the table and gave Breanne a big hug. "You are a good girl, Breanne," she said affectionately. And to Marcus she said, smiling, "It is already first light, you big oaf."

Marcus looked out the window and could see the light of the sun barely visible through the canopy of the trees. "So it is," he said laughing, "so it is."

Chapter 18
The Cavern of Echoes

Even though it was technically first light, none of them except Breanne had slept and they decided to get a couple hours sleep before they headed out. Breanne, even though she had been unconscious, was still feeling the effects of the mind lock and welcomed this decision. Iola said she would stay up and wake them when it was time. She wasn't going with them and could get some rest after they all left so she could keep watch, something they all agreed was now necessary.

"Breanne." She felt someone gently shaking her. "Wake up; it is time to get moving." It was Emiril.

"How long have I been asleep?" she asked. It felt like days to her.

"Well, you lucky kid, you got to sleep longer than the rest of us," she said jokingly. "Probably three hours now. Iola has something for you to eat, that is if you are still not full from last night?" she smiled that impish smile at Breanne, who rolled her eyes playfully.

"You know me, Emiril, I could eat a horse." She said this as a joke, and then remembered she was still not exactly sure what they *did* eat around here. She started to feel sick, man, she hoped it wasn't really horse.

Emiril did not seem to get the joke and said, "Well, you will just have to settle for rabbit stew again, we did not have time to make anything else."

Breanne felt elated. Yes, eating a rabbit was kind of sad, but lots of people eat rabbits, she was just glad it wasn't a horse. Although, she thought, Emiril didn't seem too thrown off by me saying I could eat a horse; I wonder if they do eat horses here. She would have asked Emiril, but the elf was already out the door. She looked around and saw Iola over by the hearth.

"Hurry up, slow poke," Marcus said, startling her as he came in the door. "The caravan is going to leave without you. And besides that, I have a present for you," he added.

Breanne's eyes lit up. "A present, for me," she said, obviously delighted, "What is it, where is it?" She jumped up and started to go to the door.

"Now hold on there, little lady," Marcus said laughing. "Yes, your present is outside, but you need to eat first. We have a long ways to go and you're going to need your energy."

Breanne's face dimmed. "But..." she started. Marcus squinted his eyes, and with eyebrows drawn together, shook his head no and pointed to the table. She thought about saying something else, looked at the stern, yet caring, expression on his face and said, "Oh, all right," and sat down at the table.

Laughing, Iola came over with the plate of food she had warmed up for her, set it down and told Breanne, "You know Marcus and I have a daughter, and she has to eat before she gets her presents too." She rubbed her hand across the back of Breanne's shoulders lovingly, and winked at Marcus and he smiled back at her.

The minute Iola set the plate in front of her, if Breanne had had any leftover arguments about not eating before going out, they were instantly gone. The smell made her mouth water, and remembering what the food had tasted like before, made her stomach almost leap out of her body and eat the food itself, bypassing the slowness of the chewing and swallowing process. She ate that plate and one more before she started to think about her present again. Even at that though, she had a little bit more before she pleaded to Marcus with her eyes. (I ate, now can I see it, please?) He chuckled, got up from finishing his second plate of food and told her she could go with him to see it.

Breanne nearly upset the chair, she got up so fast and hurriedly walked to the door, paused, turned around and thanked Iola for the food and then followed Marcus outside. Iola smiled to herself. It would have been nice if the girl could have stayed with them, having two girls would be fun, especially one so polite, her parents must be proud.

At first glance she did not see a present, but she was not really sure what she was looking for. She saw Marcus standing by some horses that appeared to be packed for their trip, and Emiril was adding some things to the bags on her horse. She didn't really see anything that stood out. Of course, she didn't really think it would be wrapped up, like in her world, but she did kind of expect some sort of indication that it was indeed a gift, and for her. She felt awkward and looked at Marcus, half confused, half embarrassed. She raised her eyebrows, as if to say, a little help here please.

Emiril laughed. "Marcus, you big lug, she doesn't know what is not normal here, it does not stand out to her, you need to tell her." Breanne gave Emiril a big smile of gratitude, grateful for her friend's help.

Marcus let out a big hearty laugh and slapped his knee. "You're right, Emiril," he said, "how could she know, that was foolish of me." He laughed again. "Come here Breanne."

She walked over to him and before she could say or do anything, he scooped her up with his well-muscled arms and sat her upon the big brown horse he had been standing by. "Here is your present, Breanne," he said, smiling at her.

"Are you serious?" she asked incredulously.

"Yes."

She stared at him, and then she looked at Emiril who was smiling at her. She noticed Iola had come to the door and when she saw Breanne look her way, she smiled and waved. Breanne could not believe that Marcus had just given her a horse. She had wanted a horse her whole life and she had resigned herself to the fact that she would probably never get one; they lived in town and had no room to keep a horse. She reached down and pet his neck; he was so soft. His ears flicked back and she knew he was checking her out too. She had taken horseback riding lessons once, so she knew how to ride a little, but she was no pro like Emiril and she was still a little nervous sitting up so high on a horse she had just met.

"Thank you, Marcus," she said, her voice cracking with emotion. "I can't thank you enough, he is so beautiful." She stopped and thought for a minute. "Is it a he?" she asked Marcus. It would not be good to start out their new relationship by offending the beast right off the bat. She hoped it was a boy; she didn't want to think of it being upset with her already. After all, with all this mind locking going on, she didn't know if the horse knew she had called it a boy. She looked at Marcus.

"He's a boy," he confirmed. She immediately felt better.

Emiril walked over to her where she sat on her new horse and tied a pack to her saddle. "There is an extra change of clothes in here for you," she said. "And I also put in a brush for your hair, one for your teeth and a lunch Iola made for you." Breanne glanced over at Iola again and smiled, Iola smiled back. "Don't worry, Breanne," Emiril was saying, "I will be there sooner than you think." She smiled brightly. "Oh yah, one more thing." She looked at Marcus and said, "don't let this big lug trick you out of your lunch, he has one of his own." Marcus laughed at this and Breanne did too.

"I won't," she said, "heck maybe I'll eat his."

Now Emiril and Marcus were really laughing, and Emiril told Marcus he had some competition these days. They walked over to Iola and each of them gave her a big hug. "Hey, guys," Breanne said, "I'm not so good at getting down off these things, can you help me?" The three of them turned and were once again laughing. They all three walked over and Emiril showed Breanne where to hang on to the saddle and how to swing her leg over to dismount the horse. Marcus told her she had better remember that for when his arms got too tired to help her. Now that she was down, she too gave Iola a big hug and thanked her for everything; she was going to miss her.

Next, she turned to Emiril, knowing their parting would be very hard, but Breanne had come to terms with the fact that Emiril was doing what she felt was the best thing for her, and she trusted her. They hugged each other for a long time, and then they each turned and walked to their horses. Marcus helped Breanne mount again, and then mounted his own horse. They waved good bye to Emiril and Iola and Marcus led them away from the house, which was now a place of false security. As warm and comfortable as it was, it was not safe there any longer; she hoped Iola and her daughter would be ok.

Chapter 19
The Spell of Calm

The Dark Mage grew weary searching for the horse and rider. He grew angry. His army had searched every house in Ethuanova; there was no sign of her. No one was talking either. He knew she had been with the elf Emiril, but he could not locate her either. Her powers were very strong and she blocked his mind from locking onto hers. She made sure that to him, she did not exist. This infuriated him; one day he would be more powerful than she, and then he would make her pay for being so uppity. He had known her since before the uprising, when he was a frequent visitor at the palace. She had always looked down on him. No matter what he did to win her favor, she refused to like him. Well, one day I'll show her, he thought, she will pay for being so rude, and for helping the girl.

He refocused his thoughts on finding the girl. He figured the best place to start looking was Daedhrog. It had only been one day since the messenger had encountered them, so with any luck he would find them before they reached the Elven glen.

He focused his thoughts toward the creature, and it stopped circling Ethuanova and began flying south over the immense forest, scanning the tree tops as it went, the Dark Mage seeing what it saw, the vast green carpet of forest and the old road winding idly beside it. It was too much to hope they were dumb enough to travel the open road. Emiril should know by now that he was looking for them. He knew she was too smart to think that she didn't. He concentrated his search on the forest.

Emiril waved goodbye to the others, then turned her horse and headed for Malarcis. She had to see the sorceress; only she would know how to get Breanne home, if she could get home.

She galloped all the way, her horse, an Elven breed, was unusually fast and strong. She wanted to get back to Daedhrog as fast as possible and they were making good time. She knew Marcus could handle almost anything, but the Dark Mage was very powerful and Marcus would not be able to withstand an all-out attack without help. Their only hope was for him to get Breanne secretly and safely through the forest before they were caught. Her mind was now fresh with worry and she hurried her horse, which to his breed's credit, their speed increased.

Marcus and Breanne waved goodbye to the others and headed into the trees. Breanne started to ask him why they were not taking the road, but caught herself before the words could escape her lips. Duh Breanne, she said to herself, you would be sitting ducks out there. She was glad she had stopped herself from asking the question, she would have looked foolish. Instead, she asked Marcus how long it would take to get there.

"Well, we'll have to walk most of the way, the trees are too thick to go any faster, one of the horses could trip or bump you into a tree; we wouldn't want that to happen," he said giving her a look of pain and anguish, while grabbing his head playfully, as if he had really been bumped into a tree. Breanne smiled at him, I bet he's a good dad, she thought. It's too bad I didn't get to meet his daughter. He stopped his anguished musings and continued, "It's about twenty miles from here to Daedhrog, so I figure about ten hours, eleven if we stop and have lunch; but we should be there just after dark, I would think."

"And where did Emiril go?" she asked.

Marcus looked at her. If Emiril didn't tell her where she was going, there must have been a reason. He thought about what to say. "She had to go see someone," he said carefully, "it will take her longer to get to Daedhrog than it will us, but you should see her by morning, I would think." He quickly changed the subject so Breanne would not ask any more questions; this did not get past Breanne however, but she decided to let it go for now.

Instead, she asked him another question, one that had been with her for a while now. One she thought she already knew the answer to. "Marcus, when we were in the tavern, when I first met you, you looked at me and I felt…" she didn't know how to say it. Marcus was listening intently. He had wondered if she knew, now it seemed that she did know something at least. She continued. "I don't know how to say it just right, but I felt something in my head, and I wanted to know if it was you." She quickly looked away, surveying the trees around them, trying not to meet his gaze. There, she had said it, if she looked foolish, she looked foolish. But this had been on her mind for a while now and she needed to know.

Marcus stopped his horse and waited for her to draw up beside him. He looked at her, a serious expression on his face. "Did it feel like butterfly wings?" he asked. Her eyes opened wide; she didn't need to say it. "I wondered if you knew then," he said. "You looked as if you did."

"Marcus, are you a mind reader too?" she asked, although she already knew the answer.

"Yes," he said, "I am."

They looked at one another for a minute longer, neither one saying anything. They both avoided breaking the silence, at the moment, content to think about what had just transpired. Marcus turned away and started out once more and she followed in. They rode for four hours that way, neither of them having anything to say, each wrapped up in their own thoughts. Marcus thinking about Iola and their daughter, hoping she had gotten out of town and on to her mother's all right. She should be safe in Mininthus, he thought, the Dark Mage won't be looking for her, he will be looking for us. That last thought gave him a chill. He just hoped he could get Breanne to Daedhrog with no mishaps, but he knew that was a lot to hope for. Even with the other thoughts swirling in his mind, he still came back to that nagging question he had tried not to think about, how did she know he was in her mind? Only other mind readers can feel their mind being read, but the minute he had started to read hers, she had felt it, so he had stopped. And what would explain her reaction to the mind reader in the tavern. Most people would live their whole lives never knowing their minds had been read, never having a reaction to it. He thought for a while she would die, maybe Mindoneth could explain it to Emiril.

Breanne's thoughts were about Emiril. She hoped the elf was safe and she was scared to even let the thought of her dying and Breanne never seeing her again linger in her mind. She willed it quickly away, replacing it with thoughts of picking a name for her new horse. She still couldn't believe Marcus had given him to her. She smiled, the horse turned his ears back as if listening to her thoughts, and she patted his neck. What is a good horse name, she thought? She wanted it to mean something; she didn't want the name to be silly, like when people name their dogs Spot. She thought about home, and all the people helping her to get back there. She wondered if she would ever get back to her world. On the bright side, if there was one, she figured she was now a world traveler and Jesus was protecting her. "That's it," she said to the horse, "I am going to name you 'Jesus Contribution,' after my Lord Jesus Christ, I'll call you JC for short. He helps people who are struggling in their lives, like everyone is helping me now, including you." She smiled, satisfied with her decision.

"You ready for lunch?" Marcus asked, interrupting her thoughts.

"Yes," she replied, quickly looking up. "I am starving."

"I don't know where you put all that food, young lady," he said, laughing. They dismounted by a small stream and let the horses eat the meager grass that grew by the water's edge while they dug out the lunches Iola had packed for them. Breanne once again ate like she hadn't eaten in days. Marcus thought to himself, I wonder if I ate like that at her age. And then felt sorry for his mother if he had, think of all the cooking that poor woman must have done. He made a mental note to thank her the next time he saw her.

The creature soared over the trees, making tight circles in a grid like pattern. The Dark Mage watched intently for breaks in the forest canopy. When there was one, he sent the creature down for a closer look, hoping there would be some sign of the girl.

His head ached, he felt as if it would explode. He had been locked with the creature for hours; he wasn't used to being locked for so long. If it wasn't for the creature's strength, he would have had to come back to his own mind by now, but through the locking of their minds, the creature kept him strong; like a parasite he fed off the creature's unyielding stamina. It would be dark in a few hours, and then it would be almost impossible to find her. If she made it to Daedhrog, she would be protected now and he would not be able to kill her as Ogolel had ordered. If he didn't kill her, Ogolel would be very angry; she may kill him instead; he was starting to panic. The creature could sense his anxiety as their melded minds shared information as well as emotion. It too became agitated and the Dark Mage had to fight to calm it down enough to resume the search. He had to be more careful and control his emotions. Locking minds with a creature was dangerous at best, and if he lost control now, he, or both of them could die. He focused on the tops of the trees looking for any signs of a break in the canopy; he had to find her, his life probably depended on it.

Chapter 20
Courage of the Lion's Heart

Emiril was exhausted from the long run to Malarcis, so too was the horse. They had made it in three hours; she was pleased with the time they had made and ran quickly up to Mindoneth's door. She stopped before knocking, both to gain her composer and catch her breath. She didn't want to give a bad impression. As she raised her hand to knock, the door suddenly opened before her.

"Welcome, Emiril," Mindoneth said with a big smile, arms held wide to receive her granddaughter.

Emiril's face broke into a beautiful smile and the tension she had been feeling since first meeting Breanne melted at the sight of the old elf. She stepped into the comforting embrace of her grandmother. She welcomed the feel of her arms wrapped tightly around her. She smelled familiar aromas which to her meant love, acceptance and most of all, safety.

"I have been expecting you, darling," the older elf said matter-of-factly. She grabbed Emiril by the arm, ushering her into the house, as only a grandmother can do and not offend. "Come have some tea with me. Don't worry," she said as if reading Emiril's mind. "Adwin will see to your horse, make sure he is watered, fed and ready to go when you are." She said these things as if she knew Emiril would only be here a short while. Emiril wondered what else she already knew; her grandmother never ceased to amaze her. "Thank you, grandmother," she said, following her inside and shutting the door behind her.

Her grandmother seated her at a small table beside a window and then hurried into the kitchen to retrieve a tea service, which was all ready and steaming hot. The house was much as Emiril remembered it, small with only one central room, a kitchen and one bedroom. Her grandmother had always replied when asked why she didn't make it bigger, "When one lives alone and has the love of one's family, one doesn't need as many material things." Emiril loved the way the house reflected these thoughts, paintings of her and her family lining the walls. She noticed one in particular. She had been fifty the day that one was painted, just a wee thing, having just been given her horse Tanja by her parents as a gift to celebrate her aging; she was so happy that day. Her attention was redirected to a tea cup being placed in front of her. She smiled gratefully at her grandmother. She started to say something. "Not yet," her grandmother said raising a finger; tea first." It was her way of letting Emiril rest from her long ride, and she was thankful. It had been a long two days, and she was sure it was going to be an even longer time before things were back to normal.

As they sat sipping tea, Emiril could not help but notice her grandmother was still so beautiful and at such an advanced age. Her black hair had just a hint of silver coursing through it, her face had only the slightest amount of age lines, and her emerald green eyes still shown as brightly as they did four hundred years ago. Emiril hoped she would age as gracefully as her grandmother, in fact she hoped she would live to be her grandmother's age. It was almost unheard of even among elves for one to live past one thousand let alone to one thousand and six. Her grandfather had been the oldest known elf to live; he had passed into the other side when he was one thousand and eight years. She worried about her father, he was getting up there in years and she hoped that he would follow in his parent's footsteps so that she would not be alone anytime soon. Since her mother's passing sixty years ago, she had become very dependent on her father, but it seemed more so, on her grandmother. She did not want to even entertain the thought of her passing.

She had taken several sips of the warm tea, noting that it was very pleasant and calming. She thought that her grandmother had probably added some roots of the arinal plant, known for its calming effect on people. She was grateful, she could feel the tension leaving her body and a feeling of peace replacing it; she began to wonder if the tea wasn't also charmed as well. She looked at her grandmother, but as usual could not tell anything from looking at the stoic expression on her face.

Then the silence was broken.

"I know why you're here." Her grandmother's eyes bore into Emiril's own.

Emiril looked at her, not quite surprised, but almost.

"You were right to come to me, you are up against a magic far more powerful than even you realize." Emiril looked confused. What didn't she realize? "A great deal." Her grandmother replied to her unspoken question. She realized then, her thoughts were not entirely her own. "She is from another world, yes, but not entirely." The old elf looked at her knowingly.

Emiril's eyes opened wide. "What do you mean?" she asked in astonishment.

"I sense that she is somehow a part of this world, connected to it, although she doesn't know it." She watched as her grandmother closed her eyes and sat silently seeking. She was seeking information about the girl who had found her way into a world she did not belong to, yet somehow did belong. She searched Emiril's mind, noting all that had transpired since she had met the girl. Suddenly her eyes opened, and this time *she* looked astonished. "She could feel the mind reader in the room?" she asked, seeking confirmation from Emiril, although she had seen it in her memories.

"Yes, she could, it surprised me as well. But I did not have time to think more on it then."

"And your friend Marcus, she sensed him as well." It was Emiril's turn to be surprised again, she had not known this, and quite frankly did not know how her grandmother could have gleaned that from her mind if she did not even know about it herself. But now, with this new information, she was starting to put the pieces together.

"You are on the right track," her grandmother assured her, shepherding her thoughts in the right direction. "Tell me more about what happened during her connection with the mind reader."

Emiril thought for a moment. Then concentrated her thoughts on the moment when she realized Breanne was in trouble. She thought about the girl's reaction to the reading and how they had all been afraid she would die. Her grandmother nodded her head, "Yes, yes, you were right to worry. It is most unusual for someone without the gift to know anything is happening to them during a reading, and the reaction itself, I have never encountered the likes of it before." She looked up, breaking the connection with Emiril. She had seen enough; in fact, she was troubled by what she had seen. Troubled yes, but there was something else, something she could not yet put her finger on. Could it be what they had hoped for? She would need time to think about it. She would not speak of it until she knew for sure, there was no sense getting everyone's hopes up if it wasn't true. She had to suppress a feeling of elation in herself, she just didn't know yet.

"The child is different," she said solemnly. "But not only because she comes from a different world. As I said, she is connected to this world somehow. She belongs here. The book knew it when she found it; it allowed her to enter our world. Her kind are not able to perform spells from our world, the only reason the spell worked was because of the connection she has to this world. She knew of the mind reader and of your friend Marcus because she has some sort of magical ability that she herself is not aware of. I am not sure without meeting her personally what she is capable of." Emiril raised her eyebrows. The old elf continued, "I think the reaction she had to the reading was due to the fact that her mind was led into the spirit realm and she could not find her way back. Most people who get read are not able to go to the spirit world because they are not able to do magic, and those that are able are trained, such as your friend Marcus; they can come and go safely. What happened, in a sense is, she was thrust into the spirit world by the mind reader and left there to find her own way back. She is lucky she did; no one could have helped her," she said putting Emiril's thoughts of guilt to rest. "She did not know she was even in the spirit world. She would not have known to seek help, and even if she had, she would not have known what to look for; she would not have known anyone else was there. We are lucky that the mind reader did not realize what had happened. You were right to shelter her, and as far as what he saw in her mind, even though he didn't see everything, you can rest assured it was enough to have Ogolel looking for her even as we speak."

Now Emiril was very fearful for the girl. She knew that Ogolel would stop at nothing to find her if she sensed the same things her grandmother did; and she was certain that she would sense at least half of it. The rest may have been blocked from her by her shielding the girl from the mind reader, but the information she did gain from him would be enough to put Breanne in terrible danger, as well as anyone else who happened to be with her. Her mind whirled, thinking about her friend's safety. She wondered if Iola and her daughter had gotten out in time, or had they been discovered? Were they now at the mercy of the Dark Mage or worse, Ogolel?

"They are fine." Her grandmother smiled at her. "They are safely at her mother's, awaiting his return." Emiril was grateful for her grandmother's intuitiveness and the information; she did not want to

111

worry about Iola and her daughter on top of Breanne and Marcus. Breanne and Marcus were a different story however. She knew her grandmother couldn't sense the two of them to let her know how they fared; she had placed a spell of concealment on them before they left, and along with Marcus's ability to cloak their movements, they stood a good chance of making it to Daedhrog undetected. She just had one more question for her grandmother and then she too would be on her way to the glen. As usual, the minute the question entered her head, her grandmother had an answer.

"I have been waiting for this question," she said rather bleakly. "I did not want to answer it." She looked out the window and Emiril could see great concern in her eyes. She knew she was not going to like what she heard next. "The only way for her to return to her world…." Her voice broke, she sat for a moment longer staring out the window silently; then she turned and looked directly into Emiril's eyes. It was then that Emiril could see how concerned her grandmother really was. She suddenly looked her rightful age, her eyes were deep set with worry, her face looked more drawn and wrinkled than it had previously, and Emiril could see a look of forlornness on her face. She wondered what could be so upsetting as to elicit such a transformation in the old elf. She waited for her to continue. "The only way for her to return to her world," she began again, "is to use the spell." Emiril played the thought in her mind. The spell was in the book, the book was in her world. There was no way; no one else knew the spell, only…it hit her then. Only Ogolel knew the spell. She was the only way for Breanne to return home. They were going to have to face her, that evil sorceress, the most feared elf in all the land, Ogolel, her aunt.

Her grandmother had followed her thoughts, had felt her fear and shock over the news. "Wait," she said quickly. Emiril looked at her again. "There is one light to reach for," she said, hope now in her eyes, replacing that awful look of despair. "You may not have to face her directly. There is another book." Now Emiril's head was reeling. How can this be, she thought?

Her grandmother continued, "The second book was the one smart thing Ogolel did before she stood against the throne. She made a copy of the original, just in case it was lost to your father. Our spies were only able to confirm this much. But we think that the Dark Mage has it, on the island of the ancient ancestors." Emiril shivered, a chill ran through her. She could not believe they were going to have to find this book if Breanne were going to get home. "There is one last thing," her grandmother said. Emiril braced herself for more bad news. "You will need to find the dragon pendant."

"What dragon pendant?" Emiril asked exacerbated. She hadn't heard about a dragon pendant.

"There has to have been a pendant," Her grandmother said. "The spell doesn't work without it. You will have to ask her, she will know about it, you have to find out where it is, or the spell will not work. The magic to make the spell work was derived from the soul of a black dragon; Ogolel captured it and imprisoned it in a pendant. We were all horrified when we found out about it. To think of the poor beast being a prisoner of Ogolel, locked forever between life and death. He cannot escape, and she uses his magic to work her spells. Especially the spell of Aberrant, no other dragon's magic will make the spell work; it has to be a black dragon, and the dragon Ogolel captured is the last black dragon in our world. She had the rest killed so that she and she alone could master its powers." Emiril had not known this; she wondered why she had not noticed the black dragons were gone from Ibacion. She must have known subconsciously, but never thought about it. Ogolel was indeed cruel, to have killed off an entire subspecies to hoard its magic; only a truly evil person could do such a thing. But what if Breanne did not have the pendant? She had said that nothing had passed into this world with her. She feared that without it, Breanne would be stuck here forever.

"Do not worry about that, dear," her grandmother said as Emiril started to take the tea cups to the kitchen. "You have more important things to attend to. You just get going now, and I think you had better ride as straight and fast to Daedhrog as you can, if you get my meaning."

Emiril did indeed get her meaning. She was afraid it may already be too late. She was afraid Ogolel might already know where Breanne and Marcus were, and if she did, then the Dark Mage would be there as well, with that creature of his. She shuddered at the thought.

"Use the spell of light," her grandmother said.

"What?"

"The spell of light," she repeated. "I taught it to you when you were only a girl, do you remember?"

"Yes, I do, but use it on what?" Emiril said, confused.

"On the creature, of course," her grandmother said, looking at her as if she were daft.

"Oh," Emiril said, suddenly realizing the old woman had been in her head again. "Yes ok, I was wondering what would work on it. Thank you, grandmother," she said sincerely. She did not want to fight the creature, it was terrifying, but if she had to, now she knew how. And with her grandmother being the one telling her which spell to use, she was sure it would work.

They hugged for a long moment, neither one knowing when and if they would see each other again. Then just as her grandmother had promised, she turned and saw Tanja waiting for her, looking rested and ready to go. She thanked Adwin, leapt onto the horse's back and took off at a dead run along the old road. With any luck she would make it to

Daedhrog before or about the same time as Marcus and Breanne. She did not yet know how vital her timing would be.

Chapter 21
The Book Reveals

"Are you ready to head out?" Marcus asked as he put the rest of his food away. He had decided to keep some for later as they still had a long ride ahead of them.

"Yes," Breanne said. Marcus noticed she had eaten all of her food; he was not surprised by this.

They mounted their horses and once again started out, crossing the stream and heading more southwest this time. The forest was unchanging, a dense understory of tall trees towering far above their heads, brown trunks standing guard below. The brown earth was littered with fir needles, making the ground soft and sponge like under the horses' hooves, which made their passing silent. Breanne could smell the damp earth and that musty smell reminded her of mushrooms. Birds could be seen flitting from one limb to another, watching the intruders, keeping the attention on themselves and away from their nests, which lay hidden in the branches far above the riders' heads. Occasionally a squirrel would rear up on a branch and chatter relentlessly at them, as if challenging their right to be there, in his forest, and only when the riders could no longer be seen did he return to his foraging.

The shade from the tree canopy was a welcome blessing, the temperature which would be ten degrees warmer outside the forest, was a pleasant seventy-five degrees. Breanne felt relaxed, and to her surprise, a little bit less hopeless.

"Marcus, how do you know which way to go? The trees all look the same in here and there are no trails." She peered around them in bewilderment. She had noticed that for the four hours they had been travelling, nothing seemed to have changed. It was one fir tree after another, never a meadow or any other landmark, save for the stream, to account for where they were, and she wondered how he seemed to know the way without getting lost in the monotony.

"I used to hunt here when I was a boy," he said.

"But Marcus, aren't you from the South? I mean, Emiril said men with blonde hair came from the South and people with dark hair came from the North, and you have blonde hair."

"My family did live in the South, yes," he said rather solemnly. "We left when I was a young boy. I was about six, I think. We had to leave; my family was in service to the king when Ogolel tried to take over. After our service ended, we lived in peace in our native land for quite some time after that, but then Ogolel started to kill all who had stood in her way back then, and their descendants as well. We had to leave and come up here closer to the king, where we could be protected. It was then that I met Emiril. She has been a great friend since."

"Well, how come you can read minds? Don't you have to be an elf to do that?"

"No, you don't have to be an elf, the man at the tavern wasn't an elf," he said. "A lot of people can read minds; the only requirement is that you are filled with magic."

"What does that mean, filled with magic?"

"Well, you can be filled with magic several ways. One is to be born a magical creature, like Emiril, although elves aren't the only magical creatures here. Another is to get your magic from a source, either good or evil. That is how the Dark Mage got his magic; he promised his soul to the dark spirits for it. I got my magic from Emiril; she touched my soul with hers."

"How do you touch a person's soul," she asked?

"It is hard to explain." He thought about it for a moment, then continued, "Two people go into the spirit world, and they link minds, but they also grasp one another like in a hug. Then the person with the magic is able to pass some of it to the other person. When they return to this world, one person will have some of the other person's magic."

"How much of their magic do you get?" she asked fascinated.

"Well, I guess however much they want to give you. I am not sure, but I think you could get all of it if you wanted. I know that when Emiril and I linked up, it just flowed openly from her to me, until we broke the link. So, I guess if the link was not broken, you get as much as you wanted. Emiril gave me enough so that I could learn to read minds and perform some protective spells to keep my family safe." He said this with obvious gratitude and love for the elf. They had a strong bond between them.

She thought about her family now and wondered what they were doing. Were they worried, were they frantically looking for her? Her parents would know she was missing by now, it had been two days. She felt hopeless; she was starting to feel as if she would never get home. Tears welled in her eyes; she had to stop thinking about home and concentrate on the present.

"How much longer now?" she asked Marcus, hoping to hear some good news.

"Oh, about another four hours, we are making better time than I had thought we would. I think we will get there an hour sooner than I told you earlier.

The news brightened her mood and she started to enjoy the ride, noticing now, the small patches of wild flowers that grew on the forest floor where what little sunlight filtered through the dense tree canopy found the earth.

The creature glided through the break in the tree canopy to the forest floor below. The stream bubbling happily moments before now seemed to slink by, as if wishing it could gouge a new path out of the dirt it flowed through, in order to avoid the demon creature which had invaded its happy home. The Dark Mage peered through the creature's eyes at the bank along the stream. What he saw made his heart leap, hoof prints, dozens of them, and scuff marks, as if someone had been sitting beside the water's edge. They had been there, he knew it was them, they had been careless, he was getting close. He searched until he found the direction they had left in, then ordered the creature back up into the air and turned toward his unsuspecting quarry. In another hour it would be sunset and then darkness would make the hunt almost impossible, he had to find them, he had to find them now.

Emiril and Tanja ran down the old road at an unbelievable pace, trees flew by on their left as if they themselves were running in the opposite direction, making her dizzy. She felt the need to look to her right, out at the unmoving grassy plains, to steady herself; the lack of movement brought her perspective and slowed the dizzying sensation. The horse's long neck was stretched far out in front of it; lather coated both his sides as well as his chest. They had been running at a full gallop since leaving Malarcis, five hours ago. Yet even now, the horse showed no signs of slowing and Emiril knew that her grandmother had had a hand in his miraculous stamina; even Tanja being pure blooded Elven stock, could not have lasted this long, running this fast. She had understood the message from her grandmother, that time was of the essence, that Ogolel would be looking for Breanne, and that Emiril needed to be there to prevent her undoubted demise. But she wasn't sure if she were going to make it in time; she wasn't even sure where Breanne and Marcus were. What she was sure of however, was the fact that without her help, they would die, and she wasn't about to let that happen. What she wondered now was, how long the spell her grandmother placed on Tanja would last? She silently thanked her grandmother and hoped they would get there in time. She could see the sun starting to set and reached out with her mind, trying to contact Marcus.

Breanne's lack of horse-riding experience was once more taking a toll on her backside. She tried standing up in the stirrups for a while, but her legs became tired too fast to keep that stance for very long. She slid from side to side, first sitting on one cheek, then the other. It was no use; she was going to have to accept the fact that her bottom was going to fall off the minute she got off the horse. (A little dramatic she thought, but the pain was real.) She called out to Marcus to slow down a little, her horse wanted to break into a trot to keep up with his and if that happened, it really would be the end of her bottom. (No dramatics there.) He slowed, and she caught up to him.

"What's the matter?" he asked. "We're only about an hour away. It will be dark before we get there and then you will have to stay close by me so you don't get lost, ok?"

"Ok," she said, her face grimaced in pain. "It's just that I'm not used to riding and, well, uh, my, well, my bottom hurts." She looked away quickly, her face red.

Marcus laughed softly, but not in a way to further embarrass her, she silently thanked him for that. "Well, in that case," he said gently, "we can slow down a little. We need to be more watchful anyway, we are coming out of the forest. Do you see the break in the trees up ahead?"

Breanne strained to see through the growing darkness. After a few moments she could make out the spot where the trees thinned and light could be seen just on the other side. "Yes, I see it," she said excitedly. The thought of seeing Daedhrog and meeting more elves made her thoughts of home and evil creatures all but disappear.

"Just on the other side of the trees, there is a clearing," he said, the tone of his voice echoing her excitement. "It is the last leg of our journey, then we pass through the shield into Daedhrog. And into safety," he added.

He looked at Breanne, smiling; he too was ready for their trip to be over.

"What's the shield?" she asked puzzled.

"It is a magical force that surrounds Daedhrog and keeps out evil. You'll see it when we pass through, it shimmers at night and when the sun shines directly on it, it's the only time you can see it; during the day, it's nearly always invisible. When we get there, we'll have dinner and sleep in warm beds," he said, smiling at her, "and in the morning we'll meet up with…" His face suddenly went blank, he stopped in mid-sentence. Breanne saw a distant look in his eyes; he reined his horse in and motioned Breanne to do the same. His horse pawed the dirt, irritated at being restrained. She had never seen anyone look the way Marcus did now. His face looked like a corpse, he stared straight ahead, eyes fixated on something only he could see. She felt suddenly alone in the forest. She looked around her, the dark understory suddenly became eerie and foreboding, noises that she had not heard before suddenly deafened her. She knew at any moment something dark and dangerous would come creeping out from behind the nearest tree; she was suddenly afraid.

Emiril focused all her energy into finding Marcus, she had to reach him. It was dangerous to mind link with him, it could give away their position, but she had to warn him. She hoped she was not making a mistake.

The last rays of daylight streaked across the now mostly dark sky. The sound of the horse's feet beating rhythmically on the dirt road lent an eerie kind of music to her trance-like state. At first, she wasn't sure if she would be able to find them, then she thought she felt his presence.

She strained with the effort of linking her mind to his. At last he was there, hearing her. She frantically sent images to him of Ogolel, the Dark Mage, the creature, and then she shared Mindoneth's warning with him. She waited; except for the wind whipping her hair and the labored breathing of the horse, time seemed to stand still. She hoped that what she had been trying to convey had been understood and then to her relief, Marcus acknowledged that he had gotten the message and sent her an image of where they were. She was surprised when she realized that they were only about an hour out of Daedhrog. They had been making good time; she herself was a little closer, having taken the more direct route, the old road, and of course she had been running the entire way. Breanne and Marcus had had to take it slow as they wound their way through the trees. They decided to meet at the shield on the other side of the clearing where Marcus now sat talking with her. Then they quickly broke the link. Emiril thought they had been linked for less than ten minutes. She thought that they should be safe, but she was wrong.

The Dark Mage flew through the ever-darkening sky. The last rays of sunlight played a game of hide and seek on the tops of the trees, first this tree was visible, then it was shrouded in darkness, then another tree followed suit and went from being visible to disappearing in the darkness. This is how it went as the creature, with his parasitic passenger watching intently through his eyes, flew west toward the setting sun, following a trail of disappearing trees. The mage grew ever more distraught; he could feel the sharp edge of fear as he thought about returning to his fortress empty handed. He then imagined having to tell her he had not found the girl, that she was in the safety of Daedhrog under protection of the king. He shuddered, he was scared, scared for his life. He thought about not returning to his island sanctuary, no longer the safe haven it used to be. Now it seemed more like a crypt where he would go to die when Ogolel found out that he had failed. He thought maybe he would stay linked with the creature. He did not need to return to his body, he could live inside the creature's mind forever, and they would simply continue to fly west, following the retreat of the sun, staying just inside its warming light. But he could not stay connected to the creature, he did need to return to his body, it was impossible to stay inside the creature's mind forever, eventually his soul would die. So, he resigned himself to his fate and gave the creature the order to return to the island. He was about to sever the link between them, when he felt something flutter through his mind. He recognized it as energy passing from one mind to another. He could sense the linking of the two minds, guessing whose minds those might be and he suddenly saw light at the end of his long tunnel of defeat. He honed in on the signal, his mind picking it up like radar. He couldn't believe his luck; he had been ready to give up in defeat, assuming the girl had already passed through the shield and into Daedhrog, and now this. He could scarcely concentrate he was so elated; he had to focus.

On command, the creature banked sharply, turning toward the source of the signal, the Dark Mage guiding him, his heart beating fast, his breathing rapid. They were closer to them than he realized, and they were close to Daedhrog. They would have made it through the shield undetected if they had not linked minds. How stupid of her, he thought. Emiril should have known better, she should have known that she would give them away. He was elated by her stupidity; now he would not have to face *her* empty handed, his life no longer in danger. With new found life, he urged the creature on. Only minutes from now he would have them.

Breanne watched in horror and fascination as Marcus sat riveted in his saddle. Twice she had thought about trying to wake him out of whatever trance he was in, but twice she had decided against it. Maybe it was like sleepwalking, she had always heard you never woke up a sleepwalker as it could be dangerous for them. So, she sat, waiting for whatever was happening to him to pass. The horses became more agitated as the forest went from being shaded to an ever-increasing blackness. She finally had to grab the bridle of Marcus' horse to keep it from wandering into the clearing, a place where the horse seemed much safer than the enveloping blackness of the forest. She thought the horse had a good idea, but she had remembered Marcus' remark about needing to be more careful now that they were almost to the clearing. She did not know what was in the clearing, but she didn't want to find out the hard way.

Suddenly, from somewhere deep in the blackness, which minutes before had been the pleasantly shaded forest they had ridden through, an eerie sound echoed through the darkness, reverberating from tree to tree, making the hairs on the back of Breanne's neck stand straight up. She thought maybe it was a bird, or a coyote, but she also wondered what kind of crazy creature she would be unfamiliar with could be roaming these woods at night. JC pawed the ground and snorted, sensing her unease, which in turn, was making him uneasy. She decided that she would rather take her chances in the clearing, where at least she could see a little, than stay here in the now pitch-black forest waiting for that thing to find them.

Slowly she turned the horses toward the clearing and being careful to hold onto Marcus' arm, she led the group toward the gray light. She hoped she was making the right choice. As if to reassure her of her decision, the thing in the forest cried out once more, decidedly closer this time. She had to restrain herself from letting the horses break into a trot, she didn't want Marcus to fall out of his saddle and get hurt.

As they approached the clearing, she slowed and then stopped the horses just inside the tree line. She strained to see anything in the grayish light of the clearing. The moon, half covered by clouds, could only shed enough light on the clearing for Breanne to vaguely identify trees, shrubs, and other large landmarks. All else was lost in the darkness, unable to be picked out due to the meager light. She sat there, waiting for her eyes to become more accustomed to the new light source. Suddenly she tensed, then a mere millisecond before the hand touched her shoulder, she jumped, a scream stuck in her throat. She turned her head to see Marcus staring at her, looking as if he had just woken from a long sleep. He looked tired and in the grayish light, he looked scary.

"You scared me to death!" Breanne hissed. She could feel each beat of her heart against the thin layer of skin on her chest. She thought it might well be up against her skin, confused and trying to find its way back into its rightful spot below her rib cage. She tried to calm herself now that she realized it was only Marcus and not the mysterious creature grabbing her from out of the blackness, with the intent to drag her off to its hidden lair to be eaten slowly one limb at a time, (way, way too dramatic she scolded herself).

"I am sorry," he whispered. Then he put his finger to his lips and motioned her to come closer. She leaned in, her ear almost touching his mouth. "We are in danger," he said. She could feel the adrenalin that had started to diffuse, now surge once more through her body. "Do you remember me telling you about the Dark Mage and the creature he controls?" She nodded silently. The sounds of the forest suddenly seemed distant. "I have just spoken to Emiril." Breanne involuntarily looked into his face, astonishment in her eyes. He nodded that it was true and gave her a look that implied, I'll tell you later, and she turned her head once more to hear his low whispering voice. "She has warned me that the Dark Mage is looking for us right now. He probably has an idea of where we are already, and when Emiril and I linked minds, it was dangerous; it could have given our position away. I don't know if it did for sure, but we need to assume it to be the case so that we won't be caught off guard. Do you understand all that I am saying to you?" Breanne nodded once more. Then, as she waited for him to continue, she found herself straining to hear, not Marcus, but anything. She suddenly realized she was having a hard time hearing, because there was nothing to hear, the familiar sounds of the night, the frogs, the crickets, all were gone. Warning bells started going off inside her, her body sounding the alarm that something was not right with this picture. She looked at Marcus, he too was looking around, his head cocked to one side, listening, reassuring her that she was not imagining it; he too had noticed the sudden change. She saw him look into the blackness behind them, then he looked into the clearing and finally he looked straight up above them, and his face took on a look Breanne had not previously seen on him, a look of stark terror. She felt the terror run through the man and straight into her. Her hair stood on end, her nerve endings tingled with the overload of electrical impulses being sent frantically to her brain, "warning" they said, "danger," goose bumps covered her entire body. The horses were not immune to this pandemic of terror, they broke the silence, dancing back and forth and pawing the ground. Big clouds of steam were snorted out of their nostrils. She had to fight to keep JC from running away, in which direction it didn't matter, as long as he didn't stay here. It was then she realized why Marcus was so terrified, and why the horses were acting the way they were, and why she looked like a freshly plucked chicken with all its bumps protruding from its skin. The unspeakable had happened, he had found them, the Dark Mage had found them.

Chapter 22
Breanne's Choice

Emiril felt better now that she had been in touch with Marcus. She now knew they were safe, if only for the time being. She continued down the old road for roughly two more miles, then turned off into the plain that surrounded Daedhrog. She knew where she was going even in the dark. As a child she had played in that clearing many times. She and the other Elven children had thought it great fun, due to the fact that it was just outside the shield and exposed them to danger. They would pretend to fight evil sorcerers and giant trolls (and of course they always won). What they didn't know however, is that an elder elf had been secretly watching over them the whole time. The children never did anything that wasn't monitored, especially the king's daughter. But still, they did not know they were being watched and it built upon their courage to dare the outside world and so it was allowed. However, they would never have been permitted to play anywhere else outside the shield; there were very real dangers outside the glen.

The moon was shielded behind the clouds, the meager light it had afforded no longer available which to Marcus meant they were less likely to be seen. He chose this time to act. "Remember to stay close to me, ok?" he said, looking into the girl's eyes. He hoped his fear for their safety was not as evident as he felt it was; it was actually more evident than he could have imagined. She nodded, her fear so intense she could do little else. He went over the plan one more time, making sure she knew what to do in case the worst happened and she were left on her own. "Once again," he said, "we run, as fast as we can, go as straight as you can; the shield is about six miles ahead of us. Emiril will be there waiting. If you don't see her, you will see the shield. That's how you'll know when you're safe. Don't stop until you pass through the shield, it glimmers in the night, remember?"

"Yes," she whispered, secretly afraid she might not see it at all, that she would not find it and be running forever. The thought of being lost in the dark night, alone, with an evil mage and his monstrosity chasing her made her want to turn around, find a big tree and hide beside it until daylight. But she knew she couldn't do that, the forest was no longer safe; the only safe place was the glen and they had to get there at all costs.

He continued, "If anything happens to me…" Her face turned white, unseen in the darkness. "Keep running, don't stop whatever you do. You wouldn't be able to help me anyway. Got it?" Again, Breanne nodded, she could not believe things had turned out so badly so fast. One minute she was enjoying her ride through the cool forest on her new horse with Marcus, the next minute she was preparing to run blindly for her life through the pitch-black night.

"Ok," Marcus said, "let's go." He spurred his horse which immediately took off at a dead run into the clearing, leaving the little bit of cover the forest had offered them. He looked behind him to make sure Breanne was following. She didn't have to encourage her horse, the minute he saw Marcus' horse take off, he lunged foreword. In seconds he was beside them, running neck and neck across the inky black clearing, dark shapes flying by at lightning speed. Breanne prayed they wouldn't hit a tree or fall into a hole. She prayed they would make it. She prayed the creature was not somewhere above them, searching, and she prayed JC could see better in the dark than she could.

The horses were both running hard, but Breanne weighed less than Marcus, and she didn't carry heavy weapons on her saddle like he did. It didn't take long for JC to pull ahead of Marcus' horse and she realized that she was fast outdistancing them. She became frightened, her fear of being alone in the blackness overwhelming her. She knew that it wouldn't take long before Marcus was no longer visible in the darkness that surrounded her.

She looked behind her to see how far back they were, not daring to slow down, but she hadn't anticipated running alone. It took her a moment to see them in the darkness, about forty feet behind her and falling back fast; she saw Marcus wave her on. She started to turn back around when she thought she saw something, darker than the sky, above and slightly behind them. She peered into the blackness, the wind whipped her hair into her face and eyes; she swiped it away, her eyes watering, she squinted and kept wiping them, frantically scanning the sky. Suddenly she saw two red spots hovering just behind them. She screamed out a warning that she herself could not hear, the wind whipped it from her mouth and behind her the moment it escaped her lips. She waved and pointed frantically, and Marcus, either hearing her screams or seeing her waving, suddenly turned and looked right into the face of the creature, which by this time was directly behind him. Breaking the silence it had held until now, it screamed a terrifying high-pitched screech that made the hairs on Breanne's neck stand up. Marcus' horse let out his own scream of terror and she saw the two of them veer to the right and make a circle, coming up behind the creature. They had really fallen behind now and Breanne was losing sight of them. The creature, on the other hand, did not care about Marcus and his horse, instead it was gaining on her. She could now see its shape in the darkness, the serpentine neck, the long tail, huge wings that beat with the sound of a giant bellows. But mostly, she could see those eyes, red piercing eyes. She had seen enough, she turned back around, terror racing through her body and clung to JC as tightly as she could, subconsciously urging the horse to run faster, although she did not need to urge him at all, he was as terrified as she and was running as fast as he could with the sounds of the creature urging him on. Breanne was now convinced the creature was not after Marcus because it had not even slowed down when he had performed his evasive maneuver. This had made it quite clear to her who the creature's intended victim was, it was her.

Emiril stood waiting just outside the shield. She could not stand still, she paced back and forth, starting to walk further into the clearing and then turning back, pacing once again. How long had it been since she and Marcus had linked? She didn't think it would take this long for them to get here, although she had been closer to the shield than they were and she had to account for her horse being faster than theirs, but she was still anxious. She peered into the darkness, her Elven eyes could see things better in the dark than a human's, but she could still see nothing.

She could not take it anymore and turned to get her horse ready to go look for them, when suddenly she heard in the distance the unmistakable sound of a running horse, followed by the terrifying cry of a creature. She froze where she was. Suddenly she was very afraid. She had never fought one of these creatures before, and she wondered if she were capable of winning the upcoming battle. She started to feel helpless, then regained her composure. Stop it, she said to herself, you are a great sorceress, you will win this fight, besides, grandmother has given you the weapon with which to beat the creature. She started to feel better and her resolve came back. Well, win or lose, she thought, she had to try; Breanne's life depended on it. She turned around and planted her feet on the ground, readying her mind for the spell she would use.

The horse's hoof beats grew louder, and now Emiril could also hear the sound of the creature's wings, much like the sound of a wind storm coursing through the trees as they propelled it toward her position. She hoped the creature did not know she was waiting and she would have the element of surprise, which would aid her in defeating this nightmare monster.

She looked intently into the darkness and could just see the outline of the thundering horse with a small black blur (which she knew would be Breanne) attached to his back, and flying directly behind them was the creature. Its red eyes focused on the rider; she could see its mouth beginning to open, and white teeth now visible in the darkness. The creature brought its feet forward. She knew what was coming next; she had to act and act fast. She recited the spell, holding her arm out and up diagonally from her body, hand held so her palm was raised and pointing toward the creature as if motioning it to stop. She thought about the time her grandmother had taught her this spell. "Concentrate on your inner light," her grandmother had told her. She did so now, drawing on her inner strength. She could feel the power surge through her, starting from her toes, rising up her midsection and traveling down her arm where it then burst from her palm in a stream of electrified, white, crackling light.

The element of surprise was indeed hers. The creature did not know she was there and did not try to evade the first round of light. It hit the creature at the exact moment it had been going to grab Breanne from the saddle. It screamed loudly, the force of the spell pushing it back six feet, white electricity coursed across its body. The crackling sound it made could be heard throughout the clearing, and she could tell it was in pain. Emiril wasted no time, she did not want the creature to regain its bearings. She had to give Breanne, who was thundering toward her, time to pass through the shield. She cast the spell again and again, wounding it over and over, until at last the creature fell in defeat, its death coming with a loud thud as its body crashed to the ground with a whooshing sound as air escaped its dead body.

She stood trembling in the cold night air, staring at the giant body before her, trembling from the exertion of the fight, and the cold, but most of all from exhilaration. She had just proven to herself that she could defend against one of the Dark Mage's most evil weapons, and she once more whispered a thank you to her grandmother who miles away was sitting in her chair in front of her fire, smiling at Emiril's glorious victory (Emiril had no knowledge of this).

"Well done, my brave elfin friend."

Emiril snapped her head up to see Marcus standing before her. She had been so caught up in her victory, she had not noticed him walk up, a first for her. Relief washed through her and she felt tears well up in her eyes at seeing her friend alive and well. "I see you still live," she said with a shaky voice, only this time she could not hide her sheer joy at that fact.

"I see you do as well," he said, a huge smile on his face.

They could not help themselves; they threw their arms around each other and held on for a moment or two, overjoyed that they were both alive, the creature was dead and that Breanne was safely in the glen.

"Grandmother told me that Iola and your daughter are safe with her mother," she whispered in his ear. He hugged her more tightly, grateful for her insight, his fear for them had been a burden he carried since he left their home that morning. Now he could relax; Emiril had greatly blessed him with this knowledge.

"Let's go see Breanne," Emiril said. "I had sentries positioned just inside the shield. They had to have found her by now. With any luck she will be at the palace by now."

Chapter 23
The River Crossing

While Emiril waited for Breanne to wake up, she had passed the time by making her some tea. It was an old family recipe, taught to her by her grandmother – a blend of special herbs, to both calm her and ease her pain. While Breanne sat slowly sipping the hot beverage, Emiril told her about her trip to see Mindoneth. Upon hearing of her visit with the sorceress, Breanne asked the inevitable. Did Mindoneth know a way for her to get home? Now Emiril sat staring at the girl. She didn't want to tell her what she had learned, that retrieving the one thing that could send her home, might also get her killed. Yet how could she not tell her, she had to know. She couldn't find an easy way to say it, so she started at the beginning.

"Do you remember me telling you that the book you read from was the only book of its kind?" she asked.

"Yes," Breanne said.

"Well, I was wrong, there is another." Breanne's eyes lit up and she got excited. Emiril quickly held up a hand. "Wait, do not get excited yet," she said softly, trying to lessen the blow. "We do not have the book." She felt Breanne's reaction in herself as well. Sorrow was a strong emotion and one that mind readers and elves especially could easily pick up on.

Breanne looked down at the bed in frustration. It was just her luck that the book would be inaccessible to her, but, she thought to herself, I'm not giving up. She suddenly raised her head, eyes sparkling with renewed hope and asked, "Well, where is it then? Can we go get it?"

Emiril looked at the girl, eyes sparkling, courage showing in her face. It may be possible to retrieve the book yes, but the danger was high, the journey long. Was this young girl before her really capable of going on such a quest? Could she hold up under the strain? She knew she would be well looked after, by herself and Marcus, but would that be enough, just to look after her? At some point the girl had to be able to stand on her own. She would have to have courage. If they went, the trip would have to be secretive, Ogolel had spies everywhere. They would have to choose the members of the group carefully. She would go, and of course Marcus would definitely go – she wouldn't go on any quest without him, unless he himself chose not to go, and he never did. She thought about her friend, Marcus had saved her life several times already and she knew he would die for her and now for Breanne as well. Of course, she did not want Marcus to die, she did not want anyone to die for that matter, but he would and that made him special. Of course, they would have to enlist the services of one of the dwarves; they would need a guide to navigate through the tunnels under the mountain. She would discuss it with Marcus and they would decide if anyone else would be needed. She was beginning to believe that they could do this, that they could get the book and Breanne could return home. She looked at Breanne, resolve in her face. "We can go get it," she answered her, "but," she added quickly, "it will be dangerous. You see Breanne, the Dark Mage has the book."

Breanne's blood ran cold. She could not believe what Emiril had just told her. The evil man, who had sent that horrible creature to kill her, had in his possession, the only thing that could get her home again. She shivered so violently that she spilt her tea. Emiril quickly grabbed it from her and set it on the table by the bed. She looked deeply into Breanne's eyes and recited a spell of calm – the tea was proving not enough under the circumstances, and she didn't want Breanne to feel any more anxiety than she had to. In a few minutes, Breanne stopped shivering and looked half sleepy. "Better?" Emiril asked her. Breanne nodded, apologizing and feeling a bit foolish for spilling the tea. Emiril told her not to worry about it and gave her a bright smile, then continued telling her what she had learned about the book. "Before Ogolel went to challenge the king, she made a copy of the book. I did not know this; I do not think very many people knew about that." She said thoughtfully, "So when she sent the original book to your world, the Dark Mage took the copy with him to the island of the ancient Ancestors." She stopped for a moment, thinking of something she had not thought of before. Why would Ogolel go to all the trouble to send one of the books out of their world and then keep the copy here? That didn't make any sense. If the book was so important that she didn't want anyone to get their hands on it, would the copy not be just as important, and if she was not that concerned with someone getting their hands on the copy, why did she send the original away in the first place? There had to be something she was missing. She was very confused all of a sudden; she needed to talk with Mindoneth about this. In fact, why had Mindoneth not thought of this same question, or had she? If she had, why had she not mentioned it to her? The sound of Breanne clearing her throat brought her attention back to their conversation. "Sorry about that, I was just thinking of something," she said. "Where were we, oh yes, the book is on the Island of the Ancient Ancestors. It will be difficult to retrieve, and very dangerous, but I think we can do it," she concluded, smiling.

Breanne sat looking at Emiril; hope once again alive in her eyes. Then she looked at Emiril inquisitively. "So I was wondering," she said hesitantly, "the spell that I used to get here, can it be used whenever we want to use it, or... well, can we use it a lot?" she asked.

Emiril looked at her, puzzled. "What do you mean a lot? We would only need to send you home once, and I am pretty sure we can manage that."

"Well," Breanne said slowly, "I was thinking that if you wanted to come with me, you could see my world and then you could come back here afterword." She looked at Emiril's face, trying to read her expression. She could never tell what the elf was feeling unless she specifically chose to reveal her emotions. Then all of a sudden, Emiril's face turned pale white in color, her eyes darkened and she looked panicked. Breanne sat up further in the bed startled. "What is it?" she asked, suddenly worried again.

"I forgot something," she almost yelled. Breanne had never seen her so upset before. She reached out and grabbed both of Breanne's arms and looked her straight in the eyes. "Breanne, I am so sorry, I forgot about something very, very important. Mindoneth told me that there is only one way the spell will work again. She said that there is a pendant we need to have in order for the spell to work. She said you had to have had it in your world and that you had to have had it in your possession while you read the spell, or it would not have worked." She was now even more panicked. She continued, her voice still raised and her face even more pale than before. "I forgot about it, but without it we cannot use the spell and send you home." Her hands tightened around Breanne's arms. "Do you remember a pendant; it had a black dragon on it? You said nothing came here with you from your world, but if the pendant did not come, you cannot get home. And there is no copy of it, there can never be a copy of it." She was frantic now, her eyes boring into Breanne's, trying to rip the answer from her mind.

Breanne's heart was beating fast; Emiril was so upset and that made Breanne upset. But as she listened to what the elf was saying, her heart beat slowed and she started to relax. The pendant, that was what this was about? She had the pendant. She was so relieved she hadn't forgotten it back by the stream. "Emiril," she interrupted, "wait, wait a minute." She was having a hard time getting Emiril to stop and listen to her. Finally, she reached up and put her hand on Emiril's mouth.

Shocked, Emiril stopped talking and just stared at her. Breanne took her hand away from her mouth laughing; she did look funny, almost like she wanted to both smile and get angry at the same time. Her laughter made her head ache, and she had to stop quickly. Then she looked into Emiril's eyes and said slowly and clearly, "I have the pendant." It took about four seconds for Breanne to see it register on Emiril's face, but when it did, Breanne decided that her eyes really must be able to glow because they looked as if someone were behind each one with a spot light, they were shining so brightly. Emiril broke into a huge smile, and she hugged Breanne tightly. Breanne had to try not to moan from the pain of it, not wanting to hurt Emiril's feelings.

She didn't remember falling off the horse, but apparently, according to what Emiril had told her, she had passed out after passing through the shield, and had fallen off her horse and now her whole body ached. She waited a moment longer until Emiril let her go, then she eased back against the pillows again, smiling so that Emiril could not tell she had hurt her. "The pendant is in my pants pocket," she said. In a flash, Emiril jumped up and went to a chair in the corner and grabbed her pants and brought them to her. Breanne fumbled with the strings to the pocket for a minute before she could get the knot undone, then she pulled the pendant out and held it up for Emiril to see. What she saw shocked her. In the attic, she had noticed the eyes of the dragon appeared to be shining, but here in Daedhrog, they didn't appear to be shining, they were glowing, the deepest red she had ever seen. They were so bright, she could see the reflection of them on Emiril's face as she sat gazing at the pendant with a look of reverence. Breanne wondered why the pendant would have such an effect on the elf, but she did not have a chance to ask her, as someone was knocking on the door. Emiril jumped up, startled. "Hide that," she whispered as she left the bed and went to see who it was. She cracked the door, peered out and then opened it widely. Breanne watched as a familiar face first peeked in and then come into the room. "Marcus!" she exclaimed.

Marcus crossed the room in two giant strides and hugged Breanne tightly. She hugged him back despite the pain which now seemed to be affection's companion. She thought to herself, I will be glad when getting hugged by people will no longer be torture. (Not dramatic she thought, it really hurts to be loved right now.) When he let her go, she once again eased back onto the pillows and silently thanked God she did not know anyone else here who would come in and hug her, for now at least, she was safe.

"I was worried about you, young lady," Marcus said sternly, but with a look of tenderness in his eyes.

She smiled. "I was worried about you, too," she said just as sternly, and with the same tender look he showed her.

He laughed heartily. "You don't have to worry about me, young lady, I have a way of staying alive even when the odds are stacked against me." But then he looked sullen. "Besides, it wasn't me the creature was after," he added, looking into Breanne's eyes worriedly.

"Well," she said, "good thing we have Emiril for a friend."

They both looked at her then, and Emiril could feel the love they had for her emanating from them. "Oh, I didn't do anything special," she said, feeling a bit self-conscious.

In unison Marcus and Breanne said, "You saved our lives." Then they looked at each other and laughed. Emiril joined them.

"But really," Marcus said as the laughter faded, "if it wasn't for you, Emiril, Breanne would not be here, and I don't know if I would be either. You really did save our lives. You should be proud."

"Indeed she should be," said a deep voice from across the room. They all turned, startled by the newcomer. Suddenly, Marcus and Emiril fell to the floor on one knee, heads bowed. Confused, Breanne tried to get out of bed to follow their lead, wincing uncontrollably in pain.

"Hold it right there, young one," the voice commanded, "you stay put."

She froze where she was, grateful for the order and breathing harder than she would have expected from the pain and exertion. Emiril turned and helped her back into bed. (If anyone else comes into this room, I am going to die; nothing dramatic about that, she thought as pain coursed through her.)

"Rise up you two, you show me great honor."

Breanne looked over Emiril's shoulder as the figure stepped out of the shadows. She was awestricken as, what was quite obviously the king himself, stepped over to her bedside. He was dressed in a white flowing robe made from some kind of plush looking fabric and trimmed with golden thread. His shirt was a gold color and his pants were white like his robe. He wore dark brown boots and on his head sat a beautiful crown encrusted with red stones, which she thought were probably rubies. He had long blond hair tied back and no beard. His eyes were a deep bluish-purple color, much darker than Emiril's and like hers, they too seemed to glow. But what surprised Breanne the most was how young he looked. Emiril had told her how old her father was, yet he did not look any older than Breanne's own father, and he was only forty-four. She was beginning to see why Emiril would feel bad for her kind, if the elves looked this good at eight hundred and twenty years old, she wondered what Emiril would think if she could see her grandfather – he was only seventy-two and he looked ancient compared to the king.

"My name is King Badhor," the imposing figure before her said, stretching an arm out in her direction. "And you must be Breanne, I have heard a lot about you. Welcome to Daedhrog, may you find rest, food and peace in my home."

Breanne was entranced by the sound of his voice and spellbound from staring into his eyes, but she managed to reach out her hand to shake his. She was brought back to the present when she felt his hand not clasping hers, but gripping her wrist. She followed his lead and grabbed his wrist as well. They sat that way for an awkward moment and then he let her go. She had to remember this form of greeting, it was likely something that was common here and she wanted to make sure she got it right the next time she met someone.

Next, the king turned to Emiril. "I see you still live," he said, stone faced.

"I see you do too," she replied, equally without emotion.

He turned to Marcus who had been standing at the foot of the bed. "I see you still live."

"I see you still live as well," Marcus replied with a blank face.

Breanne could not help but be both intrigued and a bit creeped out by this exchange of greetings. The thing that really made it weird for her was the lack of emotion the three were showing. It reminded her of the way the people acted in the movie *Invasion of the Body Snatchers* after the aliens had replicated them, and she wondered if they always greeted one another like this.

"It is a warrior's greeting, used only by elves when they have been away from one another and in danger of not returning. The lack of emotion represents the fact that you did not believe they would die and gives them hope and courage in the face of danger," the king said as he turned once more to look at her. "Of course," he said over his shoulder, "we do allow certain individuals the privilege of sharing in our custom, but usually only after they have saved the princesses life a few times."

Breanne could see a twinkle in his eyes, and looked at Marcus who had a big grin on his face. She noticed too that he was blushing. Wait a minute she thought, how did he know I was wondering about that.

"I know lots of things, young one," the king replied.

Breanne was visibly shocked now. She was trying very hard not to think anything. He was reading her mind, as impossible as it seemed. It wasn't like at the tavern when she felt the flutter, this was more like telepathy. Now she knew what Marcus had meant when he had told her he had spoken with Emiril. She started to wonder how he could do that and then stopped, trying to unthink the question. Too late she thought, you already thought it, dummy.

Looking quite amused, the king smiled and Breanne thought how handsome he was for being so old. "I am very old, yes," he said, "and I have learned to do many things in my lifetime. But I will not read your thoughts without your permission anymore if it makes you uncomfortable," he said gently.

She felt embarrassed by her reaction to all of this. "I'm sorry," she said out loud. "It's just that where I come from, people can't read other people's thoughts and I am not used to it, it scares me a little." She looked at the bed for a moment letting it all sink in. He waited, then she looked at him and thought, "Can you read all my thoughts?"

He looked deeply into her eyes for a moment and she felt that same fluttering feeling she had felt at the tavern when Marcus had started to read her mind. She tried not to be afraid, she stared back into his bluish-purple eyes and suddenly she felt him say, "Yes, Breanne, I can read all your thoughts, but what is more interesting, is that you can hear me, can't you?"

Her eyes opened wider and she was sure she had heard him say something to her, but she had been watching his face the whole time, his

141

mouth did not move. But she had heard him, she was sure of it. She thought, "Say something else," and continued to stare at him, concentrating on his mouth.

"You must not tell anyone about this, do you understand?" she heard him say as she sat staring at his unmoving mouth. She was becoming afraid, but at the same time, she was beginning to feel excitement too. "You must agree not to tell anyone, do you agree?" he thought to her more urgently.

"Not even Emiril?" she thought back.

"No, not even Emiril," he said.

"I agree," she told him, but before she could ask why, he turned away, breaking the connection between them, leaving her with many unanswered questions.

Chapter 24
The Dragon's Shadow

He woke beside the pond, shivering in the pre-dawn cold. Looking around, he noticed that Ogolel was gone, but the creature remained. He could see it through the mist that hung over the water. He had to force himself not to be afraid of it any longer. He knew they had subdued it, but it had almost killed him, it would take time for him to be truly comfortable around it. He sat up and felt sharp pains running up and down his back, his head felt as if it would explode. He had never been so close to death before and he wondered if it always felt this way. Shivering, he noticed his clothes were damp with dew and wished he had not passed out last night.

The creature stirred and instinctively he jumped, his heart racing. He couldn't tell if it were sleeping or just lying there with its eyes closed. Either way, he was glad it was on the opposite shore as he. The area around the pond was silent, nothing stirred in the aftermath of the night's events. Those creatures that could escape, were long gone, and those that could not, were dead. No creature would, or could for that matter, live here again – the area was ecologically damaged by the activities that had transpired and would forever be unable to support life. That did not matter to the Dark Mage however, what did matter was the fact that she had had to come and save him. He clenched his fists, ashamed, mad, hating the fact that she was more powerful than he was. The only reason she was more powerful, was because she was and elf. Having magical abilities was a natural part of being an elf, you were born with it. He was not, he had to fight for his abilities. He had to be smart and learn incantations, and he had to be strong. She was simply born and even then, she had to come to him for some of the spells she used; she did not know them, he had to teach her.

He was becoming more agitated. If it weren't for him, she would have been destroyed that day she went before the king. His spell got her out of there, his spell kept her from being turned into an old, ugly hag with no magical abilities. But she did not even acknowledge these things. She treated him like a servant. He had even kept her secret all these years. He had told no one about the copy of the book. He had told no one about the real reason she had sent the original book away and he had told no one she had killed all the dragons so that the medallion could not be replicated. The medallion by the way was his doing, not hers. She was not as powerful as people thought. He was the one behind her power, except of course in the spirit realm. He sighed. In the spirit realm, he was no match for her, she ruled supreme over all manner of creatures there. He didn't think even the king and his mother could defeat her there. She knew that as well, that is why she felt safe there, and why she spent so much time there. He thought for a moment, if someone did defeat her in the spirit world, she would be unable to return to this world, she would be forever imprisoned there, with no magic.

He thought about the events of last night and how she had helped him subdue the creature. She was a powerful mind reader, that is where her greatest strength in this world was, he thought, in fact, she was so powerful she could kill someone if she chose to. That is why he could not stand up to her; she would surely kill him. Some day he would be more powerful than her, he thought. Someday he would break away from her and be free. But for now, he had his orders; he knew what she expected of him. He looked at his new creature; the thought of Emiril killing his last one upset him even more than he thought possible. He hated her for killing it, he hated this new creature, and he was sure it hated him. The only way the creature would listen now and do what he commanded was if it felt her presence, that would mean he would have to feel her presence as well. He glared at the creature, why had it fought so hard, why had it been so powerful, he really did hate it.

He gathered his things and started towards the clearing, then facing the inevitable, he stopped and turned around. He closed his eyes, his hands trembled, as he entered the creature's mind. Suddenly he could feel it glaring at him with unseen eyes. He shivered, remembering his near-death experience. He started to retreat, and then felt her presence there as well; he stopped, finding his courage. He reached out and with renewed resolve, grabbed the creature's mind with his. It felt less powerful than it had last night, it didn't struggle. He thought he felt a hint of resignation in the creature, as if its spirit had been broken. He knew what that felt like, his spirit had been broken a long time ago, by Ogolel, when he was very young and naïve. He found himself suddenly feeling sorry for the creature; they were in part sharing a similar fate at the hands of someone he was sure they both hated. More gently now, he showed it a mental map of Ibacion, then showed it the Island of the Ancient Ancestors. Go there, he commanded, and waited. He retreated then, back into his own mind and opened his eyes in time to see the creature heave itself off the ground and take flight, its massive black wings creating a wind strong enough to rustle the tree branches. He felt a little more courageous now, but he felt something else as well, something he hadn't felt in a long time. He felt empathy for the creature, and it felt strange.

It was time to go and as he walked away from the pond, he stood up a little straighter than he usually did. It would take him a few days to get home; he wanted to gather some plants along the way for a new spell he was working on.

Chapter 25
Captured by Fear

Breanne could smell the food before Emiril passed through the door to her room. She had been resting but had awoken about a half hour ago, starving. She felt a little better, her head did not hurt as bad, but she still felt a wave of dizziness each time she tried to do more than sit up against the pillows, so she had just laid there, studying the beautiful artwork that adorned the walls. But now the smell of the food was enough to make her mouth water and she thought to herself, I could get out of bed for food (no exaggeration). The good news was that she wouldn't have to, Emiril brought her dinner on a tray which fit neatly on her lap. She eyed the plate; there was some sort of meat that in her world would be a steak. She hoped it wasn't anything too weird, but decided she was too hungry to worry about it. There was also a sort of orange root that looked similar to potatoes, and corn. She was surprised to see corn, maybe this world was closer to her own than she realized. On the tray there was a piece of bread and some more of Emiril's tea. She looked at the elf, swallowing back saliva as her mouth freely watered in anticipation, and thanked her profusely. "Really," she said, "I am starving, thank you so much. Sorry to be such a burden on you."

Emiril chuckled, "You are most certainly not a burden," she said. "It is no trouble at all."

Breanne took a bite of the orange roots, they tasted like yams; she took another bite, she was sure that they were yams. "These are really good," she said. "What do you call them?"

"They are called Antum," Emiril told her. "They grow wild in the forests around here."

"They are so good," Breanne said, her mouth full of them. She swallowed. "Where I am from, we have something just like this we call yams. We eat them at Thanksgiving and other times also."

"What is Thanksgiving?" Emiril asked.

"Oh, sorry," Breanne said, thinking of the best way to explain it to her. "In my world people live on different land masses called continents, and one time some people left a continent they lived on and went to another one. The people there were different, but in the winter, when the new people were starving, they brought them food. They became friends that day and they have celebrated that day ever since."

"That sounds wonderful," Emiril said. "Do they still live in peace now?"

Breanne thought about it for a moment, her face saddened. She looked at Emiril. "No, they don't," she said quietly.

Emiril looked confused. "What happened?"

"Well," Breanne said, "it was very sad, really. The new people, not all, but most of them, became very greedy and they wanted to take over the land and they didn't want to share with the people who were already there. They wanted gold and they wanted to have all the land for towns and raising cattle. They started to fight the people who had been there, and they killed most of them. A lot of them died from diseases the new people brought with them too, but a lot of them were killed by the new people. They made them move away from their homes and live in places they had never lived before; they killed many of the animals the people used for food; they forced them to live the way they did. They even took their children and made them live in houses where they were told they could not speak their language, and they had to wear clothes like the new people. They were taught how to work as servants in the new people's homes. The people who had been living there had lived a very long time in harmony with the earth and nature, but now they were no longer able to feed themselves and many starved. The ones who didn't had to rely on the new people to provide them with food, and if they didn't do all the things the new people told them to, they were killed. It was horrible." Breanne looked at Emiril, she was ashamed, even though she had not done anything, she still felt guilty. "The worst part is," she said, "even today the people are still not getting treated fairly. They are still fighting for their rights in the courts, and it was their land in the first place. The new people had no right to do what they did, but because they had better weapons, and so many of the people died from diseases, they were able to completely take over and now the land belongs to them and they have ruined so much of it already. If they don't stop abusing it, there will be no hope for future generations. I just don't see why they couldn't have lived the way the people who were already there did. They did not ruin the land, they respected the animals, they lived in union with the earth. It is a very sad story." She hung her head, and a tear streaked down her cheek. She had never really thought about it as deeply as she just had, and she was really upset at what the Europeans had done to the Native Americans.

Emiril looked at her in disbelief. Imagine, a people treating another so badly. Things happened in Ibacion, but on an individual level, never had one group treated another so badly. She was beginning to wonder if she wanted Breanne to return home after all.

Breanne wiped her eyes and turned back to her dinner. She didn't want to dwell on thoughts that made her sad, she wanted to concentrate on what was happening now. She took a bite of corn. "In my world we have this food," she said. "We call it corn."

Emiril's eyes fluttered and she looked shocked. "We also call that corn," she said.

Now Breanne looked shocked also. "Really?" she asked. Surely Emiril was playing a joke on her.

"Really," Emiril said, "I'm not joking."

"How can that be?" Breanne asked her. "Don't you find that odd?"

"Yes, I do," Emiril said, looking at her equally bewildered.

Breanne ate the rest of her dinner in near silence; it was hard to talk with your mouth full.

Emiril was also mostly silent. She was thinking about that morning when her father had come in to see them. Had he seemed a bit odd? When he and Breanne were talking, he seemed to be saying more in the undertones of his words than he was in direct conversation to her. Was he reading her mind? Unless he told her, she would not be able to tell. She didn't think that was the answer; even mind reading was not that unusual. It did not give her the feeling she was having now, that something had transpired without her being aware of it. The rest of the visit had been uneventful. They had filled him in on the events that had led up to them all being there, finding Breanne, the mind reader at the tavern, the creature, her visit with Mindoneth. He had been pleased to hear she was well, the information about the copy of the book and finally their plans to gain it. He had been most interested in their plans to get the book. He agreed that they would need the help of one of the dwarves, and he had also agreed that their party should remain as small as possible to keep from being detected. She had told him about the pendant, and he had insisted on seeing it. When she showed it to him, he was in awe. The look on his face was one she had never seen before. He had told her that at all costs the pendant should be kept safe. She had agreed. Breanne had asked her to carry it, as she felt that Emiril could better protect it. Everyone else agreed, and the king had commended her on making such a wise and grown up decision. Breanne had blushed and thanked him, beginning to think of him in a grandfatherly way, and his opinion of her decision made her feel good. When he left for the night, he had given Emiril and Breanne a kiss on the forehead and shook Marcus's hand, patting him on the back. Emiril was pleased that her father was okay with all the decisions she had made so far. She always wanted to please him, and when she failed and he was disappointed in her, which wasn't very often, she felt miserable. She was also glad that Marcus was here, she felt bad that he was away from his family, but she could not have felt as brave and confident if he were not here. She could not have felt closer to him if they were blood related; she loved him like a brother.

Now watching Breanne eat her dinner, she anticipated the start of their trip. They would wait one more day for Breanne to recover. She was making great progress, but then they would have to be going. The longer they waited, the more time the Dark Mage and Ogolel had to make their own plans, or worse, move the book.

"What kind of animal is this?" Breanne asked suddenly. She looked at Emiril almost afraid to hear the answer as she slowly chewed the meat, trying to get the nerve to swallow it. She hadn't tasted meat like this before in her world, but that wasn't saying much, she had only had the usual meats before, like cow, chicken, pig, nothing exotic.

"Do you like it?" Emiril asked.

Breanne hadn't even thought about whether she liked it, she had been too caught up in worrying about what kind of animal it was. She thought about it for a moment, pushing the meat around in her mouth with her tongue. "Yes, I like it," she said, and she did truly like the flavor of it.

"It is a big animal called a Romon, which looks a little like the horse, but is thinner and has horns on its head," she said putting her hands above her head, fingers splayed out.

Breanne felt better instantly; it sounded normal. In fact, it sounded like a deer. She chewed more fervently and finally swallowed the meat, now that she was no longer afraid that she was eating a two-headed, green beast.

When she was finished, she thanked Emiril again and looked at her through sleepy eyes. Her tummy was full, and she felt great, but she thought to herself, how could I be so tired, I have been sleeping most of the day. Then, as she took another sip of her tea, it dawned on her. Emiril must have put something in her tea to make her relaxed and sleepy. She asked her.

"The tea is one I drink in the evenings to help me feel peaceful and sleep well," she said. "Do you like it?"

"Yes," Breanne said yawning. "I like it, but I am so sleepy now. I wanted to visit with you longer."

"You should really sleep though," Emiril said, "you only have one more day to rest before we leave, and you need to be feeling better by then." She smiled as Breanne's eyes drooped.

"All right," Breanne said sleepily, her voice drifting into a whisper. "But from now on, I want to know before you give me this tea. I may not want to go to sleep." She had to force her eyes open to make sure Emiril had heard her, and then she was dreaming.

She dreamed about home, about her mother standing on the front porch of her grandfather's house, arms wide open, waiting to hug her. But as she ran to her, at the last moment, she realized it was no longer her mother standing there, but Ogolel, her eyes gleaming with malice. She tried to stop running towards her, but she could not slow her feet. She closed her eyes and opened them, this time she saw Emiril where Ogolel had been, looking frantic and motioning for her to come on. Breanne renewed her efforts to run to her, hoping that when she got there it would still be Emiril, and Ogolel would not suddenly reappear. She reached Emiril, who thankfully remained Emiril, and tried to understand what she was saying, her voice sounded so far off, she couldn't make out the words. Suddenly, she felt a hand on her shoulder and she saw Emiril's face turn white. She spun around and there she was, Ogolel, staring into her eyes. She screamed but no sound came out. Ogolel said something to her, she listened harder, the voice was distant, yet she could recognize it, she had heard that voice before. She turned to Emiril, she was gone. The hand on her shoulder gripped harder, she looked again, and there was her mother now, only it was not her mother, at least not entirely her mother. She had Ogolel's eyes, and her cruel mouth. She was saying something again. She could not hear her, but could read her lips, "daughter." She watched as the person in front of her fused into first one person, her mother, and then another, Ogolel. She tried to turn away and look for Emiril, but her feet would not move. She was frozen to the spot where she stood. At last, the evil face of Ogolel faded out for good, and her mother stood in front of her. She waited a moment longer, then convinced she would not change, she hugged her; her mother hugged her back.

Chapter 26
The Council of Elders

It felt great to be out of bed. Breanne felt rested, her strength had returned and only a few places on her body were still sore. She no longer felt the wave of dizziness when she moved, which made her happy. The fact that Emiril had brought her new clothes made her even happier. She held up the cloak which was a dark brown color, made from some sort of very soft leather and trimmed in black fur, which reminded Breanne of rabbit fur. It felt very soft when she rubbed it on her cheek. She had also been given dark brown pants and a shirt to match, as well as new boots, also brown. I am going to look like a giant brownie, she thought, at which time her stomach growled loudly, indicating its desire to have a brownie at precisely that moment. Put that thought out of your mind she told it; they probably don't even know what a brownie is here. Then as if hearing her bad news, her stomach clenched and suddenly she felt ill. It didn't last though, and in a few seconds she felt fine again. Well, regardless of what I look like, these clothes are wonderful, and they look as if they will fit perfectly, as if they were made for me.

"Those clothes were made to fit you."

Breanne jumped, and quickly turned around at the sound of the unfamiliar voice. She saw a small elf standing just inside the door, smiling at her. His face was delicate looking, with high cheek bones, blue eyes and very long pointed ears; his were much longer than Emiril's, she noticed. He was also much shorter than Emiril; he couldn't be over five foot six inches tall, if that. Aside from his much different features, what caught her eye was his clothing. He was wearing a brilliant blue tunic which had depictions of animals on it. She saw the Sarr bird repeated throughout the material, but she also saw what she called a deer and Emiril called a Romon, she was sure of it. Then there were other smaller animals, but it was hard to determine what they were, as well as other birds; it was beautiful. His shirt was a silver color and sparkled in the light coming into the room from the window, his pants were snow white and his boots were gray. He looked very sharp, as if he were going to a party. She smiled at him. "How do you know they were made for me?" she asked.

"Because I made them," he said laughing.

"Oh," she stammered, a little embarrassed. "I'm sorry, I didn't know."

"That's okay," he said, walking over to her now, holding out his hand. "My name is Edlin. I am the tailor to the king, at your service." He made a half bow and waited, arm outstretched.

She was pleased that she knew how to perform the type of handshake that was used here and she also made a half bow and grasped his wrist in her hand, and smiled when she felt him grasp hers as well. "I am Breanne,"

"Pleasure to meet you, Breanne," he said, "I am a bit surprised you know the warrior's way of greeting one another." He looked at her, measuring her response.

She looked confused. "The warrior's greeting?" she asked.

"Yes," he said looking at her more intently. "That greeting is used by Elven warriors and nobility. Most elves greet one another like this." He held out his hand again, this time when she reached out to him, he took her hand in his and pumped it up and down.

She couldn't believe it, she had been so excited to use the handshake the king had greeted her with, and now she found out it was all wrong, that a greeting used by common people was exactly like it would be in her world. Was she ever going to get things straight over here? But then she thought more about it – if that was a greeting used by warriors and nobility, did that mean the king thought of her as a warrior? Now she was no longer embarrassed, but delighted in the idea that she was looked upon in such high regard by the king. She smiled.

"Do you like the clothes?" he asked, interrupting her thoughts.

"Oh yes I do," she replied. "The leather is so soft and the fur trim is wonderful. I can't wait to try them on."

"I am pleased you like them. The leather is from the Romon and the fur is that of the Surl; it is the softest fur in the land," he said proudly.

"What is a Surl?" she asked.

"A Surl is a small animal that has four legs, a long tail, and a pointed snout. It lives on land but spends a lot of time in the water as well. I use Surl to make all the king's clothes. You cannot find any fur softer, believe me, I have tried."

"I do believe you. I have never felt anything so soft," she said, rubbing the fur to her cheek again.

"Well, I will let you try them on, so that we can see how well they fit. I did not have any true measurements to use, I had to go by what Emiril told me. I too am anxious to see them on you." With that said, he left the room, closing the door behind him, but she heard him call through the closed door, "Let me know when you have them on, I will be waiting out here."

"Okay," she called back. No pressure, she thought to herself, and went about changing as quickly as she could. She was amazed how well the clothes fit, how soft and supple the leather was, and how comfortable they were. She loved the feel of the fur against her face when she pulled the hood of the cloak up. I will never want to take it off, she thought.

She had been admiring the clothes when she suddenly remembered Edlin, hurried to the door and swung it open. He was standing in the corridor, leaning up against the wall, staring up at the ceiling, but upon hearing the door, he stood up and looked her way.

"Wow," he said when he saw her standing there in the dim light of the corridor, her silhouette outlined against the darker stone walls. Only her pale face could be seen clearly, peering out of the cloak's hood. He thought how beautiful she looked, and then pushed the thought from his mind. "Let us go into the room where the light is better," he told her. Upon entering the room, he again was taken by the sight of her; this time he could clearly see the outfit and her supple figure outlined by the soft cloth. The clothing fit so well, it even surprised him. He did not think he had ever made clothing to fit someone so well before, and he had not been able to measure for them either. The pants were snug but not too tight, the shirt was just the right length and the cloak would do nicely as both a garment to wear and a blanket when needed. He hated to say it, but he was impressed with himself. There was just one more thing. "How do the boots fit?" he asked her, bending down to feel where her toes came to.

"They are wonderful," she said, thanking him again.

He stood up, convinced that the boots fit properly, and found himself face to face with her. "I am glad you like the clothes," he said, "and you have thanked me enough for them, so stop already, before my head explodes with pride." He smiled so she knew he was only joking. She smiled back, and it was a beautiful smile, her eyes sparkling and she was very pretty in that moment.

"Well," he said, turning away from her before she could see the look of admiration on his face. "The clothes may not look like they would be very warm, but Romon hide is special, it protects better than other types of hides. It will keep you very warm and best of all," he turned to her once more smiling, "it will keep you dry, it is completely waterproof."

She was amazed. "Wow, that's great," she said. "I don't like being wet and cold. This is so nice of you, I can't thank..." She stopped, he had asked her to stop thanking him. "Well, it is very generous of you and I don't know how I can repay you," she finished.

"Repay me?" he said looking shocked. "You do not have to repay me; this is a gift from me to you. I just want you to be warm and comfortable; that is enough payment for me." He smiled a big warm smile and she could see a slight twinkle in his eyes.

"Wow, you look great," Emiril said as she came into room.

"Yes, she does," Edlin said without missing a beat. He turned to Emiril and noticed that she too was wearing clothing that he had made for her earlier that year. "And I see someone else is looking great as well," he said, indicating her attire and smiling sheepishly at her.

"Watch it kid, or I will tell your father," Emiril teased.

"You wouldn't," he shot back, grinning.

Breanne looked at Emiril confused.

Catching her questioning look, Emiril informed her, at the expense of Edlin, that he was just a youngling in the glen and was perhaps her age in growth and maturity. Breanne couldn't help but notice how embarrassed poor Edlin had become, his face bright red, and she thought he might be a little angry with Emiril. "But don't let his youthfulness fool you," she went on, giving the youth a broad smile. "He is one of the best tailors in Elven history," she said proudly, "second only to his father. Is that not right, Edlin?" she asked, winking at him.

Now he blushed not from embarrassment, but with pride. "Oh come now, Emiril," he said, "you are just trying to get me to make you more

157

clothes," he chided, feeling better. He turned and winked at Breanne. She giggled at the two of them.

"Seriously though, Breanne," Emiril said looking at her new clothes, "you look great. Edlin has done it again. I can't imagine you looking more beautiful, and it sure beats you wearing my oversized outfits."

Now not only was Edlin blushing, but so was Breanne, and the way the two of them were blushing and smiling at each other. Emiril started to realize that she had apparently missed something, something that was not hard to figure out. She smiled to herself, thinking, well, the kid has a certain charm.

"Am I interrupting?" a deep voice asked from the doorway.

"Marcus," Breanne hollered and ran up to give him a big hug. He swept her up off the floor and gave her a big bear hug, while shaking her to and fro. She laughed and when he set her down, he had to steady her for a moment.

"What are you all up to?" he asked looking at the three of them. When he looked at Breanne, he feigned shock and surprise, his eyes widening and his mouth hanging open. "Wow, look at you. Where on earth did you get those fancy clothes?"

They all laughed at his antics, which is what he had been hoping for.

"Edlin made them for me," she said, spinning around and showing off his handywork. "Do you like them?" she asked.

"Do I like them?" he said thoughtfully, putting his hand to his chin and pretending to think hard. "I don't know, I think that maybe, they are just about the nicest clothes I've ever seen. And you look very pretty in them," he concluded, smiling.

Once again, she gave him a big hug. "Thank you, Marcus." She smiled at Edlin, he smiled back, blushing again, but happy with his work and happy to have been here to see her excitement.

"Well, have we had the talk yet?" Marcus asked Emiril.

"No," she said giving him a look and then smiling at Edlin.

"Oh, sorry," Marcus said softly, he too smiling at Edlin.

Edlin did not need any more hints to know that they wanted to talk in private. He looked at Breanne one more time. "You really look great," he said. "I hope we will see each other again."

"Yes," she said, "me too." She gave Emiril and Marcus a sideways glance, hoping they were not staring, but was disappointed to see they were doing just that. Her face flamed bright red.

He smiled at her words, noting the awkward look she gave Marcus and Emiril. He too felt them staring and was embarrassed. He turned to them, bowed and left. Free from the tension in the room, he walked down the corridor as if walking on air. He thought that maybe she liked him, he knew he liked her. He was going to have to find a reason to come back here.

Breanne watched Edlin leave; she was flustered with all that had just gone on. He was so, so, suave, that was the word she was looking for. He was dressed nice, well spoken, complimented her, and he was handsome. Emiril had said he was about her age, she didn't know how old that would be in elf years, she didn't think she wanted to know, but she was glad he was her age; she thought she might like him. He had definitely liked her; at least she thought he did anyway.

Emiril nudged Marcus and gave him a look, tilting her head toward Breanne and Edlin. Marcus looked at the two of them and then back at Emiril. She raised her eyebrows and nodded her head. He lowered his eyebrows and cocked his head. She nodded her head again and he again looked at the two kids before them. Oh brother, he thought, we don't need more drama now. Of course, they do look kind of cute, stumbling all over themselves. He smiled and felt Emiril elbow him in the side. He looked at her, shook his head and smiled. Together they watched Edlin make his graceful exit, then they both looked at Breanne with big smiles on their faces. Breanne looked at them and immediately wished she were anywhere but there; she felt like the prize turkey at the fair. "What are you two looking at?" she hissed.

Marcus and Emiril said in unison, "Nothing."

Breanne rolled her eyes and walked over to the chair and sat down. She had never been so embarrassed, of course, she had never really liked a boy before, especially not an elf.

Chapter 27
Emiril's Burden

"Well," said Marcus, trying to break the tension in the room. "We should discuss our plans." He looked at Emiril and smiled awkwardly. He didn't know how to proceed in this situation. His own daughter was not old enough to like boys, at least he didn't think she was, and this was a new one for him. Thankfully, Emiril knew what to do and he gladly followed her lead.

"You might be wondering why your clothes are all brown," she said to Breanne.

Breanne looked at her. She wasn't mad, just a little embarrassed, more so since Marcus seemed to know about her crush on Edlen as well. But she guessed that they meant no harm in teasing her a little, after all, they were her friends. She decided that she would give them a break and let it slide this time. She smiled at the two of them, and she could literally see the tension melt from poor Marcus' face. Oh dear, she thought, I really did make him uptight. She promised herself she would be less touchy about the subject from now on.

"Why are the clothes all brown?" she asked, hoping that would further lessen the tension in the room. "I had wondered about that."

"Well, the color will match the background of many of the places we will be going, and from the air, if you lie still, you will resemble a tree, or a patch of dirt. It will be hard to pick you out of our surroundings. This will make it hard for the Dark Mage to find you." She said that last part quietly and they all felt the unspoken fear in the room.

"That is very smart thinking," Breanne said smiling. At least now she didn't feel so bad about looking like a brownie.

"So," Marcus began with new found enthusiasm, "Emiril and I have talked about our journey and we have decided that we will only take one other person with us." He looked at Emiril and she nodded in agreement. "That person will be one of the dwarves of Fayhall. They know the passages under the mountain on the Island of the Ancient Ancestors. Their people dug those tunnels and no one knows all the twists and turns except them."

"Is it really as bad as it sounds, can you get lost under there?" Breanne asked nervously. She didn't like the idea of being below the mountain. It reminded her of the old mining caves her family visited and she didn't like going into those pitch-black caves either.

"Yes, it is very confusing down there," Marcus said. "It's like being in a maze. But that's how it was meant to be. Back when our forefathers lived there, it was known for its impenetrability. No one could get into the stronghold, the walls were too high and heavily guarded and the passages under the mountain were dug in such a way as to confuse invading armies. There are even traps, you see, the passages were made as a means of escape for the people of the island, not as a means for others to get in." He noticed how upset Breanne was starting to look. "Don't worry though," he added quickly, "the dwarves know all the passages well, after all, they built them. We can't get lost down there with a guide." He smiled at her reassuringly, and then glanced at Emiril for help.

"Breanne," she said, "I have been in the passages. They are not that bad, the dwarves are excellent guides and know exactly where to go. That is why we are going to have one of them go with us. It will be alright, I promise."

Breanne looked at the two of them. What must they think of her right now? Being afraid of going under the mountain seemed stupid, after all, they were going, and they were not afraid. But it was more than just being under there and getting lost that she was afraid of, she was afraid of the dark as well, she hated being in dark places with no lights, she always had. And then there was the idea that there would be bugs down there; not just any bugs, but spiders. She shivered. She hated spiders. She needed to stop being so afraid of everything. That is what her mother had told her just before she had left her with her grandparents. Her mother was right, she did need to stop being so afraid. She would be with her friends, and they would not let anything happen to her, they had already proven that. She had to learn to trust people to take care of her and more than that, she had to learn to take care of herself. She smiled, thanks mom, she thought. "Thanks, you guys," she told Marcus and Emiril. "I will be alright; I am not afraid anymore."

They looked into her eyes and thought they really did see a change in her, a change that had happened in the last few seconds. Then they looked at each other and smiled, they were proud of the changes in her, proud that she was becoming a stronger person.

"Well," Emiril said, "I am going to go send a message to the dwarves to expect our arrival tomorrow. You, Breanne, can relax and when I get done, we will pack you a traveling bag. You coming with me, Marcus?" she asked. He nodded and they left the room.

Breanne smiled at what Emiril had said. She hoped there would be more new clothes to pack, and if there were, she hoped Edlin would come back to make sure they fit. She rubbed her hand over the sleeve of her cloak, the softness still surprised her.

"Hey Marcus," Emiril said hesitantly.

"Yes."

"Did you notice anything odd back there between Breanne and Edlin?"

"Are you joking?" he asked, looking at her.

163

She stopped walking. "What do you mean?" she said.

He stopped, turned around and with eyes open wide said, "If there had been any more tension in that room, I would have died of a heart attack from exposure."

They looked at each other a moment longer, then burst out laughing. "It really was intense," Emiril said, tears welling up in her eyes.

"Intense is not even the half of it," Marcus said, "I don't even recall there being that much tension when I met Iola, and back then I thought that had been the most tense day of my life; this far exceeds then."

They laughed a little more, then Emiril looked at him more seriously. "Well, all kidding aside, what would you think if I told you I was thinking that maybe Edlin should go with us?"

Marcus stopped laughing. He looked into her eyes. "Boy, I don't know," he said more seriously. "Do you think he would be a distraction?"

"Well, I thought about that," she said, "but I also thought maybe he would be a confidence builder too. I don't know which aspect would be stronger is the problem. What do you think?"

"It's hard to say. I think that she would definitely be distracted, but like you said, she might feel braver or at least feel the need to be braver to impress him." He smiled at that last part. He could remember how he had felt the need to impress Iola, and boy had he. He had done all kinds of crazy and sometimes foolish things to win her heart. Looking back, he thought how dangerous and stupid that had been. "What could he offer in terms of services?" he asked her.

She thought about it for a moment. He was the tailor, what else was he known for? She really did not know. She thought he was capable of performing some spells, but ordinary spells that all the elves could do, nothing special. She didn't know if he had any special skills aside from tailoring. "I do not know," she said flatly, looking at Marcus with raised eyebrows and shrugging her shoulders.

"Well, then I guess the question is, would he be a hindrance? After all, one more pair of eyes and ears is never really a problem, unless they are a hindrance," he said, looking at her questioning.

She thought for a moment. "I don't think he would be. He has never been one to cause problems. He is smart and has common sense. I think he would be able to follow directions. So, I don't think he would be a hindrance," she said finally.

"Well, in that case, I don't mind if he comes, but if Breanne is too distracted, we will have to cut him loose, agreed?"

"Agreed," she said smiling. Boy were the two of them going to be surprised, she thought. She could not wait to see the look on Breanne's face.

They continued to the great hall where they informed the king of all that had transpired and their intention of asking Edlin to accompany them. He too saw no reason as to why he could not go. Emiril then instructed the messenger to deliver her message to the dwarves concerning their arrival there tomorrow. After these things were done, Marcus went to oversee the packing of their provisions. Emiril was heading back to tell Breanne the news when her father met her in the hallway.

She smiled at the unexpected meeting. "Father," she said, bowing formally.

"Oh stop that, you silly child," he said laughing. "Come here and give your father a hug."

165

She went to him, and he embraced her tightly, holding her for a long time. She could sense his apprehension, and wished there was something she could do to make him feel better.

"You will never be able to quiet my fears for your safety, daughter," he said.

She smiled; he always knew what she was thinking. As a child, if she had done something wrong, she avoided him at all costs, and even then, half the time he still knew. No wonder she had not caused too much trouble as a child, she could never get away with it.

"And look what a wonderful young lady you turned out to be because of it," he said laughing.

"Oh stop it, father," she chided. "I can never have a thought without you being there." Of course, she would have it no other way now, and she loved him more than ever. Read that thought she thought to him. He squeezed her more tightly, and she knew he had.

"What brings you to me?" she asked him. She knew there was something troubling him and she was a little concerned.

"Let us go to the garden and sit by the pond," he said, "and then I will tell you."

She loved to sit by the pond. She had spent many happy hours there with her mother. And many more had been spent there with both her parents. She missed those times, and she felt tears well up in her eyes; she missed her mother so much. She felt her father's strong arm across her shoulder and he squeezed her tightly to his side. Thank God for him, she thought, she didn't know if she could have made it past her mother's death without him to lean on. She truly did love him.

The little frog croaked proudly, his neck expanding to twice his body size and then deflating once again. The other frogs in the pond hovered around the lily pad to watch this proud amphibian. Emiril smiled, it reminded her of her father on his thrown, with all the elves gathered round. The sound of the stream falling the short distance into the pond was soothing, and she watched as dragonflies hovered inches above the water, a tempting meal for the gold fish below. The shade from the trees was nice, as was the cool breeze, and sitting under the blue sky, she felt more relaxed than she had in a very long time.

King Badhor looked at his daughter sitting beside him in the warm sun. She was beautiful, her golden hair shining brightly, her smooth face flawless; she was the image of her mother, that was for sure. He missed her, he wished she could be here with them now, listening to the frogs and the water as it trickled along its way. He wanted to bring his daughter out here for some quiet family time. They never spent time together anymore it seemed, and even though Queen Norin was gone, her memory lingered here, comforting them, soothing them. He could see Emiril start to relax; he could feel her spirit as it rested calmly. He hadn't seen her this way in such a long time, it pleased him. This had been a good idea. He had needed to relax as well; he was getting old and he knew it. But more importantly, his daughter was going to be putting herself in great danger and that was taking a toll on him. He had already lost her mother and he was afraid of losing her as well. He was glad of one thing; at least Marcus would be going with her. He loved Marcus like a son. He had always been there for Emiril, had in fact saved her life on four occasions. He trusted him to continue protecting her, that fact alone made letting her go on this quest more bearable. He still wished however, that he could go in her place, but that was not possible. He hated to admit it, but he was no longer able to do the things he had done in his youth. His age was a burden to his sharp mind. Getting old was difficult to accept, but inevitable. He was already making preparations to hand over the running of the kingdom to Emiril. She did not know this yet, and he would not tell her until her return. She did not need the distraction while on such a dangerous quest.

"What troubles you, father?" Emiril asked softly.

His thoughts trailed off as he looked at her. "My deep love for my daughter troubles me," he said smiling.

She looked at him with furrowed brows.

"Oh daughter, how you make me proud," he continued. "You have grown into such a lovely young elf, your mother would be proud of you. You look like her, did you know?" She smiled at him. "She always told me you looked like me, but that was not true, you definitely look like her. And you are kind, generous, sometimes to a fault." He winked at her. "You are loving, smart; all the things that make a person worthy. I could not have asked for a better daughter. Surely your mother and I were blessed when the spirits gave us you." He hugged her tight, so that she would not see the tears in his old eyes. After he had regained his composer, he let her go and looked into her eyes. "I am worried for your safety," he said. "I know," he said gruffly, shaking his head, "as one warrior to another, I am not supposed to tell you that." Then his look changed to one of worry. "But I am your father first and foremost, and as a father I tell you, I am worried for your safety."

She smiled and looked into his eyes; he had not been very good at concealing the tears. She saw that his heart was truly troubled and she wanted to console him. She did not know what to say. He knew the truths behind her quest, and she knew she could not fool him into thinking all would be well – it might not be. She could only tell him she would be careful, she would follow her training, but most importantly, she would stay in contact with him. "I will be very careful, father. I am sorry to put you through such anguish, but I know of no other way, and the reason we do this is justified; she has no one else."

"Indeed, you are right," he sighed.

She leaned against him and felt tears well up in her own eyes.

"Then I will prepare you the best way I can," he said resolutely.

She waited, long minutes passed, then she heard her father's voice crack a little as he started. "Let me tell you about your aunt," he said unexpectedly. Her head snapped up, and she stared into her father's eyes, visibly shocked. He and her mother had never spoken about Ogolel to her, and when she tried to bring her up, she was told not to speak her name in their house. Everything she knew about Ogolel and what had happened came from history books, her own memory, which wasn't very much, and her grandmother. She did not dare say a word, for fear he would change his mind. She waited in silence.

"You remember your aunt a little, don't you?" he asked suddenly.

She nodded.

"I suppose you remember the day she came to the castle?" he continued grimly.

"Yes."

"Do you remember much about her from before that day?"

She thought for a moment. She could remember very little actually. What she did remember she wasn't sure was accurate.

The king saw her thinking deeply, and looked into her mind. He saw Ogolel as she used to be, before she had turned against them. She was beautiful, her long black hair shone in the sun, her blue eyes sparkled. He felt a stirring of past emotions within himself. If it had not been for Norin, he would have wed Ogolel, but Norin had caught his eye first, and it was she who he had married, with no regrets. But he had still been very much attracted to Ogolel, and he knew that she had known this. He had met Norin, and they became engaged. When Ogolel came out for the wedding, she had been away training in the art of magic, and when he had first seen her, he had almost wished things could be different, that it had been her he had met first, but he loved Norin and nothing Ogolel could do or say could change that; they were already soul mates. Ogolel did try to persuade him to change his mind, without her sister knowing of course, but he would not entertain any offers she made him. She grew frustrated, angry, oh, she knew that she had no right to be angry with her sister, but her sense of the matter was warped. She only saw the facts the way she perceived them, her sister stood in the way of her happiness, of her becoming queen, and she had never been able to forgive her for being the one he chose. Then came the day of the wedding and from that day forward, Ogolel started to change, and she became more and more bitter inside. She began to hate her sister. She watched with jealousy and rage as Norin and her new husband walked through the gardens hand in hand, stopping to exchange long and passionate kisses. She imagined them in their chambers at night, wishing it were her and not Norin wrapped in the king's embrace. She teetered on the edge of insanity, and then the day came when she toppled over that edge. The king and queen announced to the kingdom their joyous news, they were with child, there would be an heir to the throne. She couldn't take it anymore, she had to get rid of them, they made her life a living nightmare. From that day forward, she began to plot their demise. The king's thoughts were interrupted by Emiril's voice.

"I remember her singing to me in the garden sometimes, and I remember watching her get ready for a party one time. She had been brushing her long beautiful hair, and I had admired her beauty. But I don't remember much else. I guess the memory that stands out most about her is the day she came to the castle." Her voice lowered and she spoke woefully, "I will never forget that day."

"Your aunt was not always evil, Emiril." He said this while looking deeply into her eyes, and she thought she detected a hint of sadness in

170

him. "She was once a very pleasant woman. She was beautiful, intelligent and kind, if you can believe that." He looked away from her. "What changed her was jealousy." He paused, not wanting to tell her too much. She only needed to hear some of the story. He chose his words carefully. "She was jealous of your mother being queen. She was, after all, the older sister, and she thought that it was her right to be a queen before your mother. As time went on and she did not marry, she became lonely, and when your mother and I became pregnant with you, Ogolel once again became jealous of your mother having a child before her. It seemed a never-ending cycle, your mother, through no fault of her own, accomplished almost everything before her elder sister, and this made Ogolel jealous and angry. What didn't help matters was the fact that everyone in the kingdom kept commenting on how Ogolel was being outdone by her younger sibling, which of course only fueled her rage. They didn't see that Ogolel was accomplishing things in her own right; she was becoming a very powerful sorceress, one of the most powerful in the kingdom, even coming close to Mindoneth. She would have been a powerful protector of our race had she not turned against us. But eventually, she did turn against us. The day came when she could no longer stand in your mother's shadow. She started to plot our downfall, and she enlisted help. The Dark Mage was her ally in this endeavor. He was just a mortal man, but he knew many spells. Stories abound that he traded his soul to the spirits so that he could obtain other forms of magic as well. Regardless, what Ogolel knew of magic was all natural; spells, other than simple ones, were beyond her. She needed help with the more complicated ones. She began to study and learn spells with the help of the Dark Mage. That is when she wrote the book of spells."

A little bird landed on a tree branch over their heads and began to sing a sweet melody. They listened for a few minutes, welcoming the break in the conversation. It was never easy talking about Ogolel, because although she had done horrible things, she was still an elf, and family, they still loved her; they could do nothing else.

"She studied for a long time under the Dark Mage. He taught her all forms of spells, and about the physical elements needed to perform the spells. She, in return, taught him about the spirit world and how to navigate within it. They were quite the pair, powerful, and evil. But the whole time, Ogolel was plotting the demise of her sister, and me of course. She wanted to be queen, she wanted the people to respect her and recognize how powerful she was; nothing would stand in her way."

Emiril shivered. How did Ogolel expect to be queen by removing her parents? Even if she did get them out of the way, she would not inherit the throne, Emiril would. Then it hit her, Ogolel had no intention of leaving her around either. She shuddered. Her own aunt, how could she be so cruel? Tears filled her eyes. Whatever feelings she might still have for Ogolel were now gone. She now knew the extent to which this evil woman would go to rule the kingdom, and Emiril was only an obstacle to her, dispensable.

Her father once again delved into her mind as she discovered the ugly truth about her aunt. He pulled her close and let her cry, she sobbed quietly beside him. It had been many years since she had cried in his arms; he wished she did not have to now. There was nothing he could do to console her, she had to let it out. It was not easy finding out that a relative you had loved did not share the same feelings for you. So she cried, and he held her. As he sat there, he could not help but feel sorry for his daughter, and a bit guilty. Norin and he had decided a long time ago not to reveal any of this to Emiril for just this reason; they knew Emiril would be hurt. But in light of what was happening, he felt that Emiril needed to know the truth, so that when the time came, Emiril would realize that whatever Ogolel said to her, she was not to be trusted. With the knowledge she now had, she could not be fooled into a sense of family ties; as far as Ogolel was concerned, there were no family ties. Emiril was an obstacle in her way, one that she would remove without hesitation. How he wished Nolin was here to help him with their daughter's upbringing. So many times, he felt lost and confused when it came to his daughter. His only saving grace since Norin had passed had been his mother. She had stepped up and helped him every time he, or Emiril, had needed her. If it weren't for her, he was sure that he would have failed his daughter. Of course, he had never given himself the credit he deserved. He did not know it, but his mother only strengthened his decisions, she never made them for him. It had been him and him alone that had raised his daughter into the woman she was today. She was definitely her father's daughter: strong, intelligent, caring, imaginative, loving, funny, and passionate. If Norin had been alive, she would have reminded him of all the good qualities he possessed that had made her fall in love with him in the first place, and he would then see that Emiril possessed every one of them. But she was not, and he was convinced that his mother was mostly to thank for how well Emiril had turned out.

Chapter 28
Marcus's Oath

Emiril walked slowly down the corridor. She was in no hurry to talk to anyone, still in shock from her conversation with her father. The thing that bothered her the most though was the fact that she had not realized this on her own. She felt so stupid. All these years, she had known that Ogolel was trying to overthrow her parents, why had she not made the connection and realized that she too had been on the chopping block? If she had missed something so obvious, what other things had she missed? She was beginning to doubt her ability to lead the quest for the book. There were so many unanswered questions as well, questions she really should ask Mindoneth before proceeding. Why did Breanne recognize some of the things in this world, even so far as the names being the same? And what about this whole thing with there being two books and only one being sent away? She had to see Mindoneth; there was no getting around it. She would leave tonight and meet the others on the road near Ethuanova, now that Edlin was going, that would mean Marcus would able to concentrate more on keeping them safe and less on entertaining Breanne. Just then, she realized that she had not even asked Edlin if he wanted to go yet. She had a feeling what the answer would be, but she still needed to ask him and give him time to get ready to go. She turned around and quickly headed in the direction of the tailor's quarters. When she arrived, she saw that he was there working on some clothes of a beautiful gray color. She stood in the doorway a moment watching how deftly he worked. He really was the best tailor in the kingdom, and they were lucky to have him. He looked up suddenly and smiled at her.

"Are you spying on me, Emiril? Trying to learn my secrets so you can make your own clothes and get rid of me?" His smile gave him away, he never could pull off a practical joke, everyone knew the minute they looked at him that he was kidding; needless to say, he was never in charge of planning a surprise party. She smiled back at him.

"I might just do that, thanks for the idea." She laughed, entering the room. It was bigger than she had realized and piled floor to ceiling in spots with cloth of every color. Fur was also strewn about along with large spools of thread and all manner of sewing supplies. The windows however had nothing piled in front of them. There were four large ones along one wall, floor to ceiling; they must have measured twenty feet tall. The light that came in through those giant windows gave the tailor the opportunity to see the tiniest detail on the project he happened to be working on, even on a cloudy day. She strode over and looked out one of them. The view was incredible, located on the top floor, the room offered one of the best views the castle had to offer. She could see most of the glen from this vantage point, it was beautiful, and off in the distance she could see the mountains of Fayhall which brought her back to why she had come here in the first place. She turned and saw Edlin staring at her, obviously waiting to hear what she had come to say.

"What are you working on?" she asked, walking over to admire the clothes.

Edlin suddenly blushed and looked down at the floor. Emiril looked at him, confused, then she looked at the clothes more intently. They were a small sized, almost petite, that ruled them out for men and even her. Suddenly she realized who the clothes were for, and that explained why he had gotten so flustered when she had asked about them. She smiled inside; this was going to be an interesting trip. She hoped that she was making the right choice in bringing him along.

"Edlin," she said gently. "These clothes are beautiful; the colors are much nicer than having to wear all brown."

He flinched when she said the last part.

"She will love them," Emiril continued. "I am sorry I know of your affection towards Breanne, but I do and we can't change that now. What we can do, is realize that it is a natural thing and no one blames the two of you for feeling the way you do."

The two of you? Did she say the two of you? Edlin quickly looked at Emiril, his eyes glowing brightly. "Did you say the two of you?" he asked excitedly.

She thought for a moment. Oops, I let the cat out of the bag, now what? Well, the only thing to do at this point was to tell him the truth, then promise to turn him into a toad if he told Breanne she told him. "Yes Edlin, she likes you too. But you cannot tell her I told you. If you do, I will turn you into a toad. Do you understand?"

The boy smiled the biggest smile Emiril had ever seen. He looked as if he would burst with joy. Wow, he really did have it bad, she thought. Wait until I ask him if he wants to come along, she thought; I may need to get the doctor in here.

"You are right," he said.

Emiril looked at him, confused.

"The clothes," he said, indicating the beautiful gray clothing, "They are for her. I thought she might like them. Do you think she will like them?" he asked hopefully.

"I don't think she will like them," Emiril said slowly.

Edlin looked heartbroken.

"I know she will love them," Emiril said, patting the young elf on the back. "Edlin, these are so very beautiful, there is no way she could not like them. And you can give them to her when you tell her you will be coming with us." She slipped that last part in there, wondering if he would catch it.

"Oh thank you, Emiril, I was wondering if she liked gray. I have been working…" he stopped in mid-sentence. His mouth dropped open and he stared at Emiril, clearly in shock.

He got it, she thought.

"Emiril, did you just say…did you say that I would be going with you?" he was shaking, she could see it in his hands. "Going on your quest, is that what you meant?" he continued.

Emiril grabbed his shoulders and looked him in the eyes. "Do you want to?" she asked.

"Yes." He almost screamed in her face. "Of course, oh my gosh, I have dreamed of going on a quest my whole life. Are you serious?" He looked at her with lowered eyebrows, almost aggressively. "This isn't some kind of trick, is it? You are really asking me to go, right?"

Emiril smiled. Poor kid, she thought. "No Edlin, it is not a trick, and yes Edlin, I am really asking you if you want to go."

His face lit up, "Oh my gosh, when are we leaving?"

"You, Marcus and Breanne will leave first thing in the morning, I have to leave tonight. I have something else I need to do first." She trailed off for a moment thinking of the many questions she hoped to have answered before she met up with the others tomorrow. She brought her attention back to Edlin when she heard him saying something. "Sorry, what did you say, Edlin?"

"I asked you what I should bring with me."

"Oh, well two sets of clothes, one brown set like the ones you made for Breanne, and a weapon if you have one." She looked at him quizzically. "Do you have one?" she asked.

"Oh yes," he said. "I have my father's sword; he gave it to me."

"A sword?" she said a little surprised. He was so small in stature. "Do you know how to use it?"

He looked at her with a mixture of emotions on his face, a little shock with some indignity. "Of course I know how to use it," he said, maybe a little harsher than he intended. "I have trained with the sword since I was little. My father thought that just because we were tailors did not mean we shouldn't also be able to help protect our king if he needed it." He felt a little sorry for the harshness of his words and looked down.

"Edlin, I am sorry," Emiril said softly. "I did not mean to imply anything in what I said. I was just a little shocked because I have never thought of you or your father as warriors before. Not that you wouldn't be great ones," she added quickly, "but you have never done anything but tailoring and so I have always thought of you in those terms. I bet you're a great swordsman though. I can't wait to see what you can do with your father's sword."

Edlin looked up at the last words she spoke, his eyes gleaming. "I really am good," he said quietly. "Not to brag of course," he added hastily.

Emiril surprised even herself when she gave the boy a great big hug. She had always been fond of him, and she felt bad that she had unintentionally hurt his feelings.

"Well, it's settled then," she said, holding him at arm's length. "You will be going with, not as a tailor, but as a swordsman, and I expect I will feel safer for it," she added. "Now the only question left is who will tell Breanne." She said this with a sly smile on her face, knowing the reaction she would get from him.

His eyes lit up and he almost stuttered his words. "Can I tell her, Emiril, please? I am almost done with her clothes and I can tell her when I take them to her." He waited almost jumping up and down with anticipation.

Emiril pretended to think about it, then, before he had a heart attack where he stood, she let him off the hook. "Ok, you tell her," she said, smiling.

"Oh thank you, Emiril," he said in a gush. "I will finish these clothes right away and then go tell her."

"Alright, Edlin," Emiril said, "but don't forget, you are not leaving until tomorrow. Do not kill yourself working too hard."

"I won't," he called over his shoulder; he was already back to work on the clothes, wasting no time.

Emiril laughed inside; boy he really had it bad. She turned to go, she had to find Marcus and tell him of her decision to meet with Mindoneth before joining the rest of them on their journey.

"So, I will be leaving shortly and will meet the rest of you in the morning in Ethuanova," Emiril told Marcus.

"Alright, but I still can't believe Edlin is a swordsman," he said, trying not to be so skeptical. "I know that sounds mean, but he is so small, and he is a tailor."

"So what if he is a tailor," Emiril said. "You are a human, and look what you can do." She laughed at his surprised expression.

He was almost offended by what she said, then he realized why she said it. He had said something just like it about Edlin. So what if he was a tailor, that wasn't all that made up Edlin. He could be any number of

179

things besides being a tailor, he very well could be a swordsman. He would have to withhold judgment until he saw the boy use the sword. After all, no one should be judged by their looks alone. If that were the case, many people would be overlooked for the great qualities they possessed; it wasn't fair to do that to people. He felt bad about what he had said.

"Well, it will be great to have another sword along," he told Emiril, hoping she caught the apology in that statement. And of course, being his friend for many years, she did.

"Ok, I have told Edlin he is going, you that I am going, now I need to speak to Breanne. I will see you tomorrow. Be careful, and remember to watch the skies. I don't know if he has any idea what we are planning, but I do know he is looking for her. If you get into any trouble, send me a message and I will come right away." She looked at her friend and hoped it would not be the last time she saw him, alive that is.

"We will be fine," he assured her, "tell Mindoneth hello for me."

"I will," she said as she walked away.

Breanne had her things laid out on the bed and she was looking them over. There really wasn't much there. She had the brown outfit Edlin had made her, (she didn't want to wear it until tomorrow), she had a hairbrush Emiril had given her, there were a few things she had picked up since being here, a pretty rock, a stick that was gnarled and would make a nice carving, and that was about it. Pathetic, she thought. The only thing she owned that wasn't here, Emiril had, and for good reason, it needed to be kept safe, and she did not have the ability to defend it the way Emiril could. Besides that, after she had seen the dragon's eyes glow the way they had, and after hearing the story and now knowing the dragon was real, she didn't want to carry it any more. So what she had to pack, she could fit into one very small bag. At least she would be travelling light, she thought. Not like poor Marcus, who had to carry all those heavy weapons. She looked up from the bed. Where was Emiril? She had told her she would help her pack; it had been a very long time since she had left, and she was still not back. She wished she had been wearing her wristwatch when she came here; it was hard to keep track of time without clocks. The only time she could even remotely sense what time it was, was when it got dark and when it got light. The rest of the time, she just wandered around feeling lost. She hadn't realized how dependent on time her world truly was until now, and she still couldn't decide if it was a good thing, or a bad thing. She thought about Edlin, disappointed that he had not come back either. She had hoped there would be more clothes, then she could have had an excuse to see him again. Was she being silly, she thought? She wasn't even from this world and she was going home. And more than that, he was an elf and she was a human. She sighed, he was cute though, and nice, and charming, and…. Oh what was the use, she was a fool. Maybe he didn't even like her, maybe he was just being polite, and she misunderstood his intentions, like the handshake, she had had that all wrong too. She thought he liked her, but she really knew nothing about the ways of elves. She could make a fool of herself and then she would be so embarrassed. I will just have to stop liking him, she thought resolutely. After all, I am leaving and I might never see him again. That thought stung. She felt sick to her stomach. Man, I have it bad, she thought. But really, I need to stop liking him, for my own good. She had made up her mind, and she would stick to it.

She heard footsteps in the hall. Emiril she thought, and hurried to the door. Coming out of the doorway, she ran full force into Edlin. They bumped hard, and Edlin dropped what he had been carrying. Breanne rubbed her elbow which had hit the wall when she bounced off of poor Edlin.

"Oh, I am so sorry," she exclaimed. "I thought you were Emiril, I didn't know you were so close to the doorway, or I wouldn't have run out so fast. Are you alright? Let me help you with your stuff." She was so embarrassed.

Edlin was a bit dazed, but found getting a word in this conversation nearly impossible. Finally, Breanne stopped talking for a second and he quickly jumped in. "I am fine, do not worry about it, I understand. I can get the stuff, and let us go into the room, if it is ok with you." He looked at her, and they both laughed.

"Yes, please come in," she said meekly. "Are you sure you don't want help picking up your stuff?"

"Thank you, but I can get it," he said. "I will be right behind you."

"Ok, sorry," she said as she went inside, her face a bright red. Man, she thought, he finally comes back, and I almost kill him. Way to go, she thought. She went over by the window and waited for him to catch up. As he walked into the room, she was once again taken by his good looks. She knew in that moment, that she would have a hard time not liking him anymore. And then he smiled. Ok that's it, she thought, I am never going to be able to not like him. I am in so much trouble. She smiled back at him, and his knees went weak. He almost dropped everything again. Oh man, he thought, keep it together, Edlin, keep it together.

"Can I lay these on the bed?" he asked.

"Oh yes, one minute," she said as she hurried to the bed to remove the few items she had laid out. "Here you go."

He walked over and she backed up to give him room. He carefully sat the bundle at the foot of the bed, then began to lay them out one at a time. Breanne stood there in awe, staring at the beautiful clothing he proceeded to lay out before her. The first item was a cloak, gray in color, and like the brown one, had fur trim around the hood, but the fur on this one was black. The cloak itself had silver stitching around the edges and silver stitching was used to create the most wonderful woodland scene on the back of the cloak. There were trees, animals and a small stream that appeared to flow straight out of the garment. It was the most beautiful thing she had ever seen. Next, he laid out a white shirt, also with sliver stitching. On the front of the shirt, where pockets would be if she were at home, there were two more scenes like the one on the cloak, only they were in miniature, but the details were just as perfect. She couldn't believe he had been able to create them so perfectly, they were so small. The shirt looked as if it were made of silk, it shimmered in the light, the sleeves were long and buttoned at the cuff and buttons ran down the front of the shirt as well. The buttons themselves were made from what appeared to be silver and were in the shape of birds in flight; each bird had some sort of blue gem for an eye. He laid out a pair of pants next, they were a gray color and looked to be made of some sort of soft material. There was no special stitching on the pants. To complete the outfit, he produced a pair of boots, ordinary, yet the blackest black she had ever seen. She felt that if she looked hard enough, she would see her reflection in them. She stared at this beautiful ensemble. Clothes here are so much better than home, she thought. I can't believe Edlin made these, they are so beautiful. I wonder who they are for. She had an idea who they were for, but she dared not get her hopes up, if they weren't for her, she would be so very disappointed. But she secretly prayed they were for her.

"Edlin, these are so beautiful. I have never in my life seen such beautiful clothing. Where I come from, our clothes are dull and boring. I am so impressed with your skills."

Edlin rose at least a foot off the ground with each compliment she paid him. By the time she stopped talking, he had to regain his composer before he could talk. "Well, I am glad you like them," he said, "they are for you." He heard her catch her breath and then breathe faster. Smiling on the inside, he continued. "A person cannot have only one set of clothes. When I made sure the first set was going to fit properly, I made you a second set." He stared at her, watching her reaction to his news.

She turned to him, tears in her eyes. "I don't know how to thank you, Edlin," she said quietly. "This is by far one of the nicest gifts I have ever received in my whole life." A tear slid down her cheek, and she quickly wiped it away. She thought about saying something more, but she truly did not know what to say that would express her gratitude the way she wanted to.

Edlin looked at her and saw the tear on her cheek. He had hoped she would like the clothes; he had not anticipated that she would like them this much. The last time he had felt this happy about his work was when his dad had been alive, had complimented his skills and that was the happiest day of his life. Now this day was a close second. No one else had ever made him feel this good about his work before, and he was grateful to her for it. He smiled at her, and took her hands in his. "That is the nicest, most sincere thank you I have ever had, and that means a lot to me. You are very welcome, and I am only too happy to have made you so happy with my modest gift."

She smiled back. Modest gift! Was he crazy? These clothes were not a modest gift. She wanted so badly to try them on.

As if reading her mind, Edlin broke in, "Would you like to try them on; I can go out in the hall."

"Oh yes, I really would love to put them on, if you don't mind waiting," she said.

"No, I don't mind," he said, already halfway to the door. "In fact, I want to see them on you just as badly as you do." He stopped walking, oh that didn't sound good, he thought. He turned to her, yep that sounded bad, he said to himself again, as he looked at her face. She had a look of stunned shock. Quick do something, he thought. "I did not mean that

184

the way it sounded," he stammered quickly. "I only meant I want to see them on you to make sure they fit well, like the last ones." He looked at her to see if she believed him. She smiled. Oh thank God, he thought. "I will be out there," he said, pointing to the door.

He entered the hallway and saw Emiril walking towards him. Oh good, a distraction to take her mind off of what I just said, he thought.

"Edlin, fancy meeting you here," Emiril said, smiling.

"Oh, stop it," he hissed. "I gave her the clothes, and she is about to try them on."

"Oh good, I want to see how they look. They are so beautiful. Is she dressing yet?"

"I didn't shut the door, so I don't think so."

Emiril peered in. "Want me to wait out here?" she asked a surprised Breanne.

"Emiril, no, come in here, please, and shut the door."

Emiril winked at Edlin, entered the room and closed the door behind her.

"Look what Edlin brought me," Breanne said quickly. "Aren't they the most beautiful clothes you've ever seen? I was just about to try them on."

Emiril smiled at the girl's excitement. "They are indeed beautiful," she said. "I will turn around while you put them on."

"Ok, thank you," Breanne said, quickly adding, "I am so glad you're here. Where have you been, if you don't mind me asking?"

"I don't mind you asking, in fact, I was going to tell you anyway."

"I'm almost done."

185

"I was on my way back here to help you pack, when I ran into my father in the hallway; he wanted to talk. We talked for a while and then I had to talk to…" She stopped, she had almost said Edlin. "I had to talk to Marcus about our trip. And now here I am."

"And here I am," Breanne said behind her.

Emiril turned around. She could not believe her eyes. "Breanne, you look so incredibly beautiful. If I didn't know you, I would swear you were an elfin maid."

Breanne looked at Emiril and smiled. "The clothes are so amazing; I can't believe how well they fit. And the pants are so soft, here feel," she said, walking over to Emiril and raising a leg.

Emiril felt the material and she too was shocked at how soft they were. "Wow, Edlin must be using a new hide of some sort, I have never felt pants so soft. He really went all out for you this time." She smiled at Breanne.

"What do you mean?" Breanne said sheepishly.

"Oh, you know what I mean, don't give me that innocent look."

Breanne's hopes began to rise. "Emiril, do you think Edlin likes me?" she asked hopefully.

Emiril looked at Breanne. Is it possible she really does not know? It was quite plain to her. Well, she is young, maybe she really does not know. Well, I let the cat out of the bag and told Edlin, I suppose it will not hurt to tell her, she thought to herself. "Yes, Breanne, Edlin likes you, but," she said sternly, "if you tell him I told you, I will turn you into a toad."

Breanne was too happy to care about being turned into a toad for her lack of silence. All she cared about was the fact that Edlin liked her. She had been right. She was so happy.

186

Emiril watched Breanne as she soaked in the knowledge of Edlin's affection for her. She was so happy. Man, it was nice to be young, she thought. But she was also worried for her as well. What would happen when she had to go home? The poor kids would be heartbroken. But maybe it would still be worth it to them. After all, you cannot help who you fall in love with. She interrupted Breanne's new found happiness. "Do not forget what I told you about turning you into a toad. I will, you know."

Breanne looked at Emiril as if she had just walked into the room. She had been so caught up in the wonderful news; she had literally forgotten the elf was there. "Oh sorry, Emiril, I won't say anything, I promise."

Emiril smiled. "Good, now do you think you should let him back in?" she said tilting her head toward the door.

"Oh my gosh," Breanne almost screamed. "I forgot. Oh, I'm so nervous now, what should I say, or not say, how should I act? Oh, this is terrible. I don't know what to do." She looked at Emiril, sheer terror written on her face.

Emiril laughed. "Breanne, calm down, nothing is different. He has liked you from the moment he met you. Just act the way you have been acting. You do not need to do anything different. Understand?"

Breanne relaxed a little. "You're right," she said a little more calmly. "Nothing has changed; I always thought he liked me anyway. I will let him in and act like nothing is different." She smiled at Emiril, but her smile was not very convincing.

When she opened the door and looked out, Edlin was sitting on the floor, head on his knees. Had she left him out here so long he fell asleep, she thought. Then she felt bad. "Edlin, are you awake?"

His head snapped up, "I am awake," he said quickly. "I am awake."

Breanne chuckled even though she felt bad.

"Wow, you look great," he said, standing up and stretching. "I was worried you were having problems getting the clothes to fit properly."

"I am sorry, Edlin," she said sincerely. "I am afraid I owe you an apology. Emiril and I got caught up talking about how lovely the clothes were and I lost track of how long it had been since you came out here. Do you forgive me?" She smiled her best smile.

Even if he had been angry, which he was not, that smile would have calmed any ill feelings. He smiled back at her. "I am not angry. I am just glad you were not having a problem with the clothes." He followed Breanne into the room.

"Hello Edlin," Emiril said.

"Hello."

"Poor Edlin fell asleep in the hallway waiting for me," Breanne told Emiril. "I feel so bad."

"Oh, I did not fall asleep because of that," he said quickly. "I was already tired. I was just passing the time."

"Well, come sit down," Emiril said, pulling out a chair from the table by the window.

He walked over and gladly sat down.

"Well, here they are," Breanne said, showing him the clothes in the light of the window.

"They look very nice on you," he said. "Of course, I knew they would," he said then immediately turned red as both Breanne and Emiril gave him a brilliant smile.

"What are the pants made out of?" Emiril asked him. "I have never felt anything so soft."

"Oh, that is a new invention of mine," he said. "I am using Romon hide, but I am curing it in a new way. It is a slower process. I have to scrape the hide more often to keep it supple. Then when it is done, well, this part might make you feel ill, do you want to hear it?" he asked.

Breanne and Emiril looked at each other and nodded.

"Alright," he said, "but don't blame me if you feel ill. I soak the hide in mashed brains for a few days. It softens it and gives it more flexibility." He looked at the two of them to see if they were feeling squeamish. Emiril looked good, but he could not tell about Breanne. She looked different, but not necessarily squeamish.

"You know, I think the Native Americans used to do something like that in our world," she said. "I think it is a very smart idea."

Edlin smiled. He really liked her and this was just one of the reasons.

"So Edlin, how are you coming along with your packing?" Emiril asked suddenly. She wanted to move this thing along, she had to leave soon.

Edlin gave her a startled look. Emiril nodded at him, indicating that he needed to tell her now. He turned to Breanne who had been watching the two of them and wondering what they were being so secretive about.

"So, guess what?" he asked her, a hesitant smile on his face.

"What?" she said, not quite sure how she should be feeling about the news he was going to give her.

"Well," he looked at Emiril, who once again nodded encouragement. Why was this so hard, she thought? It was not like he was asking her to be his life mate. Breanne waited, finding her patience running thin. "Well," he said once again. "Emiril stopped by my shop today and asked me if I wanted to go with you guys.... on your quest tomorrow." There,

189

he said it. Now she would either be happy he was going, or upset. If it was the latter, he was leaving the room and fast.

Breanne was shocked. Could it be true, could he really be coming with them? She looked at Emiril, who once again nodded, this time to reassure Breanne that he was telling her the truth. "How wonderful," she said more exuberantly than she intended. Keep it cool she told herself, don't seem too happy. "It will be nice to have someone more my age to talk to," she said more calmly and then gave Emiril an apologetic look. She didn't want Emiril to think she was not good company. Emiril lowered her eyebrows and shook her head in a do not worry about it way. Breanne felt relieved.

"I am glad you are ok with me coming," he said. "Not that you would not be per se, but I am glad that you seem happy about it." Oh shut up, he told himself.

"Oh, I am happy about it," she said, then quickly wished she hadn't.

Ok, time to save these two before they die of embarrassment, Emiril thought. "Well Edlin, you probably have some packing to do, and I know Emiril does, so maybe we should let you get to it, and you two can meet here in the morning, around six, I would think."

"Yes," Edlin said quickly, jumping up, relieved to be given the chance to leave before he said anything else to embarrass himself. "I will be here at six, and now ladies, goodnight." He left quickly, turning once at the doorway to bow slightly, which made Breanne like him even more, if that were possible.

"You going to be alright there, kid?" Emiril asked Breanne.

Breanne didn't look at Emiril, she was replaying the little bow Edlin had made in her mind, while staring at the door. "I will be fine. I wish I hadn't seemed too eager though, do you think he noticed?"

Emiril thought about Edlin being all wrapped up in his own emotions to even notice Breanne's. "Not a chance," she said, and meant it.

"Oh Emiril, he is so cute, isn't he?"

"Yes," Emiril said, "he is cute, that is true."

Time to tell her, she thought. "You, Edlin and Marcus will be traveling to Ethuanova together and I will meet you there."

Breanne snapped back to reality at the sound of Emiril's words. "You're leaving? Why do you have to leave?" she asked sadly.

"I have to go see Mindoneth again. I have to talk to her about our quest. If it were not important, I would not go, but it is. But you will see me tomorrow afternoon."

This was not the first time Emiril had left her in the care of Marcus, and last time, not that it was Marcus's fault, things had gone terribly wrong. She was a little hesitant, she knew Emiril would not leave her if it wasn't necessary, but more importantly, she knew Marcus would protect her with his life. "I understand," she said, and she felt good because she really did understand and she was not upset. Before she came here, and even right after she came here, this news would have made her very angry, and scared; now she was taking it all in stride. She was growing up, and growing up felt good. "Just be careful," she added. "I want to see you again." She gave Emiril a big smile.

Emiril too noticed Breanne's new reaction to the news. She did not get scared or angry and that was really great. She really was growing up. She was proud of her.

"Well, let us get you packed up," she said. And the two of them packed what few things Breanne had in a bag Emiril had brought with her, and Emiril told Breanne it would be alright to wear her newest outfit the following day, which made Breanne very happy.

After they had packed, Emiril made sure Breanne understood the plans for the following day. She told her Marcus would meet her and Edlin at six the next morning and that she would see her some time tomorrow afternoon. She then answered any wayward questions Breanne had, and told the girl goodnight.

She left quickly, she had to get started, it was a long ride to Malarcis and more than that, she had questions that needed answering.

Chapter 29
Edlin's Confession

Breanne could not believe how things had turned out. She lay in her bed wide awake. She knew she needed to sleep, but she was not tired one bit. She kept thinking about the next day when Marcus, her and Edlin would be riding out on a grand and very scary adventure, and Emiril would not be with them. Well, she would, but not right away. She thought she would be more upset about that fact than she actually was, and she knew why she wasn't. Even in the privacy of her room, with no one around, she blushed. She couldn't help it. She liked Edlin so much; she had never felt this way about a boy before. She grew sad, wishing her mother were here to share in her excitement. She missed her family so very much. Tears welled up in her eyes at the thought of her mother smiling and hugging her when she told her about Edlin. She laughed when she suddenly pictured a big scowl on her father's face. He would insist on meeting him to check him out to make sure he was a stand-up guy. She wondered what they would say if they ever found out for real and realized he was an elf. Suddenly she laughed out loud; she didn't dare think about what would happen if they found out the age difference between them. She giggled even harder when she pictured her mother fainting and her father's mouth wide open. Then she started to cry. She cried for several minutes, that deep down, stomach hurting kind of crying that you can't control or stop even if you want to. When the flow of her tears slowed, she wiped her nose and eyes and tried to think of anything but home. She knew she was homesick, but she had not realized just how homesick she really was.

Suddenly there was a knock on her door that startled her. It was very late. Who could be up at this time of night? Maybe it was Emiril, she thought. "Come in," she called out.

The door opened to reveal a familiar face, although not Emiril's. It was King Badhor. He smiled at her and his face almost looked eerie in the dim light of the candle. "Can I come in?" he asked softly.

She sat up further in the bed, clearly shocked by his arrival. "Yes," she said and she could hear in her voice the recognizable sound of her previous cry. She hoped he did not.

As he entered the rest of the way in, and turned to shut the door, she noticed he carried a steaming mug. He crossed the room and grabbed a chair from the table by the window, approached the bed and sat down in the chair beside her. "I brought you something," he said softly, fatherly she thought, like Marcus; he too must be a good dad.

She smiled and reached out for the mug, thinking about Emiril's tea and its calming properties.

"Oh, it's not something as fancy as that," he chuckled. "I am afraid I am too old school for such things. This is simply the best thing I could think of to help one feel better." He smiled slyly at her. "Warm milk," he finished.

She was stunned, first because she realized he was reading her mind again, and second because this is the exact drink her mother would bring her when she was having a hard time sleeping at home. She looked at him through puffy red eyes and smiled a smile which relayed without words the depth of her gratitude and love she felt for the old elf at that moment. "How did you know?" she asked.

"Oh, old people have their ways." He smiled. "And do not forget, I am a father, I have instincts about these things." He patted her free hand gently.

She sipped the milk which tasted exactly as she remembered. Her body started to relax as she felt the warmth of the liquid slide down her throat and into her stomach. She took a deep calming breath and exhaled slowly. She could not tell him how much she had needed this and how grateful she was at this moment in time. Or could she? She knew he could read her mind, so she looked at him and without using words, just emotions, she thought her feelings to him so that she could accurately relay to him how much this meant to her.

He thought, what insight this child had. She was so smart in the ways of magic, even though she did not know she possessed any magic. He thought back to her the love he had come to feel for her in the short time he had known her. She was like a second daughter to him already, and he could not explain how that could be. It was as if they were connected on a deep level.

He thought about her uniqueness and about the fact that she had no clue of it. After their first meeting, he had gone back to his chambers and consulted Mindoneth. It had been a while since he had spoken with her and it had done him good on many levels. But they had been in agreement about the girl, there was something that connected her to this world, and they had to figure out what that was. He had asked her if she thought the girl was the one. She had been startled by his question. She had wondered that herself, but now her son had also brought up the question. Maybe it was true, maybe she was the one, but it was still too early to tell. They would have to decide though as they would need to prepare her just in case she was the one. If she was the one, and they did not prepare her, she would not stand a chance when the time came. They had finally decided it was in everyone's best interest to go ahead and take the chance and prepare her. If they didn't and she was beaten, they would all be beaten and they would be the ones to blame. He had had very little time to prepare for this tutorial and he hoped it would go well.

"Breanne," he started, "do you remember when I told you not to tell anyone you could hear my thoughts?"

"Yes," she said, a bit frightened and not sure why.

"Well, there was a reason for that. Not very many people can do that. In fact, not all elves can do that." He looked at her, trying to determine the effect his words were having on her without reading her mind. He could see a look of understanding on her face. He waited to read her mind. "Do you know why I am telling you this?" he asked, watching her face closely.

She looked into his eyes. He could see her thinking deeply, and then he felt it. She had entered his mind. This is what he had been waiting for, he had to refrain from reading her mind first and opening the door to his own mind, so that he would know for sure if she could do it on her own, and now he knew she could. He continued to watch her face as she unconsciously sought the answers she needed. He watched as her face went from confusion, to realization and then to fear. It was at that moment that he took control.

Quickly and deliberately he stepped into her mind. He saw her eyes open wider when she realized she was no longer alone.

"Breanne," he thought, "do not be afraid. You have learned a great many things in the past few seconds and I am going to explain it all to you now. Do you trust me?" She nodded but the fear was still present. He could not expect less. "All right, here we go."

He used his mind to explain to her that she was somehow connected this world, in a way that he did not fully understand yet. He told her that she possessed magic and that was what had allowed her to enter this world. If she had not possessed magic, simply reading the spell would not have brought her here. He went on to explain that when the man in the tavern started to read her mind, he had unknowingly taken her into

196

what is known as the spirit world. Then, when he fled her mind, he had inadvertently left her there. It was by her own strength and power she had returned alive. He further told her that only people who possess magic can enter the spirit world. "So you see," he told her, "it is by no accident you are here."

He waited a moment to let all he had said sink in. She was taking it quite well, he thought.

She looked at him, "Do you know how I got this magic?" she thought.

"No, we are not entirely sure about that," he said, hiding some of his true thoughts on the matter.

"But you have an idea," she thought matter-of-factly.

He was surprised so much that he physically flinched. "Why do you say that?" he asked out loud.

"I see it in your thoughts," she said quietly.

"Do you really?" he said, trying very hard to conceal the thoughts she must be reading.

"Yes."

He could not believe this. Never had anyone except his mother, and Norin on rare intimate occasions, been able to read any thought he did not wish them to. And then it hit him, there was one other person who could. He stared at the girl in disbelief. It couldn't be, he turned away from her just in case, he didn't want her to see what he was thinking. He got up and strode across the room. He was in shock.

Breanne was suddenly afraid she had done something wrong, that she had upset the king. She had not meant to, she was sorry. She started to feel as if she would cry again. "I am sorry your majesty," she said softly, "I did not mean to upset you."

Her voice broke his thoughts and he turned to her, a soft look on his face. "Oh child, I am sorry. You did nothing wrong, absolutely nothing wrong. I am just thinking, that is all." He looked at her. How could it be? Could it be?

"Breanne," he asked her, "have you ever read anyone's mind before you and I spoke yesterday?"

"No, I didn't know I could do that," she said hesitantly.

"And have you ever had anything else strange happen to you before you came here?"

"No, not really, not anything I would call magical." She looked at him, hoping she was answering the questions the way he wanted.

"Breanne," he said turning back to her and bracing himself. "Can you tell me what I am thinking now?" he used everything at his disposal to conceal his thoughts.

She was frightened and just stared at him; she did not want to upset him again.

"It is ok, child, I want you to do this," he said encouragingly.

She nodded and looked into his eyes, then felt herself enter his mind. She looked around and could see that he was very upset. She felt his confusion, and also a hint of excitement, but what caught her attention was the fear that she felt. She wanted to do as he asked, but she didn't want to upset him, so she looked at his excitement and read that thought, hoping it would be something innocent. She concentrated on it and slowly the thought seeped into her own mind. 'She is the one, she has to be. No one else can do the things she does. She has to be the one the prophecy speaks of...' She had been talking out loud, repeating the thought to him, when she felt the connection suddenly rip apart. She opened her eyes. The king stood across the room, his back to her and she thought to herself, I must have upset him again. Oh, this is so terrible, she thought. She wished at that moment she were anywhere but here. She wished Emiril were here, or even Marcus. She didn't understand what was going on and she did not want to do this anymore. She began to cry.

He could not stop shaking. He had to. Never in his life had he lost his composer this badly. Instinctively he reached out to Mindoneth. He needed her wisdom, but mostly he needed her comfort. Instantly he felt her presence. She had been waiting for him, knowing he would come. He felt his anxiety start to dissipate. He began to feel calm. She wasted no time on questions, but instantly read his mind, and in mere seconds she knew everything which had transpired. She too grew excited and yet fearful. But unlike her son, she remained in control. "Go to her," she said softly, "comfort her. Do not worry about your thoughts, do not try to conceal them." He did as she instructed.

When he reached her bedside, she was sobbing quietly into her pillow. He felt badly for the way things had gone and for losing his composure. Gently he touched her shoulder. She looked at him through tear filled eyes. She saw the softness in his face once more, and sat up. He hugged her tightly, she hugged him back.

"I am so sorry for all of this, Breanne," he said in a loving voice. "I am sorry I got upset, I was not upset with you though, you did nothing wrong."

"Good," Mindoneth told her son, "Now tell her everything. I believe she is the one."

He was shocked to hear her say that, but at the same time, he also knew it to be true. He waited until her sobbing had stopped, then he handed her his cloth to dry her eyes. When she was composed again, he let her go. She leaned back in the bed again and instead of sitting in the chair, he sat on the edge of the bed. What he had to tell her would come as a shock to her and he wanted to be close in case she needed another hug. Maybe he thought, I might need the hug.

Chapter 30
Breanne's Doubt

Emiril wanted to travel more secretively than she had before. She knew the Dark Mage would be watching with the utmost intensity for any movement in or out of Daedhrog, so that didn't leave too many options for her to choose from. She didn't want to use the open road, and skirting around the swamp of confusion would take too long. She thought about the fact that he would be watching all of those places. He wouldn't, however, necessarily be watching the place where he found them last. He would not expect them to retrace their steps; he would consider that too obvious and would never think they would be so stupid as to return to the same place. Well, that was exactly what they were going to do. She would make sure that Marcus got the message. It was actually brilliant. They would sneak out right under his nose and he would be too busy looking for them elsewhere to notice. She smiled; she still had it.

The going was much slower than before, especially because it was dark. It was true elves could see in the dark, but not as well as one might think. She still had to be careful and then there were all the trees to contend with. Once again, she was impressed with the good time Marcus and Breanne had made the other day.

Time wore on and the night got colder as she wound her way through the forest. She kept a close watch above her, and when a patch of sky appeared between the tree tops, she was extra careful, scanning the heavens for any sign of movement. She didn't expect to see any though, she felt safe. She was sure if anything was near, she would feel it before she would see it. It was near dawn when, for the second time in less than a week, she rode up to the steps of her grandmother's house.

Adwin startled her by appearing seemingly from out of nowhere. "Take your horse, my lady?" he said quietly, almost whispering. He too seemed to know she was on a secret mission, so to speak in regular voice tones didn't quite fit the mood.

"Yes Adwin, thank you," she said, matching his whispered tone.

He was leading the horse off in the direction of the barn when the front door opened and a small silhouette appeared in the opening. "Well, here you are again, granddaughter," the voice said softly. "More questions that need answers, I fear." The latter was said with a touch of resolution.

"Yes," Emiril said, almost sternly as if talking to a child. "This time, I need to know everything you know."

Her grandmother sighed. "Yes, yes you do. Come in then, we do not have much time. The sun will be up soon."

Even though she knew her grandmother well, it still seemed a surprise when she entered the house and saw hot tea on the table, waiting for her arrival, an arrival she had not told her grandmother to expect. She was grateful though, and hot tea would certainly hit the spot right now.

She didn't need to be reminded to drink her tea first and ask questions later. So, she sipped the hot beverage as quickly as she dared (she thought perhaps her grandmother made sure to bring it to a full boil before serving it, just to make the peaceful moment last), once again looking at the many paintings around the room. One painting in particular caught her eye. It was one of her mother and father when they were first married. They were seated in the garden on the same bench she had just sat on with her father. They looked so happy, her mother's smile so beautiful. The artist who painted them was a master at small details, she could even see the twinkle in her mother's eyes as she smiled lovingly at her father.

She took another sip of her tea, but nothing came out. Startled, she looked in the cup, had she been lost in the moment that long and not realized she had drunk all her tea? She looked up at her grandmother who was smiling tenderly at her. She blushed, embarrassed that she had seen her try to drink tea that was not there.

"More tea?" her grandmother asked smiling mischievously.

Emiril smiled back at her. "It looks as if I have run out," she said and started laughing. Her grandmother laughed along with her.

When they composed themselves, poured more tea and wiped the tears from their eyes, they once again became serious.

Her grandmother surprised her by talking first, but Emiril was even more surprised by what she said. "I have spoken with your father," she said bluntly.

Emiril's mouth hung open as she tried to think of something to say and couldn't.

"We talked about your young friend. And I have a lot to tell you, so just listen, no questions until I am done. Ok?"

Emiril nodded, too stunned to speak.

Her grandmother paused for a moment, then she began.

"When you were here last and we spoke about Breanne, there was something about her I couldn't quite put my finger on. I knew that somehow she was connected to this world, but I didn't know how. After you left, I thought about it for a long time. Then your father and I spoke about her and he brought up some good points I had not considered."

Emiril was thinking to herself that she wished her grandmother would just spit it out. It was all she could do to keep from yelling it out loud.

"Patience child, I'm getting there," her grandmother said and smiled at her.

Emiril was immediately embarrassed; she couldn't have a single private thought around this old elf. She looked down at the floor to avoid the look of self-content on her grandmother's face.

"As I was saying, your father and I talked about her and I have come to a conclusion about this girl." She stopped. Several minutes passed. It was as if she was reluctant to say what that conclusion was. She cleared her throat. Emiril continued to look at the floor. She did not want to offend her grandmother with the thoughts she was thinking right then. However, if she did not spit it out soon, she might not be able to help herself. "She is the one the prophets spoke of."

Emiril's eyes flew up and met her grandmother's stare. They both looked shocked; Emiril for hearing what she just heard, and her grandmother for saying it. But it was said and it couldn't be taken back.

"Are you sure?" Emiril asked when she once again found her voice.

"Yes. I was not at first, but I am now," her grandmother said resolutely.

Emiril got up and paced the floor. She started to say something two or three times, but changed her mind. She did not know what to say. She never thought she would see the day when the one the prophets spoke about would be found. She stopped pacing, turned to her grandmother and asked her, "Is there a chance you could be wrong? I mean no disrespect of course," she added quickly.

"I have considered everything and I do not think I am wrong. I believe she is the one."

"And father knows all of this?"

"Yes, he and I have spoken and he is in agreement."

"I should be with her then," Emiril said almost in a panic. "She will need to be told; she will need training. We cannot go on this quest now." She was once again pacing back and forth, her agitation growing.

"Emiril," her grandmother said loudly.

Shocked at the tone of her voice, one she almost never used, Emiril stopped in her tracks and looked at her grandmother's smiling face.

"Sit," her grandmother said sweetly, motioning to the chair which Emiril had recently vacated. "Have another cup of tea."

Emiril sighed. Great, she thought, now we have to have more tea before I can say anything more about this. Reluctantly she sat while her grandmother poured the tea. She was glad that the tea had cooled some, as she was able to drink it faster than she could earlier, but it still took some time to get it down. If her grandmother had felt she hurried too fast, she would have poured them another cup; she had done it before.

Finally, she sipped the last drop from her cup. She looked at her grandmother. Was she always right about everything, she thought. The tea had calmed her considerably and she had been given the opportunity to think over all she had learned in the time it had taken to drink it down. She smiled at her grandmother who smiled back knowingly.

"All right then." Her grandmother started. "You need not worry about Breanne, she is in good hands. Your father is with her." Emiril was surprised, although, had she not gotten so upset in the first place, she would have guessed that on her own. "He will tell her everything she needs to know and you will teach her how to navigate the spirit world when you two join up once more."

There were so many things Emiril had wanted to say before her grandmother insisted they have another cup of tea, but now she couldn't think of one thing that her grandmother had not covered in those two short sentences, so she sat there, silent.

"Do you remember what the prophecy says?" her grandmother asked finally.

Emiril looked at her, thinking. "Yes, I think so. Well, not word for word, I mean, but yes."

"Well go on then," she said, "tell me what you remember."

"Well, the first part is about the rise of evil in the land, and we know that to be Ogolel." Her grandmother nodded in agreement. "And then it talks about one who will come not from our world, yet of our world, and destroy the evil one. That part had always confused me, and still does actually. How is she part of our world, have you been able to figure that out yet?"

"No, not exactly," her grandmother admitted. "Your father and I are still working on that part, but she is connected, I can feel it, and he can too."

"Well, we know she has never been here before, at least she does not remember being here before," she said thoughtfully.

Her grandmother looked at her and thought about what she had just said. Of course, she thought, she has been here before, now I need to figure out when. "Emiril, you are a genius," she said smiling at her.

"What?" Emiril said, looking confused.

"I was trying to figure out who she was related to, who could have left our world. I never thought that she could have been here before and not remember it. You have just opened up a whole new realm of possible answers to who she is."

Emiril smiled at her. "It was the tea," she said and then she and her grandmother broke into laughter.

After they once again regained their composure, Emiril asked, "How young would you have to be to not remember anything?" She thought for a moment. "I remember back to when I was about four, but then nothing."

Her grandmother looked at her thoughtfully. "Well, I am so old I would never be able to remember that long ago. But I suppose you are right, you would have to be really young to not remember something."

"So, what do you think then," Emiril asked, "she was about three years old or younger when she was here last?" She looked at her grandmother to see if she thought that sounded right, but was startled by the look on her face. "What's wrong?" she said standing up to go to her.

Her grandmother put up her hand, hesitated, then sat back down.

"What is it?" she asked her heart pounding.

"Emiril," her grandmother said looking at her with big haunted eyes. "I know how she is connected to this world." Her haunted eyes echoed in her voice as well. Goosebumps rose on Emiril's arms. "How?" she asked, not really sure she wanted to know.

"I cannot tell you."

Emiril's eyes flew open, surprised at what she had just heard. "Not tell me? What do you mean you cannot tell me?" she asked almost yelling.

"Do not get angry, Emiril," her grandmother said softly. "What I mean to say is that I cannot tell you now, I am not sure yet if it is safe for you to know."

Emiril looked at her more stunned than ever. "How could it not be safe for me to know?" she asked, her feelings of anger a bit dulled.

"I really do not know yet," her grandmother said beginning to sound impatient. "I am sorry, Emiril, but I really think I could put you in harm's way if I say anything more right now. You are just going to have to trust me. As soon as I talk to your father, I will know if I can tell you. Until then, you are just going to have to be patient."

Emiril sighed. "I am sorry," she said softly, "I know you are protecting me. I should not have gotten upset." She hung her head, feeling ashamed for her outburst.

Her grandmother smiled at her. "I will let you know as soon as I feel it will not put you in danger, I promise. And right now, I do not know if it would help you anyway."

A ray of sunshine found its way through a small opening in the curtain by the table. They looked at the ray that splashed on the table, both contemplating what they knew and what one of them did not know. Today would start an adventure that was now much more than either of them would have guessed in the beginning, and if she was right, her grandmother thought, it would be the adventure of a lifetime for them all.

Chapter 31
Through the Hidden Door

Why did she want to see him? He hated it when she summoned him. It usually meant he had done something that she felt was wrong. What had it been this time? He had been watching for them. He searched day and night. It was not his fault they hadn't moved. If they had, he would know. His new creature, the one whom he had hated when it was first born into this world, had proved to be special. He had begun to like it, and that fondness had grown into a strange kind of kinship between them, a kinship built upon the shared fear and loathing, loathing of her. Together, they were less afraid of her; together, they found someone in whom they could trust. They had truly become soul mates. Never had he been so connected to a creature. He could read its thoughts before the creature was done thinking them, and the creature responded to his commands even before he realized he was giving them. It was as if they had been made to be one conjoined soul, instead of two separate ones. His thoughts broke off as he neared the chamber of solitude. He stopped just outside the door and cleared his thoughts. There must not be even one stray thought in his mind to reveal his true feelings for her. If there were, he could lose his life, and he did not wish to lose his life today. After taking a few more deep breaths and thinking on such subjects as herb gathering and spell ingredients, he opened the door and went in.

As usual, the silence was eerie. He whistled softly to keep his mind from slipping towards madness. He sat down in the chair and reluctantly closed his eyes, allowing his mind to open itself up as if for bait.

He sat for only a moment when the pain of her arrival was upon him. He grimaced and sweat instantly poured forth from every pore of his body. He could feel her rummaging through his mind. She was like a bull in a china shop; she didn't care what she broke. He ran behind her, straightening things she left a mess. If she didn't stop soon, he would not be able to fix things, and he would go mad, lost forever in a broken mind, sitting in a room with no light and no sound.

At last she stopped. He froze. The last thing to straighten tauntingly close, he dared not reach for it.

"Why have you not caught her yet?" she said low and purposefully.

He could hear the evil as it slithered over every word she thought to him. The sound was as uncomfortable as nails on a chalk board, and if he had been aware of his physical self at that moment, he would have realized that all the hair on his body was standing on end.

"I have been searching for her day and night," he thought back and to his dismay, it sounded a bit whiney to him.

"Searching day and night, and yet you don't have her," she hissed back.

"Your highness, please," he thought frantically, a hint of fear mixed with the whine. "I can't find her if she hasn't left the safety of Daedhrog."

She was silent. He waited. Outside, his physical self started to tremble, he was unaware.

"I had better know the second she leaves that place," she said and he felt the brush of her spirit behind him.

"Of course, your highness," he thought and she could sense the fear in his voice. It made her happy and she left.

He stayed where he was for several minutes. He needed to regain his composure before returning to his body, and he needed to set right the last thing she had messed up. He grabbed it and at once, a fear greater than any he had ever known before filled him. The last thought of his she had seen was one that was supposed to be buried deep within his mind. His life was in danger now, that much he knew. When and where he would meet his end eluded him however. He stared at the thought, wishing he had been more careful. She would never let him live, now that she knew how much he hated her.

Chapter 32
The Amulet's Power

How much he should tell her was still in question. He did not want to tell her about her mother, but if he did not, he would take the chance that she would tell her and then Breanne might not fulfill her quest. Everything hung in a balance now. If she was truly the one, a fact of which he was sure of, then only she could vanquish Ogolel from their world. If she knew the truth, however, would she be able to go through with it?

"Breanne, tell me about your mother," he said softly.

"My mother?" she asked startled.

"Yes, is she a good mother to you?" he asked.

Her eyes lit up as she thought of her. "Oh yes, she's a wonderful mother," she said truthfully. In fact, her parents were the epitome of what parents should be, kind, fair, and loving. She couldn't have asked for anything more when it came to her parents.

"Good," he said. "Do you think she loves you?"

Breanne gave him a look of astonishment. What kind of questions were these? "Of course she loves me," she said almost defiantly.

He chuckled. She was a good daughter, he thought, sticking up for her mother the way she was. "All right," he said, raising his hand in a truce. "I am sure she is a great mother. I just needed to hear that from your own mouth. Now, the reason I asked you all these questions is because I want you to think about something."

She smiled and nodded, the irritation she had been feeling faded.

"What if someone told you that your mother was not your real mother, what would you say?" he watched her face to see her reaction.

Breanne stared at him. He saw no emotion on her face at all. He reached into her mind only to find it empty. His eyes grew wide, how could she empty her mind from him? He tried again to peer into her thoughts, nothing. He began to worry.

"Breanne, are you ok?" he asked hesitantly.

Then, in a flat voice, she asked him, "Are you asking me a hypothetical question, or are you trying to tell me something?"

Right then he knew that he was going to have to be candid with her. She was far too intelligent for anything else.

"Breanne," he began hesitantly, then more confidently, "I think that you are not who you think you are. I believe that you were born in this world and then sent to live in your world when you were very young. I think the family that you know there, are not your real family. I believe you were adopted by them."

She looked at him incredulously.

"Also," he added, "I believe I know who your real mother is."

They sat in silence for a while, he letting her soak in all he had just told her. Again, she just stared at him. He did not try to read her mind again, her powers, which she had recently been made aware of, were obviously growing, and whether she knew it or not, she was able to use them quite effectively, in this instance to close herself off from him. This was another strong piece of evidence that he was right in his guess as to who her mother was.

After several more tense moments of silence, she spoke.

"I know who she is."

He flinched.

"I dreamt of her." She stared deep into his eyes, and he could feel himself being drawn to her. He let it happen.

He found himself in her mind. She was showing him the dream. He watched as she was confronted by Ogolel. He watched her read the word daughter on her lips. Then he saw the dream version of Breanne turn to him, her eyes pleading with him. He had never seen thoughts manipulated in such a way. He watched as she turned once again to her mother and he felt himself being pushed back out of her mind.

When he was back in the room again, he looked at this frail young girl before him. Who was she? He knew now beyond any doubt that Ogolel was her mother, that much was obvious, but who was her father? How did she come to possess powers which were fast proving to be greater than his own, and did he dare say, greater than even the great Mindoneth's. There was so much he still did not know.

Breanne broke the silence, her words hollow sounding, melancholy. "I think I am the daughter of Ogolel."

He just looked at her. He didn't know what to say. She looked back at him.

Finally, he spoke. "Breanne, you may be the daughter of Ogolel, but that does not make you Ogolel. You are a great person. I know it must be hard to hear all of this right now. Your world as you knew it is no longer and will never be the same again, but you have a whole new world before you and you still have your old one, it is just different."

She looked into his face and he saw a glimmer in her eyes. Feeling more confident, he continued, "You will always have your parents. Ogolel is nothing more than someone who gave you life. She did not raise you, care for you and teach you, your parents did that, and they will always be the ones you think of when you think of your family."

He smiled. "And guess what?" he asked her, a look of happiness on his face.

"What?" she asked still upset.

"I do not know if you have thought about this yet, but Ogolel is my wife's sister." He looked to see if it was registering with her. Not yet. He continued, "That makes her Emiril's Aunt, and that makes you and Emiril…"

"Oh my gosh," Breanne shouted loudly. "That makes Emiril and I cousins. Doesn't it?"

He laughed heartily, feeling better that she was coming out of her depressed state. "Yes, yes it does."

"And that would make you my uncle," she said, her eyes wide.

He hadn't thought about her relationship to him, only her relationship to Emiril, but yes, he was her uncle. That would explain why he had felt so strongly for her the moment they met; he must have sensed that she was related to him then. He smiled even bigger, "Yes Breanne, I am your uncle."

"I knew there was a reason why I loved you so much," she said. She leaned forward and gave him the biggest hug ever. Happily, not everything she had just learned about herself was bad.

"Now Breanne," he said firmly, "you still need to keep some of this a secret, the part about Ogolel being your mother."

She looked at him, confused. "Do I have to keep it a secret from Emiril?" she asked.

"Especially Emiril," he said sternly. She detected an unspoken warning in his voice.

"I don't understand why Emiril can't know," she said impatiently.

He looked at her, trying to think how to explain it. "The reason you cannot tell her is because she cannot keep it a secret the way you can. Ogolel can see into people's minds, and she can see into Emiril's mind, if she is not careful. If she were to find out about you before we are ready, it would be bad."

"But what makes you think she can't read my mind?" she asked quickly.

He looked at her, not sure he wanted to tell her. "Because," he said finally, "I could not read your mind." He watched her expression to see if she understood the full implications of what he had told her.

She thought about what he had just said. Emiril had told her how powerful her father was. He was one of the most powerful elves ever. If she had blocked him from reading her thoughts, what did that mean? Was she just as powerful as he was? Or maybe she was more powerful. She was a little hesitant to ask, she didn't want to offend him. "So how come I can block you from reading my thoughts?" she asked finally. "Is it because Ogolel is so powerful?"

He thought about it for a second. "No, I do not believe that is it. She is not more powerful than I am, there is something else, something more about you that we do not know yet."

She sat thinking about all of this. Just a few days ago, she was a normal young girl passing the time at her grandparent's house while her parents were on vacation. Now, she was in a different world, she was a different person, and she possessed magical abilities. So much had happened to her in such a short period of time that she had a hard time believing it to be real, but it was real. All of this was real and she was doing her best to accept it as quickly as it was being thrust at her. She had to admit though, that even as some of this was shocking and frightening, she was finding a lot of it exciting as well. It was like being in a movie. One never thinks the things that happen in movies are real.

Stuff like that doesn't happen, but in her case, it was happening and she was glad, even if she was still homesick.

"Well, a lot has happened here and we need to talk a little more about what this means for you," the king said resolutely.

"I think I already know," Breanne interrupted.

He looked at her, surprised and hopeful. If she did know then maybe she was accepting of her fate and she would be able to accomplish what the prophets said she would.

"What do you know of the prophecy?" he asked her.

She looked at him solemnly. "I don't really know about the prophecy," she said almost hauntingly. "But I do know what I am supposed to do. I think I've known for a while." She looked into his eyes, and he could see in her, whatever it was that made her so powerful, staring out at him. It was as if it, the power, were in her, looking out through her eyes like windows and it made the hair on his neck stand up. "I am the one who will kill Ogolel," she whispered and her words were almost hypnotic.

He didn't know what to say back to her at first. He knew what she was supposed to do as the chosen one, but to hear her actually say it, and with that presence about her, he was at a loss for words. He did the only thing he could think of, it was rather instinctive; he hugged her. He held her for a long time and she welcomed it. In his arms she could pretend that this was just another day at home and he was her father, but armed with the knowledge that he was her uncle, a revelation that made her extremely happy, she could feel even more comfort from his loving embrace.

After a long while, he let her go. "You are a brave girl, Breanne. I know this is probably all very shocking for you, but you are handling it very well. I want you to know that if you do this, which it sounds like you are willing…" He watched her reaction to his words very closely, and she showed only resolution in her face. "The only place Ogolel can be defeated is in the spirit world. And even then, the only one who can defeat her is someone who is blood related to her. For the longest time, we thought it was going to have to be Emiril. She does not know this, we never told her. Her grandmother and I thought it was best not to say anything until the signs of the prophecy were revealed, but they never were. You see, Emiril could not fulfill the part about not being from this world. We had about given up hope that the prophets were right, and then you showed up." He smiled at her. "You fulfill everything in the prophecy: you are not from this world and yet you are, and you are blood related to her. You are the one, Breanne, the one this world has been waiting a long time for. You need to know, Breanne, there is only one way to defeat her, you must take her powers from her and ban her to the in-between."

Breanne sat up further. "I know about this," she said excitedly. "I know how to take her powers."

Once again, he was surprised by this young girl. "You do? Who told you?"

"Marcus did," she said, remembering their conversation that day in the woods. "We weren't talking about Ogolel; we were talking about how he got his powers." The king's eyebrows raised; he had never heard that story. "Marcus told me that to get someone's powers, you must go into the spirit world and embrace each other, then the person with the power can transfer some of it to the other person." She looked at him, the expression on her face was one of cunning, and he thought she resembled a soldier about to spring a surprise attack. "One other thing he told me was that if you didn't unlock your embrace, you could take all of someone's magic from them." She looked at him intently, waiting for his reaction.

"Well, that is it then," he said matter-of-factly. "We will take her magic from her and leave her in the in-between."

"What's the in-between?" she asked.

So, there's one thing Marcus did not tell her about her thought. "The in-between is the place between two worlds. Just as you leave one world and enter the other, you go through an area we call the in-between. In the case of Ogolel, if someone were to take her into the spirit world and remove her powers, then bring her only part way back and leave her there, she would be in the in-between, and she would never be able to leave it."

"Would it be difficult?" she asked nervously. "I mean, could you get her to the in-between and then leave her there without much of a fight?"

He looked at the girl; he knew it would not be easy. This was going to be by far the hardest thing she had ever done. But he also knew she could do it. He could sense it, and that she had whatever it was that he had seen within her, that look in her eyes. It was something he had never seen before, and no matter what anyone said, he knew it had been looking back at him, as if it were another entity living within the girl.

"I think it will be hard," he said truthfully, but just as truthfully he said, "But I know you can do it. I have no doubts about your abilities."

She smiled at him, and then looked worried again. "How will I get to the spirit world and back again? The one time I went there I was almost lost."

"Emiril is going to teach you how to come and go safely," he said reassuringly, and he could see she liked that idea very much.

Breanne yawned and rubbed her eyes. The king noticing this, suddenly realized it was very late and she had to get up early in the morning.

"Well, young lady, we have talked for a long time and now I am afraid you are falling asleep." She smiled. "I will let you get some rest and I will see you first thing in the morning." He looked at the window and sighed. "I am afraid that will not be long off. I am sorry about that."

"It's alright," she said. "It wasn't your fault, we just had a lot to talk about."

He smiled at her and watched as her eyes drooped a little lower. "Well, goodnight then," he said as he got up and headed toward the door. Then he stopped and turned to her. "I am very proud of you, Breanne. You are handling all of this like at true member of the royal family and I couldn't ask more of you."

"Thank you..." She paused then decided to say it anyway, "...Uncle."

He smiled a big smile. "I rather like the sound of that, Niece," he said happily.

He then turned and left her to drift off into a deep sleep. She did not dream that night.

Chapter 33
Whispers in the Dark

Edlin was up before the sun. He had packed everything the night before, but he wanted to go over it all to make sure he did not leave anything behind. He was so excited, he was sure he would overlook something. He rummaged through his bag and decided everything was there, the same as it had been the night before. He sat down on the bed. It was at least another hour before sunrise and then another hour until he was supposed to meet Marcus and Breanne. But he was too excited to sleep anymore, in fact, he had hardly slept at all.

He picked up the sword once more. He looked into the gleaming blade and by the flickering candlelight saw himself in its reflection. His father would not believe it, him, going on a quest with the princess. Never in his wildest dreams would he have thought this would happen to him. The biggest dream he had ever had was to be able to make clothes for the royal family. That is not to say that he didn't want to dream big, he just never thought it would come true. He held the sword up, its blade shimmering in the candlelight. I will make you proud, father, he thought.

He put the sword back in its sheath and made sure to lay it on his bag. It was the last thing he'd want to forget; he didn't want to think of how embarrassed he would be if he did. Breanne would think he was a fool. And Marcus, well, let's just say Marcus would never look at him as a man for the rest of his life, but worst of all, he would never be able to look Emiril in the eye again. He touched the sword again and silently thanked his father for teaching him how to use it.

He lay back down on the bed. Morning would come slowly.

Bang, bang, bang. The sound came again. It was annoying and yet he could not find the source of it. He looked here and there. Bang, bang, bang. "Would someone please make it stop!" he shouted.

"I will not stop, young man, and you had better get up or I might just leave you here," the voice said gruffly.

Edlin opened his eyes to bright sunlight, which was suddenly blocked out by a towering figure. He blinked several times, trying to remember who he was and where he was.

"Are you awake, sleeping beauty?" the figure said in a less gruff tone.

Edlin blinked his eyes several more times and the figure began to take shape. "Marcus?" he asked sleepily.

"Yes, it's time to get up, or do you not want to go?"

As if someone poked him in the back, Edlin jumped straight out of bed and stood swaying on his feet in front of Marcus. "Oh Marcus!" he said loudly. "I…What…I mean, I must have fallen asleep. I am so sorry." He shook his head to clear it and almost fell over in the process.

"Easy boy," Marcus said laughing. "It's alright, I see you're ready to go and if you're anything like I was at your age, you've been ready all night." He patted Edlin's shoulder. "Let me guess. You woke up, if you slept at all, before the sun, couldn't think of anything else that needed doing, laid back down to wait for sun up and fell asleep. Does that about cover it?" he said, smiling at the open mouthed Edlin.

"How did you know?" Edlin asked in awe.

Marcus laughed heartily. "I've been there many times my boy, many times."

"Then you're not mad?" Edlin asked relieved.

"No, boy, I'm not mad, you're ready. Now, if you hadn't been ready, I would be tanning your hide right now." He gave Edlin a look that proved he was only half serious.

"Well, I am ready," Edlin said quickly, gathering up his things, making sure to grab the sword. "And you are right, I have been up most of the night, and did fall asleep waiting until the sun rose. You were right about everything," he said, standing in front of Marcus, ready to walk out the door. "Thanks for not being mad," he added quietly.

Marcus gave the young elf a broad smile. "You're welcome, Edlin, but seriously, all good swordsmen have been there before, including me. Now let's go get Breanne. I can't say for sure that she will be ready, she is a girl after all."

Edlin smiled at that last remark. I bet he wouldn't say that if she were here, he thought, and definitely not if Emiril were here. He chuckled to himself as they started off to Breanne's room, imagining the reaction that comment would have gotten from Emiril.

When they reached Breanne's room, the door was open. They peeked inside to see her and King Badhor sitting at the table by the window. They looked like they were just finishing up breakfast. Great, Marcus thought, and gave Edlin a look. Edlin knew exactly what he was thinking, (now we'll never hear the end of us being late) and gave the same look to Marcus. Marcus shrugged his shoulders in resignation and motioned Edlin in. "After you," he said. Edlin gave him a look of, gee thanks, and then walked into the room, putting on his best smile. Marcus followed, smiling as well.

"Sorry we're late," Edlin said, bowing before the king. Marcus too bowed low as he approached the table.

King Badhor looked at Edlin. My how that boy has grown, he thought. And he sure has turned out to be a handsome young fellow. It is no wonder Breanne is taken with him.

"Please sit," he said, motioning them to two empty chairs at the table. "We saved you some breakfast. Adventurers need to eat before they start out, you never know when your next meal is going to come." If anyone had been looking, they would have noticed the sadness that passed, as quickly as it came, from his eyes, but no one noticed and King Badhor hid his emotions from the excited trio.

The two late comers sat down and eagerly dug into the left-over food. It was still warm at least, but they would have eaten just as voraciously if it had been cold. As they ate, the king and Breanne made small talk. He told her about the castle and how long it took to build, and she told him about houses in her world and how they were so much smaller. He asked her if they had castles in her world and she explained that in Europe they did, but they didn't really use them anymore, except of course for the queen of England. But that was the only real castle in use that she knew of.

When Marcus and Edlin were done eating, they got down to more serious conversation. The king told them about the dwarves, that they were a nice enough race, if you didn't make them mad. He then told them that inside the Island of the Ancient Ancestors, they would need to be careful and watch for traps, but mostly they needed to stay together and not get separated from their guide, or else they may never make it out. He also told them that this quest was one of the most important ever taken in their world and how brave and honorable they were. This made Edlin feel very proud and important, which did not go unnoticed by Marcus. Maybe it was a good thing that Edlin was going on this quest after all, he thought. It will do him a world of good to get out of the castle and become a man. The poor boy had been lost since his father passed. Marcus decided he would do everything he could to teach Edlin how to be a man, and a warrior.

When the king had finished instructing them about their trip, he stood and embraced each of them. Breanne a little longer than the others, then he excused himself and left the room. As he was leaving, he thought to Breanne, "You can get in touch with me anytime, but check with Emiril first to make sure it is safe." He turned and smiled at her, then he was gone. Breanne hoped that would not be the last time she would see her Uncle.

"Well, I guess it's time," Marcus said, sounding official.

The other two looked at him, their faces a mixture of excitement and apprehension. It took Marcus handing Edlin his bag to get their feet moving, but as soon as they were, they made good time getting out of the castle to their waiting horses.

"Oh JC," Breanne cried out as she saw her brave horse for the first time since their terrifying ride to Daedhrog. She ran up to the beast and gave him a big hug. The horse seemed to be just as happy to see her and whinnied and stomped his feet, rubbing his massive head against her. She scratched his ears and patted his neck. "I am so glad to see you," she said to the horse. "I have missed you."

Marcus looked at Edlin and shrugged his shoulders. "I think a man and his horse have a different kind of relationship," he told him. "More laid back, I would say."

Edlin looked at Marcus' horse standing patiently by, looking neither happy nor upset to see his master, and smiled. "It would seem you're right," he said and turned to his own mount. Well, really it wasn't his horse; he was given this horse by Emiril when she had decided he would be coming with them. It was a good-looking horse though, about sixteen hands, brown and sturdy looking. He stroked its nose, and the horse

225

snorted softly then nibbled his fingers. "You will do fine," he said, then put his bag on the horse's saddle, making sure it was tied down good. He wasn't quite sure how to put the sword on though, and much to his relief, Marcus came over and showed him the proper way. There was a trick to it apparently, so that it would not fall out, yet would be easily retrievable if necessary. Edlin thanked him and realized he was growing to like this man he was now truly getting to know, after so many years of being around him.

After they were all squared away and last-minute goodbyes were said to well-wishers, they officially started their quest.

They rode single file, passing out of the castle walls, and winding their way through the town's streets. Breanne had been unconscious when she was first brought to the castle, and this was the first time she had seen Daedhrog. It was beautiful. The houses were all white, two story, Victorian looking places, with spires and balconies. Each yard was planted with colorful flowers and shrubs which were trimmed in fantastic shapes and picket fences sectioned off each yard. The streets were white cobblestone and towering trees with many shade giving branches lined the sides. To her eyes it looked so clean and pure. She had never seen anything so beautiful. Occasionally someone would wave to them as they passed by, and children would follow them for a block or two whispering amongst themselves and pointing. She heard birds singing in the trees, but could not get a glimpse of them. She felt so good here, she suddenly didn't want to leave, but she knew she had to. She had to help the people who lived here; she was the only one who could keep this peaceful place from falling into the hands of the evil sorceress Ogolel, and she was going to do her best to make sure that didn't happen.

Soon they left the town behind them and broke out into more open terrain. The fields were green with tall grass and trees dotted the landscape every so often. Up ahead in the distance Breanne could see what had to be a forest, and she started thinking about the route she and Marcus had taken to get here. She spurred her horse to catch up to him. "Marcus?" she asked, "Is this the way we came to Daedhrog?"

He looked at her and smiled, surprised she had figured it out so soon. "Yes, it is," he said. "Emiril and I figured that the Dark Mage would be watching all the routes out of Daedhrog except the one we came here by. It would be the last thing he would expect us to do, so we are doing it." He smiled a mischievous smile at her.

"That's brilliant," she said, smiling back.

"I'm actually glad you came up here though," he said more seriously. "I want to talk to you before we leave the safety of the shield." He looked back at Edlin who was just as busy looking at his surroundings as Breanne had been. Edlin had never left Daedhrog before, and this was all new to him as well. When he was satisfied the youth was not listening, he went on. "When we leave the shield, you can't leave your mind open, and you can't try to read anyone else's either." Breanne looked surprised that he knew. Catching her surprised look he told her, "I know what I need to know to keep us all safe." She nodded. "So, do you understand what I told you?" he asked her, his face showing how serious this issue was.

"Yes," she said solemnly. "I will do as you say. I don't want to bring that creature back upon us." She shivered, remembering her brush with the creature, and death, the last time she was outside the shield.

"Ok, good." Marcus went on. "I spoke with Emiril this morning and she is going to meet us near Ethuanova. We can't go into town because there will be spies there looking for us." He looked at her for a moment, a look of concern on his face. "How are you holding up?" he asked her, the concern also resounding in his voice.

She smiled at this man who had been slowly taking a place of great importance in her life. He reminded her so much of her father, he made her feel safe, even when they weren't necessarily safe at all. "I am doing alright," she said truthfully. And she was doing alright, more so than she would have been, if she had not learned all the things she had the night before. At least now she knew that she had the capability of protecting herself, a little at least. And she also knew that she was at least part elf. She certainly didn't have the ears of an elf, but she had some elfin blood in her, and if she were part elf, she would more than likely be able to do some of the magic that Emiril did. In time, Emiril would teach her how to use her powers. Then she really would be able to protect herself.

"Good," Marcus said, sounding a little relieved. "Now we just have to keep an eye on Edlin."

"Hey, I heard that!" Edlin said sounding hurt.

"Oh, Edlin, hi," Marcus said, surprised.

"I will have you know, sir," Edlin said sounding official. "I am really good with a sword and do not need to be looked after, in fact." He added, "I will be looking after Breanne and Emiril just as much as you will be." Breanne couldn't help but notice that his head was thrown back and he sort of had his nose up in the air. He looked like a stuffy aristocrat and it was all that she could do not to laugh. If she did laugh, she would crush his spirit, and he might never speak to her again. She looked at Marcus and could see he felt bad that Edlin had heard him say that.

"You know I was just teasing," Marcus said quickly, eyeing Edlin to see if he was buying it. "Why, I was just telling Breanne that it was nice to have another sword around; kinda takes some pressure off of me." He looked at Breanne. "Wasn't I, Breanne?"

"Oh, yes, you were," she added quickly. "And he also said that it would be nice to have another man to talk to, instead of only having women for company." She smiled at Marcus and he looked back at her gratefully.

"Really?" Edlin said, looking at Marcus, then back at Breanne.

"Really," they both said simultaneously.

"Well… all right," he said still looking a little out of sorts. "But really, I can use a sword, my father taught me. And," he added looking at Breanne with soft eyes, "I will protect you, Breanne, honest."

Breanne felt her stomach do several flip flops, and she could not suppress the foolish smile that lit up her face. Marcus rolled his eyes and gently nudged his horse to walk a little faster, trying to get out from between them. Oh brother, he thought, so it starts.

For the rest of the time it took to get to the edge of the shield, Marcus rode ahead of the two young people. He could hear them talking nonstop and was glad that he was not obligated to participate in their conversation. He was too old for the kinds of conversations young people who have a crush on each other have. He missed Iola; he was still not used to being away from her for long periods of time and didn't think he ever would be. He also missed his daughter; she grew so much every time he left. He felt as if he was missing out on her whole childhood, and that was something he could never get back. A glimmer in the distance brought his attention back to the present. They were almost to the edge of the shield, and once they passed through it, they would no longer be under the protection of Daedhrog. The time for idle conversations was over. He stopped his horse and waited for the others to catch up.

Chapter 34
Ogolel's Command

When Breanne and Edlin caught up, Marcus looked at them very seriously. "We are about to pass outside the shield," he told them. "Once we do, we will be vulnerable to attack." He didn't want to scare them, but he wanted them to know exactly what the situation was. "The Dark Mage will eventually realize we have left the safety of the glen, and once he does, he will be relentless in his search to find us, and if that happens, we all know what can happen. I for one don't want him to find us, at least until we meet up with Emiril." He smiled at his last statement, as did Breanne and Edlin. "So, from this point on, there will be no more idle chatter, we have to be quiet and stay alert."

Emiril looked ahead of them to the spot where they would be passing through the shield. She shuddered, knowing the likelihood of running into the creature so soon was very slim, but she couldn't help but be a little scared. Marcus saw her apprehension and wished there was something he could say or do to make her feel better, but if the truth were known, he too was a little apprehensive about leaving the safety of the glen. Edlin on the other hand was very excited about leaving. He had never been this far from the castle in his life and the thought of leaving the glen altogether was very exciting to him. He, of course, had never seen the creature, yet.

"Well, let's get moving," Marcus said resolutely. "Daylight will be gone before we know it, and I don't feel like camping in the forest tonight."

Breanne remembered the animal she had heard in the forest after it had gotten dark the last time, and she did not want to spend the night in

230

there either. "Yes, let's get going," she said nervously. "I don't want to be in the forest after dark either."

Single file, they left the glen, each one thinking different thoughts about their quest.

They had ridden half the day when they came upon the same stream she and Marcus had stopped at to have lunch on their first trip through these woods. Breanne wished they could stop again as she was once again feeling the saddle in her backside, but Marcus had already told them there would be no stopping until they were safely through the forest.

Edlin had ridden behind Breanne thus far and with Marcus in front, she felt somewhat safe, (safer than she would have if she were riding in the back). But she had lost that magical feeling the woods had given her the first time she was a visitor here, with its tall swaying trees, gentle breezes and warm earthly smell. Instead, all she could do was think about evil creatures lurking above her and hiding behind every tree, waiting to pounce on her and tear her limb from limb. (A little dramatic, maybe, but not by much, considering how close she had come to losing her head the last time she was near these woods.) She rode silently, praying that they would make it all the way through before nightfall.

Edlin could feel the tension emanating from the other two, but he had no experience with which to associate their feelings, so for him, the ride through the forest was a pleasant, wonderful adventure. Never had he seen so many trees in one place, never had he smelled the damp, earthy smells of a forest. He would look straight up and struggle to see the tops of the enormous, green, giants which surrounded the travelers. The coolness of the forest was pleasant and he loved listening to the chirping of birds as they flitted here and there, sometimes stopping on a nearby branch to chastise them for riding too close to their nest. He saw squirrels running from tree to tree carrying fir cones to stash away for their winter feast. He did not know how lucky he was, that he could enjoy this trek, when his two companions were riding in fear, unable to enjoy the wonderful sights and sounds around them.

Just before nightfall, Marcus turned to Breanne and smiled. "We are nearing Ethuanova," he said, and Breanne could see that the tension had left his face. Seeing Marcus relax, and with the news, she too relaxed. Now that she was no longer worried about being killed in the woods, she had the opportunity to think about other things, and one of those things was the fact that Emiril was going to teach her to navigate the spirit world. She was a little nervous because of the last time she was in the spirit world, but she had to remind herself that this time, she would not be alone, Emiril would be with her, and she would not abandon her there. But then she thought, what if Ogolel is there? I will have to remember to ask Emiril about that when I see her. Her thoughts were interrupted when JC came to a sudden stop. She looked up and noticed that she had run upon Marcus' horse standing in the middle of the trail. "Sorry," she whispered to Marcus. He smiled back at her and motioned for Edlin to come closer.

When they were all as close as they could get to one another, Marcus whispered lowly, "We are very near town, but we can't go any closer, there are spies all over looking for us, and they will surely be in Ethuanova as well. We will wait here for Emiril, but we must be very quiet. We can't attract any attention to ourselves, understood?" The other two nodded silently in agreement. "Ok you can dismount, but no fires and no talking."

Quietly Breanne slid from the saddle, her backside feeling very tender. She looked over to where Edlin was just slipping down from his mount and smiled when she noticed him rubbing his backside as well. At least I'm not the only one, she thought happily, then felt bad for Edlin.

Edlin walked over to where Marcus stood, scanning the darkness around them. He whispered something to him and Marcus replied just as quietly. Breanne wished she knew what they were talking about. Then Edlin turned and walked her way. When he was very close to her, he leaned over and whispered in her ear, "Marcus said we can talk if we whisper like this. He added though, that if he hears us, we will have to be quiet again." He leaned back and smiled at Breanne. She smiled back. Even in the dark he was handsome, she thought.

This time she leaned over to Edlin, "How was your ride?" she asked, hoping he had enjoyed it more than she had.

She turned her head and he whispered, "It was really great. I have never been outside the glen before. I cannot believe how much I have missed." When he said the last part, Breanne could detect a hint of sadness in his voice. She felt sorry for him, but at least he was here now and would have the chance to see and do many things while on this trip; that is, if we make it very far in the first place, she thought.

Suddenly they heard a twig snap in the darkness to their right. They froze. Marcus came quickly to where they were. He put his finger to his lips. They didn't need to be told, they were already as silent as they could be, hearts pounding. Another twig snap and the rustle of leaves. There was definitely someone or something out there.

"Do not shoot me with that arrow, Marcus, or my father might get angry," a voice whispered.

Everyone, including Marcus breathed a sigh of relief; it was Emiril.

"You need to teach your horse to be more quiet Emiril, or you might be dead right now," he chided.

"If you were anyone else, the horse would be far away and you would be dead by now," she shot back.

They embraced, both noticeably happy to see the other.

"And how are you two doing this fine evening?" she asked Breanne and Edlin.

They smiled at her. "Even better now that you're here," Breanne said in an excited whisper.

Emiril smiled and hugged the girl. "I missed you too," she said lovingly. She looked at Edlin. "And you too," she said, giving him a big smile.

"Did you check out Ethuanova?" Marcus asked her.

She looked at him and nodded. "Yes, there are strangers in town, just as we thought there would be. But they are hanging out in the tavern, I did not see anyone out walking around. I think we could sneak over to that old abandoned house without any problems. You know the one on the south end of town?"

"Yes, I know it," he said. "Ok then, you lead the way."

Slowly and quietly, they made their way around the town to the abandoned house. They put the horses in the stable and went inside. Emiril hung the curtains, which they found lying on the floor, back over the windows, and Marcus secured the doors. When they were sure that all was secure and no light would escape the windows, they lit some candles Breanne and Edlin had found in one of the kitchen cabinets.

The place had been empty a long time from the looks of things; there was an inch of dust covering everything, and cobwebs hung in every corner.

"Well, it isn't home, but it will do in a pinch," Marcus said lightheartedly.

"Can we talk now?" Breanne whispered.

"Yes, just not real loud," Marcus replied.

"Good, I was getting tired of whispering," Edlin said, relieved.

They all laughed.

"We can't make a fire," Marcus said sadly, "but we have some dry rations and they will do for tonight, I think. But first," he said looking around at the messy cabin, "we should clean up a little, and I mean a little, I'm not doing any real chores." He cautioned everyone and then winked at Breanne.

"And when do you ever do real chores?" Emiril asked him, giving him a sly look. "I think I should ask Iola how many chores you do. I think hers and your counts might be a bit different from each other," she said, smiling brightly.

Breanne and Edlin just laughed as they turned chairs upright, dusted the table off and spread a blanket over it.

"Well, that looks a lot better," Emiril said, sounding pleased.

"Well done you two, now let's eat," Marcus said. "I for one am starving."

"Me too," Breanne said emphatically.

"Me three," Edlin joined in.

"Well, I had a big dinner..." Emiril said teasingly. The others glared at her, Marcus picked up an old wooden bowl that was lying on the floor and pretended he was going to throw it at her. "Just joking," she said quickly, "just joking."

When they had all finished their rations, which didn't fill any of them up, and had washed them down with some water, they got up and claimed sleeping places, each one dusting and tidying up their chosen spot, even Marcus. Then they sat and visited for a while. When Breanne and Edlin's eyes began to droop, Marcus and Emiril told them to get some sleep and moved back to the kitchen table to catch each other up on things they didn't want the other two knowing right now.

Emiril told Marcus about her visit with Mindoneth and how she would not tell her everything she knew yet. Marcus agreed that was unusual and that whatever it was, if it could put them in danger, Mindoneth was right not to tell her, Emiril was still a bit put out by that, but she knew Marcus was right and so had her grandmother been right. Marcus told her of their uneventful trip through the forest, which he admitted had been a little stressful after the last time. Emiril asked how Edlin was doing and Marcus told her that so far, he was doing remarkably well. When they had finished filling each other in on all the day's events, they too went to bed; they were all going to have a very long day tomorrow.

Chapter 35
The Shattered Spell

Morning came fast to the travelers, and after packing up their things, they settled for another meal of dry rations, after which they were ready to move out. After first determining that no one was around to see them, they retrieved their horses and headed back into the woods, traveling in an easterly direction. It would take them two more days to reach Fayhall, and they had to hurry, time was not on their side. The Dark Mage would know before too much longer that they were not in Daedhrog any longer, and then it would not be safe to travel in the daytime.

The pace was quick and no one had time to visit. They rode all day, stopping only once to water their horses. As night drew near, they could see the Spires of the Sarr Birds rising in the distance. If it had been just Emiril and Marcus, they would have pushed on through the evening and made it there by morning, but Breanne and Edlin were not seasoned warriors and would not be able to keep up the pace. So, Marcus found them a nice out of the way spot amongst the trees to spend the night.

Unlike before, they could not have candles, so they ate their rations in the dark. After they were finished, it became clear that no one was in the mood to visit. They were all exhausted by the day's hard ride. Instead, they all agreed it was best to turn in and they went right to sleep. All except Marcus, who took the first watch; later he would wake Emiril, and she would take the second watch.

Morning dawned beautiful and bright with the birds singing and the air warm. Breanne stretched and sat up, looked to her left and froze. Standing about ten feet from her was a creature she had never before laid eyes on. Her breath came fast and her heart began to pound. It was looking right at her. The cool air it breathed out of its nostrils came out like puffs of smoke from a chimney. Its tail waggled and its ears flicked forward and backward, listening to the different sounds of morning. Breanne tried not to be afraid of the creature, but she was having a hard time. It was so odd looking, sort of like a deer, except it had one eye, right in the middle of its forehead, and it had so many antlers coming off of its head that it looked more like a porcupine than a deer. It blinked its one eye and continued to stare at her.

"Isn't it beautiful?" a voice said from behind her. It was Marcus. "If we weren't on this quest, it would make a great breakfast."

Breanne shuddered to think someone could eat that creature, she felt sick. "What is it?" she asked.

"It's a Romon," he whispered back.

Her eyes grew huge, her stomach turned. She felt like she was going to vomit. "It's a what?" she asked loudly.

The Romon, startled by her sudden outburst, turned and ran off.

Marcus looked at Breanne just as startled as the Romon had been. "It's a Romon," he said hesitantly.

Breanne groaned audibly.

"What's wrong with you?" Marcus asked her, not sure whether to be concerned or irritated.

Laughter suddenly filled the air. It started out low and then got louder and heartier.

They turned to find the source of it. Emiril was sitting on her blanket holding her stomach, laughing uncontrollably.

"Now what's wrong with you?" Marcus demanded, growing more irritated and confused by the minute.

Breanne was still feeling sick and did not know whether to be upset with Emiril's laughing or not.

"What is going on?" a sleepy Edlin asked. "What happened?"

This made Emiril laugh even more, and then Marcus started to chuckle simply from watching Emiril laugh, and before long, they were all laughing and only Emiril knew why, although Breanne half suspected the reason, and she was right.

When the laughter subsided, Marcus spoke first. "Ok, now in the name of King Badhor, tell me what is wrong with you," he said, pointing at Breanne, "and why you're laughing," he finished, now pointing at Emiril.

"Ok, ok," Emiril said, "but stop, before you get me laughing again." It took a few more seconds before she could go on. "I am laughing, not at you Breanne, but because of your reaction to seeing the Romon. I am sorry," she said when Breanne shot her a hurt look. "I really am, but it was funny, you have to admit it." She smiled her most gracious smile at Breanne, who begrudgingly smiled back. She had been right, Emiril was laughing because of her.

"WHAT!" Marcus all but hollered, startled birds flew off, chirping loud warnings.

"Ok, no need to shout," Emiril said quickly. "I was laughing because poor Breanne has never seen a Romon before, and when she saw it, she obviously found it to be unappetizing and that is what she ate the other night. There, I have said it." She looked at Breanne, "I really am sorry for laughing, Breanne."

Breanne just sat and stared at Emiril. Had she overreacted to the appearance of the creature? It had after all tasted really good. She couldn't help but think about the fact that the creature had only one eye. It was the weirdest thing she had ever seen. And what about all those antlers? Never had she seen such an odd assemblage on a deer. It did taste good (maybe I am exaggerating she thought). She smiled at Emiril, "I guess I must have looked awfully funny to get you to laugh," she said, chuckling.

Emiril flashed her a big smile. "Friends again?" she asked gently.

"Friends again," Breanne said warmly.

"Ok, you two," Marcus said with a voice of authority. "If you don't mind, it's time to get going, we have things to do today."

They both nodded and they all broke camp.

"How long until we reach Fayhall?" Edlin asked after they had been riding for an hour.

"We will be there around nightfall," Marcus replied.

"Have you ever been there?"

Marcus looked at the youth, his eager face so innocent. He remembered back to when he was about Edlin's age, well, not his elf age, but about sixteen in human years. He had been just as eager for adventure as Edlin was now. Time does fly, he thought sadly. Now he wished that adventures would not come and he could stay at home with his family. His face drew up in a grimace as he thought they would be skirting the town of Caspiata where Iola was. She would be so close, yet he could not go to her; she could not even know he was close, it was far too dangerous. He would have to pass by without so much as a word. His heart ached.

"Well, have you?" Edlin asked, far too excited to see the melancholy mood Marcus was in.

"Oh, sorry Edlin, yes I've been there," Marcus said, his mind traveling back through the years. "It was about ten years ago. I was on a quest then as well. We rode to Fayhall to seek assistance from the dwarves as we needed to enter a cave which was home to a black dragon." He noticed Edlin's eyes, that looked as if they were glowing, he was so excited. "You see, the dragon had taken a young lass and her family was willing to pay handsomely to get her back. But none of us had been inside a cave before, especially not a dragon cave. So we made a deal with one of the dwarves that if he led us through the cave, he would get a cut of the money the lass' family was paying us to retrieve her, and, if we slew the dragon, he would get a cut of the dragon's treasure as well." Marcus studied the young elf's face, looking for signs of fear. There were none and this pleased him. He continued his story. "This one dwarf named Gilund took us up on our offer. He was a great guide and led us right to the dragon's lair. We were able to sneak up on the beast and slay him. The lass was saved, and we all split the treasure. It was a grand adventure." His face was once more at ease, the pain of missing Iola lessened by the memories of his youth.

"Wow," Edlin exclaimed, "I hope I get to slay a dragon someday."

"Well, unfortunately there are not many dragons left these days," Marcus said sadly. "The people have killed all but a few, and I have heard that the dragons no longer mate now that the black dragons are extinct."

Edlin looked at Marcus, clearly shocked. "I did not know that," he said, sounding sad and disappointed. "I cannot believe how people can be so thoughtless as to destroy a whole species. If our world loses all its dragons, it will lose a piece of itself and never be the same."

Marcus thought how insightful the youth was. "You're right, Edlin, it will lose a piece of itself if the dragons go extinct, but unfortunately, if they won't breed, there isn't much people can do about it. They should have thought about the consequences of their actions beforehand."

The little group stopped by a stream to have lunch, each one thinking about the upcoming meeting with the dwarves and the subsequent trek through the mountain. And each one seemed to have different feelings about the whole thing. Emiril was worried about how she was going to keep Breanne safe and teach her the spirit world without sending up a beacon as to their position. Breanne worried about her friends and the danger they were in because of her. Edlin hoped he would be true and fight with honor if the need arose. Marcus worried about keeping them all safe; it was his job to make sure they all came back alive. And all of them worried about where and when the creature would show up, and if it did, whether they would be able to fight it and win. After about fifteen minutes of nibbling on dry rations and deep thinking, they unanimously decided to press on.

The sun had just passed below the mountains and darkness had fallen when Breanne's attention was drawn to the night sky. She wasn't sure what had caught her attention, but she was sure she had seen something. She scanned the sky, not wanting to look away in case it showed back up again. After about five minutes, she was about to give up, when she saw it again. Her heart began to pound, and her breathing became rapid before she could convince herself that it was not the creature. What she saw was not a black shadow against the black sky, it was colorful, beautiful. Then it dawned on her what it was. She spurred her horse to catch up to Emiril.

"Emiril," she shouted and then covered her mouth with her hand, Emiril turned, startled. Breanne uncovered her mouth, this time she whispered, "Emiril I saw one." Although she whispered, it was still loud in the still night air.

Emiril looked at her, confused. Breanne pointed toward the mountains and then Emiril realized what she was talking about. "You saw a Sarr bird?" she asked the excited girl.

"Yes, up there," Breanne pointed to one of the closer peaks. "It was beautiful, just like in the story, it glowed gold and green." She was so excited she could barely sit in her saddle.

"That is a good sign," Emiril told her. It is said if a person sees a Sarr bird, good luck will follow them for days."

Breanne smiled even brighter. She hoped it was true as it would be one of the only things she had to contribute to this quest.

"Where did you see it, Breanne?"

She turned to see Edlin, who appeared to be just as excited as she was. "Up there," she said, pointing to the spot.

"I hope I get to see it," he said eagerly. "I have never seen one before."

Breanne was somewhat surprised to hear that. "I thought all elves had seen a Sarr bird," she said.

"No, not all," he told her. "Most elves have only heard of them in stories which is why it would be really great if I could see it too. I could tell all my friends that I had seen one for real." He scanned the sky where Breanne had seen it.

"There, look quick," Marcus said. He had been listening to their conversation and he too had scanned the area Breanne had seen it in.

They all looked into the night sky, and just where Breanne had indicated, they saw what looked like a glowing golden orb, with a hint of green.

For a moment no one spoke, they just watched as the majestic Sarr bird flew around in circles in an upward spiral. It was truly one of the most magnificent things they had ever seen.

Breanne suddenly remembered the feather Emiril had told her about. "Emiril, you forgot to show me the feather you found," Breanne said with a hint of sadness in her voice.

"Yes, you are right, I am sorry," Emiril told her. "I will show it to you when we get back, I promise."

"You have a feather from a Sarr bird?" Edlin asked incredulously.

Emiril smiled at him. "Yes I do, and before you ask, yes, I will show it to you as well," she said, laughing softly.

"Thanks, Emiril," Edlin said, genuinely pleased.

"Well, let's pick up the pace," Marcus interrupted. "We are almost there and I for one would like to sleep in a real bed tonight." The others agreed and spurred their horses into a faster gait.

After they had ridden another hour, the trail began to climb. Breanne found herself struggling to stay upright in the saddle. She had to lean farther and farther over JC's neck to keep from falling backward. She couldn't see a lot in the dark, but from what she could discern, the terrain was now more rocky than woodsy. The sound of the horses' hooves was no longer the soft plod it had been when they had traveled over the fir needle strewn forest floor. Now it was a dull thud and high-pitched clicks from the rocks that littered the path. She thought to herself, if we keep making this racket, we are bound to get eaten by the creature, or something else that may be lurking nearby. (And that is no exaggeration, she thought, shivering a little.)

They climbed for what seemed hours or perhaps days, or months, but she knew it had been a shorter time than it seemed. She watched the sky for another glimpse of the Sarr bird, but she didn't see it again. She became bored and tired; it was all she could do not to fall asleep. If it had been daylight, she would not have been so relaxed and bored on their steep ascent to Fayhall. If she could have seen the terrain around her or the one hundred foot drop off to her left, she might have refused to even continue up the mountain. Luckily though, she could see none of that and the climb to Fayhall was an uneventful one.

The small group finally reached a level area about the size of a football field. In the darkness, the sides of the cliff appeared as big black impenetrable walls. There was no sign of a continuing trail or a doorway with which to enter the hall. For all intents and purposes, they were marooned on a cliff face high in the mountains. Breanne started to get nervous, scanning the sky for any sign of the creature.

"Hang on a minute," Marcus told them. "I will find the door."

Door? Breanne thought. She watched as Marcus dismounted and approached the face of the cliff. He stopped in the middle and began to run his hands over the smooth rock face. He searched for several minutes when he suddenly stopped. He reached down and picked up a rock and used it to bang three times on the area he had chosen, then quickly stepped back and waited.

Several minutes passed and Breanne was starting to wonder if there really was a door. Then from somewhere on the other side of the rock face, she heard what sounded like stone grinding on stone. The noise was a low rumble at first, but it quickly turned into a loud roar. JC started to prance around and Breanne was having a hard time controlling him. She watched as the illuminated outline of a square appeared in the rock face. The rock face itself seemed to be moving toward them at a slow crawl.

JC whinnied in fright, backing away from the noise. Breanne tried to calm the beast, but to no avail. She tried to coax him over to Emiril, but the horse was having none of it. He began to back more quickly toward the edge of the cliff.

"Emiril," Breanne shouted! Her shout would have been louder had she been able to see over the ledge into the deep chasm below.

Marcus heard her terrified cry and turned to see the girl and horse dangerously close to the edge. In an instant he was running toward them. He could see the whites of the horse's eyes and hear his heavy breathing.

Breanne saw Marcus running toward them. She didn't know whether to get off or stay on the horse. She could not see over the edge, but she did not want to find out what was down there the hard way. She clung to JC's mane and prayed Marcus would reach them in time. On the other side of the ledge, the door mechanism had changed direction, and now was moving to the left, revealing a large opening in the mountain side. She could see torches on one of the walls, and then she felt JC's hoof lose its footing as it slipped over the edge. The surprised horse faltered, having no concept of space and boundary in its frightened state. He took one more step backward, his hind leg thrashing the air, trying to find solid ground where there was none. He began to go from panic to sheer terror. He whinnied louder than before, and his other three legs started to tremble. Breanne knew it was only a matter of seconds before they would fall over the cliff. She closed her eyes and prayed.

Marcus grabbed the horse's bridle just before the frightened animal took another step backward, the step that would have sent him and Breanne into the hundred-foot chasm below. He pulled the horse forward, away from the edge. JC was terrified and at first refused to budge, but Marcus pulled harder, talking to the horse and he began to respond. Breanne opened her eyes when she heard Marcus' voice. She felt the horse move forward, and she began to cry. When they were a good ten feet from the edge, Marcus told her to get down, and she gladly obeyed. She ran up to the big man who had just saved her life and clung to him, now sobbing. He put one arm around her and handed the reins of the horse to Emiril who was standing beside them. He hugged

Breanne for several minutes, letting her cry. When her sobbing turned to sniffles, he held her away from him and looked in her face. "You all right now?" he asked, smiling reassuringly.

Instinctively she smiled back. "Yes, I think so," she said hesitantly. "Thank you, Marcus, you saved our lives." She threw her arms around him again and hugged him harder than she had ever hugged anyone before. He chuckled and told her she was welcome.

"Ahem,"

They all turned to see a short man with a long beard standing behind them.

"Gilund, my old friend," Marcus said surprised and pleased. "I didn't know you would be meeting us here."

"Well, when I heard my old friend Marcus was coming, do you think I would have allowed anyone else to meet him at the door?" he replied with a huge smile. He then looked at Breanne who was staring at him through red eyes. She had never expected to meet a dwarf in her lifetime, and here she was only mere feet from one. "And I am sorry about the door frightening your horse, my lady," he said more solemnly. "I am glad you are not hurt."

She smiled at him. "Thank you," she said and then quickly added, "It wasn't your fault though."

"That's mighty gracious of you, my lady," he said bowing low.

He then turned his attention to Emiril. This time, he bowed even lower, and for a dwarf, that is very low. "Welcome to Fayhall, Princess Emiril, our kingdom is at your disposal."

Emiril returned his bow, although she wasn't able to get as low as he did, but she did good, Breanne thought. "You are most gracious," she said.

247

Next, Gilund turned toward Edlin. He looked the youth over from head to toe. "Welcome, young one," he finally said. "Your years are few, but I detect a good heart in you."

Edlin blushed a deep red and smiled ear to ear, glad the dwarf had complimented him in front of Breanne. He gave her a sideways glance to see if she had caught the exchange of words, and was even happier to see she had. "Thank you, master dwarf," Edlin said using a title of high respect for the dwarf, who like Edlin appeared to like the compliment. For he too smiled from ear to ear, then clapped Edlin on the back, which was also a sign of respect in the dwarven race. Marcus was amused by all the ego building the two were doing, and was happy about it as well; it would make their requests easier to listen to.

"Well, let's not stand out here all night," Gilund said heartily. "Please come in."

No one needed to be asked twice. It had been a long hard ride here, and coupled with what had happened to Breanne, they were all tired and hungry for real food. They gratefully followed the dwarf inside.

Chapter 36
A Light in the Storm

The torches that Breanne had seen flickering on the walls during her ordeal had been but a mere few of the many which lined the walls of the tunnel they now found themselves in. The tunnel itself was long and somewhat narrow, approximately twenty feet wide, the ceiling, however, stretched past the torches' flickering lights and she could not tell how high it reached. She could smell the musty odor of damp earth and she was chilled by the cool breeze that blew steadily towards the cave's opening. She retrieved her cloak from her saddle and wrapped it around herself. Instantly she felt warm and cozy, the dampness not able to penetrate the well-made garment. She silently thanked Edlin once again for making it for her.

Marcus appeared at her side. "Let me have your horse," he said quickly. "They are going to shut the door." Breanne immediately handed him the reins; she didn't want any part of the frightened reaction that was bound to come from him. Marcus quickly led him ahead of the others so that he would have room to control the animal. No sooner had he done so, then the now familiar sound of the door, this time working in reverse, filled the small tunnel. The noise which had been loud before was now deafening. Inside the narrow passage the sound reverberated off first one wall and then the other, only to bounce around, having nowhere else to go, reverberating again and again until it finally ceased to exist. Poor JC, Breanne thought as she covered her ears, he will really freak out now.

She leaned around Marcus' horse, which Emiril was holding and looked ahead. She could just make out Marcus' body pressed against the frightened animal, holding him close. She was surprised when she saw the horse standing calmly under Marcus' touch. She could see Marcus' arm moving as he stroked the horse's neck. He was leaning close to the horse's head and Breanne knew he was talking to the animal. The door seemed to take forever to close, but finally she heard it shudder as it reached its final resting place, and then there was silence. She waited a moment longer then removed her hands from her ears. She could hear water dripping steadily from somewhere overhead.

"Well, that went better than expected," Gilund said as he suddenly appeared next to her. "It looks like Marcus has a gift with animals." He gave her a broad smile then headed to where Marcus stood still caressing the horse.

"It's kind of creepy in here now that the door is closed," Edlin said softly, studying her face to see if she felt the same way. He was relieved when he saw that she too had a fearful look about her. He took a step closer to her, and without thinking, she took one towards him. His presence made her feel safer.

All of this was not lost on Emiril who had been watching the pair out of the corner of her eye. Good, she thought, it is just as I had suspected, they do seem to bolster each other's courage. This will be a great help when we start through the passages on the island. She was glad she had decided to bring Edlin; it was one of her more brilliant ideas. She couldn't help but smile at her decision.

"Ok, follow me," Gilund called from up ahead. "If I go too fast let me know, and whatever you do, don't stray off the path, it just may be the last thing you do." His words sent shivers down Breanne and Edlin's backs.

Breanne and Edlin glanced at each other and each knew what the other was thinking, there was no way either of them would be straying anywhere.

The cave grew steadily colder as they marched deeper into the mountain. Breanne wasn't sure, but she got the sensation they were angling downward on a very slight incline. Every so often, moonlight would filter into the cave through ventilation shafts bored into the ceiling. Other than those few spots, if it weren't for the steady stream of torches that lined both walls, it would have been pitch black. So black that if you held your hand in front of your eyes, you would not be able to make out the outline. She didn't want to see it first hand, she was glad for all the torches. She glanced over at Edlin walking so close to her that now and then she felt his cloak brush hers. She was glad he was on this trip, as much as she had come to love Emiril and Marcus, Edlin made her feel more at ease. She couldn't explain why, but she was glad that he was there.

Breanne was beginning to wonder if the tunnel would go on forever, when up in the distance, she saw light, more light than the torches gave off. It appeared there was some kind of an opening up ahead.

"It is about time," Edlin said and she could detect a hint of relief in his voice, relief that she felt as well.

"I wonder how deep in the mountain we are," she said, her voice echoing her anxiety.

"I would think at least a quarter of a mile." Startled, Breanne and Edlin turned to see Emiril close behind them.

"That far," Edlin asked incredulously.

"I have heard the heart of Fayhall lies one mile deep within the mountain," Emiril said reverently.

If Breanne had been nervous about being underground before, now she was downright scared. What if there was an earthquake, or a cave in? How were they going to make it out in an emergency? They didn't even know the way. (Definitely not overreacting she thought.)

Emiril must have sensed her growing fear for she patted her on the shoulder. "It is ok, Breanne, Fayhall has been here for years and nothing has ever happened here. Besides, dwarves are the best miners ever, they would not have built it if it was not safe."

Breanne smiled at her friend. I hope she's right, she thought.

Just before and to the right of the doorway with the light spilling from it, there was a side passage which was lit similarly to the one they were in. As they approached the passage, an old man appeared. Breanne hadn't noticed him before. She watched as Marcus handed him JC's reins. She felt fear creep through her but decided to trust Marcus' judgement. As they drew nearer, Emiril gave both hers and Marcus' horses to two other dwarves who had been waiting in the shadows. Edlin passed his mount on to a dwarf who Breanne could not quite see well enough to decide if it was male or female, she was leaning toward female.

"We are about to enter the great hall," Gilund told them. "The king is waiting to greet you. Please address him as Great One, it is a dwarven custom." Then he turned and strode through the lighted doorway.

The light was very bright, and after being in the torch lit tunnel for so long, Breanne had to get used to the brilliant glare before her. She was glad they were walking as a group, because for the first twenty steps, she was effectively blind, her only saving grace being able to follow the others. As her eyesight began to return to normal, she was instantly in awe of her surroundings.

The immense amount of light came from many sources: there were many candled chandeliers hanging from the ceilings, sconces with more candles burning lined the walls, even more lamps scattered on tables and hung from posts, and to add to the already well-lit room, there were several fires burning in open fire pits. Breanne wondered how, with all these candles and fires burning, the air still felt cool and smoke did not fill the air. She discovered the answer when she looked up. Near the center of the room, in the ceiling, there was a large ventilation shaft. From what she could see of it, it was perhaps ten feet wide, and looking straight up into it, she was hard pressed to see the stars at the end. What Emiril had said about Fayhall being a mile deep in the mountain appeared to be true, perhaps both in depth and into the side of it as well.

The hall was filled with many dwarves, some sitting at tables having conversations, some walking by with trays of food and still others were coming and going, their purpose unknown. Breanne noticed that most but not all of the male dwarves seemed to have beards, the length of which seemed to be a personal choice, as some were long, some were short and still others were in between. The female dwarves so much resembled a beardless male dwarf, that they were only distinguishable by the fact that they had a definite feminine aspect that seemed to be shared among all females, regardless of species. She was surprised that she saw no young dwarves among the adults.

As they neared the opposite side of the room, Breanne noticed a large, rather plain wooden chair that sat upon a riser. In the chair sat a figure who, to Breanne, appeared to be very imposing. He had bright red hair and a long red beard that, while in a sitting position, reached the tops of his boots. He was surrounded by females, and some males, who appeared to be close to him as they laughed heartily and patted each other on the back.

As they drew even closer, she noticed the red-haired dwarf had very bright blue eyes. She guessed that this was unusual as he was the only one she had seen so far with this particular eye color. She assumed he must be the king and tried to remember what Gilund had instructed them to call him. It wasn't your highness, that, she would have remembered. Oh, she hoped she wouldn't be the first one to speak to him. If someone else went first, they would say it and then she could follow their lead.

253

With her luck though, she would be the first and she would look like an idiot if she couldn't remember what it was. As they drew closer, she started to panic. Think, Breanne, think.

The small party stopped and Gilund stepped forward, bowing low. "Hail great one."

That was it, Breanne thought, great one, now don't forget again.

Gilund continued, "Our guests have arrived. May I present to you, Princess Emiril from Daedhrog, daughter of King Badhor and Queen Norin."

Emiril stepped forward and bowed low. "Great one, thank you for your hospitality."

The king nodded at Emiril.

Gilund went on, "May I also present Lord Marcus, warrior of renowned legend and friend to all dwarves."

Marcus stepped forward and raised a fisted hand to his heart, nodded his head slightly and then stepped back without uttering a sound. Breanne watched as the king also raised a fisted hand to his heart and nodded to Marcus as well.

Gilund presented Edlin next. "Presenting young master Edlin, brave warrior in training, and master tailor to the king."

Edlin stepped forward, and with fisted hand over his heart bowed instead of nodding. Breanne thought perhaps only full-fledged warriors nodded and warriors in training bowed. She would have to ask Marcus about that. As she watched Edlin step back, she suddenly realized it was her turn next, and to her horror, she also realized, she didn't know what to do. Did she bow and talk, bow and not talk, just nod…! Her heart started to pound, she looked at Emiril, trying to get her attention.

Gilund stepped forward. Breanne stepped closer to Emiril, psst... Emiril turned, thank God, Breanne thought. "What do I do?" she mouthed.

Emiril smiled, "Bow and step back" she mouthed back.

Breanne nodded.

She heard Gilund announce her. "May I present Breanne, friend of King Badhor and all of Ibacion."

Breanne stepped forward and bowed deeply, then rose and started to step backward when she heard the king speak. She froze where she was, her heart now in her throat. She glanced at Emiril who shrugged her shoulders. Great, Breanne thought, it couldn't just be easy like everyone else's introductions, now what.

"Breanne, friend of King Badhor, how is it that you are also friend to all Ibacion?"

Breanne felt weak, she didn't have the faintest idea what to say and to make matters worse, she thought she detected a hint of sarcasm in his voice. Her mind raced, she couldn't think of anything, the seconds ticked and they seemed like minutes to her. Then Emiril stepped forward, and Breanne felt her heart beat return to normal.

"Great one," Emiril began bowing again. "If I may..." she paused, waiting for the king to acknowledge her. He only stared at her, a look of disdain on his face. She continued, "Breanne is not from our world." There were audible gasps from around the room. The crowd gathered around the friends started to grow. "She is an honored guest of King Badhor and she is the one of whom the prophets spoke, therefore, she is a friend to all of Ibacion." There were many more gasps from the throng now gathered to hear what was transpiring and loud whispers passed between them.

Breanne watched the scene as if it were a movie being played out before her. She felt disassociated from it all, it was beginning to weigh heavily on her, all this stuff that was happening to her. She was accepting of it, but it was still very hard to grasp: elves, dwarves, dragons, creatures, and most of all Ogolel. Was all of this real, were her parents truly not her real parents? Was she even here at all, or was she in a coma for some unknown reason, lying in a hospital bed with her mother and father sitting beside her, crying? She looked at Marcus, he winked at her, then she looked at Edlin, his face was a bit ashen, and she smiled at him. He smiled back and his smile made her feel a little better. She then scanned the crowd around them. The dwarves were short, with very masculine features, square jaws, piercing eyes, but contrary to the ones she had seen in story books they were not ugly. The only thing that struck her as strange was how much the females looked like the males. She smiled at some of them, and some of them smiled back, the ones that didn't, she quickly looked away from. Her attention shifted back to the conversation between Emiril and the dwarf king.

"What proof have you, that she is the chosen one?" the king asked.

"I offer no physical proof," Emiril stated, sounding resolute, but she has been identified by none other than the great Mindoneth herself." She said this last part more loudly and with her head held higher than it had been previously.

Now the gasps and whispers were even louder, and Gilund had to quiet the crowd.

The king looked shocked, which made Breanne happy. He was not a very likable guy, and she relished the thought of him being as uncomfortable as he made her feel, but then the look of disdain turned into a deeper, uglier look, one of hate.

Emiril stood her ground, she knew the king was known to be intimidating and she had prepared herself to deal with him before

256

coming here. This reaction, however, was over the top. She knew if she showed the least sign of weakness, he would jump on it. He kept staring at her with those cold blue eyes, hatred seeming to radiate from within him as he waited for her to falter. She stood strong.

His scowl deepened. She was making a fool of him, in his own court. If Mindoneth had truly identified her as the chosen one, he could not go against her, he would be a fool to even try. It could start a war between the two races, which could eventually encompass all who lived in Ibacion. He had to think of a way to save face, and fast. "Why do you come to Fayhall?" he asked in a tone that was deep and forbidding.

Breanne began to wonder if they would make it out of there alive. She had not expected such a cold welcome.

"We come to ask for assistance in traversing the passages under the mountain on the Island of the Ancient Ancestors," Emiril shot back in a tone equal to his.

"Why do you wish to enter the passages?" he asked in the same evil tone.

"We are on a quest to fulfill the prophecy and rid the world of evil."

Murmurs, louder than whispers could be heard.

"What business is it of the dwarves to help you in this matter?"

"If you do not help us, Ogolel will grow stronger and stronger and she will conquer all of our lands." At the mere mention of her name, the king visibly flinched, and the room exploded in the loudest gasps yet. Once again, Gilund had to quiet the crowd.

The king stared at Emiril for the longest time. His face showed how much he disliked this elf standing before him, he didn't try to hide it. He heard the murmurs in the crowd and knew she had forced his hand. If he did not do as she asked, his subjects might get angry and there could be an uprising, but on the other hand, if he gave in to her request, it looked like she had forced him to bend to her will, which in a sense she had. He was seething with anger He had to find a way out of his predicament. Then it came to him, and he was pleased with his idea. It would not make things completely right, but at least he could save some dignity. "We will grant your request," he said with a wry look on his face, "but, you may only take one guide." He glared at Emiril, now for the part of his plan which would allow him to keep his dignity. "Furthermore, you must take your guide and leave, now. There is no refuge here for those who will bring the wrath of the evil one upon us."

The room grew silent, no one knew what to say.

This time, Emiril was the one who was shocked. It took extreme self-control not to show it. She could not believe that the king would treat her, the daughter of the Elven king, with so much disdain. She was very angry and wished she could communicate with Mindoneth right then. Ogolel or no Ogolel, she wanted to tell her all that had happened, and although she knew it wouldn't happen, she wanted to think Mindoneth would punish the dwarf king by bringing some sort of curse down on him. But, Mindoneth would not do something like that and she knew it. Regardless, she could not speak to her right now anyway, they were too deep in the mountain, the rock blocked all forms of mind reading. Because of that fact, she had been waiting until they got here to teach Breanne about the spirit world. Ogolel could not sense them if they were here, now she did not know what she would do.

She was still staring deep into the dwarf king's eyes/ Her father would hear of this, mark her word, he would hear about how the king of the dwarves had treated the princess of Daedhrog. And then there would be retribution. She did not look away until the king began to squirm in his chair and finally glanced at his servant standing beside him. She immediately turned so that when he looked back at her, which took less than two seconds, he saw only her back, she had won again.

The crowd parted as Gilund led the party out of the hall. Some of the onlookers wished them luck and God speed, others sneered at them, clearly some were closer to the king than others.

Emiril leaned over to whisper in Marcus' ear, "Will Gilund be going with us then?"

"I don't want to speak for him, but I think it would be a fair guess," Marcus whispered back.

Breanne walked behind Emiril, looking furtively around her, afraid that some of the dwarves more loyal to the king may try to attack them. She did not realize that they would never do such a foolish thing, if they did, they would all perish. King Badhor and Mindoneth were far more powerful than all the dwarves put together and that fact brought about the disdain the dwarf king felt for the elves. Little did he know, he had just sealed the fate of his people by the way he had treated the daughter of the Elven king.

Chapter 37
The Betrayal

Gilund led them swiftly from the great hall. "The horses have already been taken to the mouth of the cave," he whispered softly. "We must hurry." Although Gilund knew the dwarven king would never issue an attack on the party, he was not as sure about the dwarves most loyal to the king. He didn't want to think they would be so stupid, but he simply didn't know.

Breanne, immediately picking up on his anxiety, started to feel panic rising in her. Maybe her fears of being ambushed were not as farfetched as she had thought they might be. The others also detected a sense of worry in the dwarf's voice and hurried along as fast as they could without breaking into an actual run.

In most of Breanne's experiences, the return trip from somewhere always seemed much shorter than the actual trip there, but in this case, it seemed to take twice as long to get to the mouth of the tunnel than it had taken to reach the great hall. As she hurried through the passage, every shadow seemed to be hiding a concealed assassin who at any moment would jump out and in one swift move, end their lives. (Exaggeration, maybe, but she didn't know if it could happen or not.) Consequently, she tried to stay in the middle of the tunnel, not getting too close to the walls, which made her feel safer.

Suddenly the tunnel was filled with the unmistakable sound of the door to the outside being opened. As she hurried along, Breanne once again covered her ears, blocking out the horrifically loud noise. Poor JC, she thought suddenly, Marcus was not there to calm the horse, and she wondered how he was doing. As if someone had heard her silent thoughts, her question was quickly answered by the sound of a horse whinnying in terror; the noise unbelievably, could be heard over the loud rumble of the door. She felt her heart sink and tears welled up in her eyes. Poor JC, she thought. She remembered how scared she had been when she had been transported from the attic to Ibacion, and she wished she could be with the horse now. Again, the tunnel echoed with the terrified cries of the horse.

Her pace quickened, as did that of the others, until they were moving at a fast trot. The flames of the torches mounted on the walls began to dance in a rhythmic motion, more violently than would be normal. Breanne knew it must be from the air entering the mouth of the tunnel, her pace quickened even more. She was now at a slow jog; the others, knowing why the girl was in such a hurry increased their pace to keep up.

At the exact moment the noise from the door stopped, Breanne felt the first hint of a breeze on her face. She lowered her hands and ran now, as fast as she dared in the shimmering light of the torches. Up ahead, she noticed the cave was not its usual inky black. It appeared grayish and she knew that what she was seeing had to be the mouth of the tunnel.

She could hear voices as she ran the last few yards, and she was unaware that she was now running at a full sprint. At long last, she broke out of the dark cave and emerged in the fresh night air. She searched the moonlit ledge for her beloved horse. She located him about twenty feet to her left and her fears for the animal were laid to rest. He was no longer crying out in fear and appeared to be much calmer. Still, she went to him, and thanking the dwarf who had taken care of him, she gave him the biggest hug ever. The horse draped his head over her shoulder as if hugging her back and whinnied softly. She felt his love for her flow through her, and she returned the thoughts to him.

They were standing there together, silhouetted against the rock face, when the others emerged from the cave. Marcus was relieved when he saw the horse had calmed down. He had been scared that the dwarf would not be able to control the animal and, in its terror, it would run over the ledge. He silently thanked God it had not.

Emiril too was relieved to see the animal calm, but more relieved to see Breanne safe. She would have to tell that girl never to run ahead of them again. She searched the sky for any signs of danger, and was relieved to see only stars.

"How is he?" Edlin asked softly.

Breanne turned quickly, a little startled. "Oh Edlin, I'm sorry," she said, "you startled me." She saw the genuine concern in his face. "He is fine now, thank you for asking. I was so worried about him when I heard him scream," she added.

"Yes, I know, so was I." Then he smiled a little. "You run really fast, you know, I tried to keep up with you, but I could not." He looked at her sheepishly.

She could see he felt a little embarrassed about not being able to keep up with her. "I think it was the adrenaline," she said quickly. "I don't normally run fast at all. I bet if JC had not been in trouble, you would have beaten me out of the cave."

He looked at her gratefully, knowing she had given him an out, which he willingly took. "Yah, maybe you are right, concern for a loved one, or in this case, an animal you love, can make you able to do things you normally could not."

"Well, concern for oneself should make you less likely to burst out of a cave into the open where God only knows what may be waiting to eat you."

Breanne and Edlin both jumped and turned quickly. "Oh my gosh, Emiril," Breanne said, louder than she wanted to. "You almost gave me a heart attack."

"Me too," Edlin said, sounding just as shaken as Breanne.

"Good," Emiril said sternly. "You need to learn that rushing out into the open like that can get you killed. You have to stay with the group, is that understood?"

Breanne hadn't thought about her safety when she had run out of the cave, she had only thought about JC and getting to him. She thought now, about what could have happened to her if the creature had been out here when she came bursting out of the cave. She didn't want to think about it anymore, she was truly sorry for not thinking first. She looked solemnly at Emiril. "I won't let it happen again. I promise." She gave her a small smile, at which point Emiril's heart melted and she smiled back, no longer able to be irritated with the girl.

"Alright then, I just do not want you to get hurt," Emiril said softly. Then she turned around and walked over to where Marcus was talking with Gilund.

"Did you talk to her?" Marcus asked as she walked up.

"Yes, she will not do that again," Emiril replied. "What are you discussing?"

"Well, Gilund has decided to be our guide," Marcus said grinning, obviously pleased that his old friend was going to be the one they entrusted their lives and the fate of Ibacion to.

Emiril's face lit up. "Oh, very good," she said enthusiastically. She too was pleased to have someone who Marcus trusted guiding the group.

"We should get started right away," Gilund interjected. "I know the king was not all too pleased with the way things went this evening, and let's just say, some people would be more than happy to cheer him up, if you get my meaning." He glanced back into the cave, a worried expression on his face.

Emiril's anger flared anew upon hearing what Gilund had to say. She had never been as angry, well, not since Ogolel betrayed the kingdom, but this time, the king of the dwarves had overstepped his bounds. She had no idea what would cause him to behave in such a way, they had always been allies with the dwarves. Regardless, she was going to make sure he paid for the way he treated her, and the way he treated the prophet's chosen one, that alone would be enough for him to lose his throne. She wanted so badly to contact Mindoneth and tell her all that had happened, but any sending of thoughts would tell the Dark Mage that they had left Daedhrog and for now, he did not know this, a fact of which she could not believe their luck on. So, she put aside her anger and focused on the task at hand.

"I don't know if you want to start tonight or wait until morning, but if you want to wait, I know a place we can go," Gilund told them.

Marcus looked at Emiril and he knew she would be able to go on if need be, but he also knew that the children needed sleep, right now. They were running on pure adrenaline, but all too soon, they were going to calm down, and when they did, they were going to be more tired than ever. "I think it would be best if we got some rest, what do you think?"

"I agree," she said quickly, "those kids have not slept in a long time, and it is just a matter of time before they start to feel it."

"Then it's settled," Gilund said. "I will take you to a place that I know of not too far from here where we will be safe." He turned and walked over to the dwarves who were waiting to shut the door. When he came back, he told them that they needed to hurry because he had told the dwarves to give them a ten-minute head start before they shut the door, to enable them to get JC far enough away that it would not spook him, and the clock was ticking.

They all hurried then, none of them wanted a repeat of the door episode.

The five travelers rode single file down the narrow path that four of them had just hours before traversed. As Emiril and Marcus had predicted, now that the excitement of the night was drawing to a close, Breanne and Edlin were beginning to wane from exhaustion.

"It's not too far," Gilund called over his shoulder. He too had a sense that the two youngest travelers were going to need some sleep; he had noticed them nodding off already.

Breanne was beginning to feel the effects of too much excitement combined with not enough sleep. She could hardly keep her eyes open, they seemed to have a mind of their own. They would slowly close, and she would force them to open again. This went on for what seemed an eternity, until she heard their guide call back to the group that they had arrived at their destination. She jerked her head up, from where it had been nested on her chest, and surveyed the area. It was still quite dark and she could see nothing that stood out.

"Do you see it?" asked a groggy Edlin.

She glanced at him and smiled, knowing that look on his face. She was just as tired, but she hoped she didn't look as haggard. "I don't see anything," she told him.

The two watched as Gilund dismounted and walked over to a large bush growing in the side of the mountain. He started pulling the bush aside and was joined by Marcus and Emiril. In a few short minutes, they had revealed a dark opening, which thanks to the bush, had been previously hidden from view. Then Gilund lit a torch and went inside, followed closely by Marcus. Emiril remained outside to keep an eye on

Breanne and Edlin. Minutes passed and Breanne began to wonder how far into the mountain this cave went. She hoped it was not as deep as the last one, she did not like the idea of being so far under the mountain. A few more minutes passed and she was beginning to think it was going to be just like the last one, when she saw a flicker of torch light; they were coming back. She breathed a sigh of relief.

"Ok," Gilund called out, "come in, and bring the horses too."

They slowly filed into the cave, which was hard to do when there was only one torch to light the way. JC pranced nervously, anticipating the loud noise which had accompanied his last excursion into a dark hole in the side of a mountain, but soon calmed when the anticipated noise did not arrive. After they had all entered the cave, Gilund and Marcus repositioned the bush to once again cover the opening. Now that they were concealed within the cave, Gilund lit two more torches, handing one to Marcus and one to Emiril.

"Follow me," he told the group, "and like before, stay on the main path." He started down the dark tunnel, the scene eerily reminiscent of their last tunnel excursion.

Unlike last time, however, they had only gone a short distance when an opening appeared to their right. Gilund stopped. "Put the horses in here," he directed.

One by one, the horses were led into the darkened alcove. When Breanne approached with JC, she peered into the semi-lit room and was amazed. It was a much bigger area than she had anticipated, about forty feet in length and twenty feet wide. The ceiling was high, too high for her to really grasp the exact measurement, but there was plenty of headroom for the horses who wandered in and sniffed the unfamiliar area cautiously. Breanne thought she heard a trickle of water from the back end of the room, and when Marcus entered with his torch to unsaddle the horses, she looked further into the darkness. What she saw

266

was a small steady stream of water which flowed out of a hole in one of the cave walls. It ran down the wall and through a little trough on the floor that had undoubtedly taken thousands of years to create, then flowed out of the room through a small fissure in the opposite wall. The room was perfect for keeping the horses in; she was sure that JC would be happy here. She helped Marcus and soon the horses were all unsaddled and they went to rejoin the others. After Marcus and Breanne left the makeshift horse corral, Gilund placed a rope across the opening about waist high. It would not keep the horses in if they really wanted out, but it was enough to keep them in if they were content. She looked in once more and smiled, they definitely looked content. JC was already on his back all four feet in the air, no doubt scratching his itchy back where the saddle had been on far too long this time. She turned and followed the others who were starting to walk away.

Gilund led them further into the cave. Breanne noticed it was not as well taken care of as the last one, and the smell was mustier. Without torches lining the walls, she could not see more than ten feet in front of her. She could only imagine how dark it would be without the three torches they did have. The sound of her boots suddenly caught her attention. They were making a squishing sound with each step she took; the ground must be very moist beneath them. A few feet further and she detected a steady wooshing noise. It sounded familiar, yet in the cave the noises were almost alien when they reached one's ears after bouncing around so much. Some familiar noises could terrify a person when distorted this way. A few feet more... yes, she did know that sound, it was the sound of water, rushing water like a river, or at least a large stream. Suddenly, a blast of cool air washed over her, and she shivered violently. She looked ahead and thought she saw light.

"Do you hear water?" Edlin asked.

She glanced over at him. How long had he been there beside her? She had not realized he was there. Man, elves were quiet, they would make good stalkers back home. (No exaggeration.) "I think so," she replied.

The light up ahead grew brighter and at last they left the narrow passage and entered another room. It was by no means as big as the great hall had been, but it was big enough. Breanne guessed it had to be as big as a football stadium. And the light source was moonlight which was streaming down through a hole in the ceiling roughly sixty feet above them. Outside, the moonlight would have appeared dim, even though it was full tonight, but in here, in the pitch black of the cave, the moonlight was like the sun shining down on them. It illuminated almost the entire room, and in the middle of the room was where the noise of rushing water was coming from. Like liquid silver carrying diamonds, the underground river coursed its way through the mountain, sparkling and gleaming, its noise like a song beckoning the thirsty travelers. Water was never so good as when it was drank from a pure clean source, and it didn't get any purer or cleaner than an underground river.

They looked like animals at a watering hole, each one leisurely taking in their fill, and when they were satiated, they filled their canteens, thinking how good the water would taste tomorrow when the only thing available would be tainted surface water.

At long last, Marcus got up and stretched. He surveyed the cave; the opening above had allowed for seeds blown by the winds to find their way into its depths. With plenty of water available, the seeds had taken root and thrived, many generations later. The cave floor boasted a number of plants and flowers and a nice plush carpet of grass covered the area directly under the opening and a few feet beyond, in the center of the room there was even a tree. It was a willow tree rising up twenty or so feet toward the sky. It was a small paradise, hidden from the rest of the world. He imagined how beautiful it must be in the daylight.

"How did you ever find this place?" he asked Gilund.

"Hunting," Gilund replied.

Marcus lowered his eyebrows at the dwarf. "What do you mean hunting? What were you hunting?"

Gilund looked at Marcus. "Well, it's kind of a long story, but since we aren't going anywhere, I'll tell you. (Truth was, Gilund enjoyed telling stories, especially ones about himself.) On the day in question, I was hunting a bear that had been killing some of the sheep the lowlanders bring up for grazing in the spring. They had asked me if I would keep an eye out for him. Days passed and I began to think the creature had left these parts. Then I saw him one day, coming up the trail. He had just killed himself a lamb and was bringing it back to his lair when I spotted him. I followed him for a ways until he rounded a corner and when I came around it, he was gone. I couldn't see him anywhere; he wasn't up ahead on the trail, it was too steep to go down the one side and he wasn't climbing up the other side, he was just gone. I couldn't believe it. I ran ahead as far as I thought he might have gone if he had suddenly broken into a run, but he wasn't there. I looked over the edge to see if he had maybe fallen, but he wasn't down there either. I knew I would have seen him scrambling up the mountainside, so I was, as you can imagine, beginning to think I had gone mad. It was a very hot day and I thought maybe I had a touch of sun fever, so I sat down by this tree to get out of the sun and have nice cool drink of water, and when I did, I felt a nice cool breeze coming from behind it. I started moving some branches around and that's when I saw there was a cave behind it. Aha, says I, that's where that rascal of a bear got off to. I chuckled to myself, then started to laugh real hard, that bear almost had me believing I was mad.

Well, after I came to my senses again, I knew I had to go in after the beast; after all, he was killing sheep, and a lot of them too. So, I got a torch, drew my sword and followed him in here, just the way we came, and when I got to this big room here, there he was, leisurely eating his lamb by this here river. I knew I couldn't sneak up on him with all this open area, so I waited by the entrance there for him to come out. It took two days for him to get hungry enough to come out again. I nearly froze to death the first night, I only had on my spring clothes and no coat, and spring nights can get below freezing, especially in this cave. But the second night is when he decided it was time to eat again. He got up, stretched and lumbered toward the opening. I got my sword ready, and waited until he took two steps outside the doorway, then I drove my sword straight into his side, deep into his heart. Poor beast never knew what happened, he was dead before he hit the ground. This here cloak is made from his hide."

He held up a brown cloak made from animal hide, the fur still intact on the outside. Hanging over each shoulder were the legs of the bear. Whoever had fashioned the cloak had been clever, using the bear's legs in such a way, that with an added button on one, they could be clasped together, holding the cloak tight, eliminating the need for a string. Gilund then held up the hood of the cloak which was fashioned using the bear's actual head, so that when the hood was worn, it looked as if the bear was staring right at you. "The really great thing about the cloak is that if you get down on your hands and knees, you look like a bear. I have snuck right up to other bears and they don't even know the difference until it's too late. I never go hungry in the winter," he said, smiling.

Breanne and Edlin sat staring at Gilund. The story was unlike any they had ever heard. Breanne thought it was gruesome and macabre, but admittedly awesome at the same time. Edlin thought it was the coolest thing he had ever heard and as soon as he could get his hands on a bear hide again, he was going to make himself a cloak just like Gilund's.

Emiril was amused at the kid's reaction to the story. It was obvious Gilund had a way with words and knew how to captivate his audience; after all, she had been captivated by the tale as well, but now, it was time for the kids to get some sleep. She stood up and surveyed the area. "Gilund," she asked, "do you have anywhere in particular that you sleep?"

Gilund looked up at the elf. She was a commanding figure, and handsome as well. Then he too surveyed the area, trying to remember if any one particular spot was more comfortable than the other. "Ah, no, I guess not," he said finally. "You can choose anywhere you like. But you don't want to sleep directly under the tree." He looked at the willow. "She's mighty pretty, but first thing in the morning, well, birds, if you catch my meaning."

Emiril looked at him, she did not want to know the rest of that story, all she could think was, it was a good thing there was a river close to wash up in. "Ok," she said, "no one sleeps under the tree."

Breanne and Edlin gave each other a look and burst out laughing.

"That is enough out of you two," Emiril chastised. "Now find your spots and get some sleep, we have a long day ahead of us tomorrow." She did not add that they needed to have their minds clear and alert for danger, afraid if she did, they would not get any sleep at all.

It didn't take long for Emiril to hear the steady breathing of the two kids. She, Marcus and Gilund sat near the river; they had been waiting for this moment to discuss tomorrow's plans.

"We should reach the sea by tomorrow night," Marcus told them. "I have a friend who will take us to the island. He is a fisherman, and he goes out that way regularly. Any other vessel may cause suspicion."

271

"Good," Emiril said. "I am still so furious about what happened at Fayhall, I was counting on staying there tonight, so that I could teach Breanne to navigate the spirit world. I cannot do that now. The only reason I could do it there is because of the depth of the hall, the rock blocks anyone's ability to pick up on the activity."

Marcus thought for a moment. "Emiril," he asked, "you say that the rock blocks people from picking up on the activity, but what about after you go into the spirit world. What if Ogolel was there, wouldn't she know you were there as well?"

"That is a good question," she said. "I think she would. I was hoping she would not be there, which is why I was going to do it at night, hoping she would be asleep. I know that was asking for a lot, but I did not have any other choice. She needs to learn before she confronts her, or she will not stand a chance."

Marcus nodded. "You're right," he said. "Look what happened the last time she got caught in the spirit world unprepared, we almost lost her."

"Well, if it's any consolation," Gilund interjected, "one of the tunnels under the mountain on the island goes down just as far as the great hall does."

Emiril looked at him stunned. "It does?" she asked incredulously.

"Yes, one of the tunnels was built to lure the invaders down under the mountain. There is only one way in or out, the idea being that once the invaders got down there and figured out that it didn't go anywhere, they would have to turn around and come back out. By that time, the army would be at the entrance waiting for them. They would either have to surrender, or die. It went down a long way, giving the army plenty of time to get set up."

Emiril gave Marcus a huge smile. "How fortunate, we will be able to train her after all."

"Yes," Marcus said, but he sounded a little worried.

"What is it?" she asked.

"Well, Gilund said there was only one way in or out. What if the trap gets sprung on us when we go down there?"

Emiril paused a moment. "Well, you, Edlin and Gilund could stay at the top and wait for us."

Marcus looked surprised. "But what if something happens to you while you are down there, or in the spirit world, who would help you?"

Emiril looked exasperated. "Ok, how about you and Gilund stay up top, and Edlin will come with Breanne and I, then if something goes wrong, Edlin can come and get you." She paused, then seeing Marcus about to say something quickly added, "When you come down, Edlin can stay at the top with Gilund and protect the passage."

At this point Gilund started to chuckle.

Marcus gave him a look that said, 'What!'

"You sure you don't have two wives?" Gilund asked and then began to laugh in earnest.

Marcus' eyes opened wide, then he looked at Emiril, and she started to laugh as well. Shrugging his shoulders, he said rather demurely, "Well, maybe I do, maybe I do."

Through his laughter, Gilund said, "I don't think Iola is gonna want to hear that." His laughter doubled, Emiril had to stifle hers and shush him before they woke the kids. Marcus was a good man and took it all in stride, even laughing himself.

When the laughter subsided, Emiril looked at Marcus. "You know I was only playing with you, Marcus. I trust your opinion and value your friendship more than anyone else. I would not have come on this quest if you had not come. You are my best friend."

Marcus looked at his friend and felt his heart swell. She really was a good friend, and if he had not already been married to Iola, he would have asked her, but just being friends was enough for him. "Thank you, Emiril. I know, I just want to make sure you and Breanne are safe."

"And I would not have it any other way," she said gently.

"AAAAHHHH you two, stop right now before you make a dwarf cry. The penalty for that is death." He said that last part gruffly, but his eyes were soft. He could see the depth of their friendship and wished he had a friend who was as close to him as these two were to each other. The truth was, he never really fit in with the rest of the dwarves, they just seemed so shallow and crude. He wanted more out of life than living in a tunnel and mining rock for a living. That was why he had gone on the first quest he and Marcus took and why he had volunteered to go on this one as well.

Breanne moaned in her sleep. The three of them looked in her direction. "Poor lass," Gilund said. "I suppose she's dreaming about the wicked witch herself."

"I do not know," Emiril said sadly, "but I fear dreams will not be as scary as the real thing."

Gilund and Marcus looked at her, the full impact of her statement fell heavily on them. She was right too, the most terrible thoughts of Ogolel could not begin to match the real thing.

"Well, on that cheery note, let's get some sleep," Marcus said, standing and stretching. He was not sure he would be able to take his own advice.

Soon the cave was filled with the sound of sleeping beings, all except one. His own prediction coming true, Marcus could not find sleep that night.

The sound of birds, hundreds of them filled the cave. Breanne opened her eyes to bright sunlight, the birds so loud that they were almost a nuisance rather than beautiful. Apparently, they had found this cave and it offered them a refuge from normal predators, so they told their friends, who told their friends and so on. She sat up, looking around to see if anyone else was disturbed by the noise. Apparently so, Edlin was lying on his stomach, his cloak pressed tightly over his head. Emiril was also sitting up, looking at the host of birds that were so thick they almost blotted out the entire tree. She did not see Marcus or Gilund however, and wondered where they had gotten off to.

"Emiril," she hollered above the din. Emiril could not hear her. She wanted to get up and go to her, but she was a little nervous she would spook the birds and they would fly about the cave. She didn't want to get hit in the head by a bird. "Emiril," she yelled louder.

Emiril thought she heard something above the roar of the birds. She turned and saw Breanne looking her way. As soon as she saw Emiril looking at her, she waved her arms at her and gestured to the birds, next raising her hands palms up in a gesture asking what she should do. Emiril motioned for her to stay put. She too didn't quite know what to do in this situation. It was very possible the birds would panic and then, if they did not fly out of the cave, they would have birds everywhere.

At that moment, Gilund and Marcus strode into the room. Gilund had a rabbit slung over his back, and Marcus carried some eggs and greens. They both stopped just inside the doorway. Marcus's mouth dropped open, not able to believe the sight before him.

"Don't move," Gilund said.

"I don't intend to," came the quiet response.

"Now do you see why I told you not to sleep under the tree?"

"Clearly, now how do you get them out of here?"

"Like this." He motioned for Emiril and Breanne to lie down and cover themselves with their cloaks. As soon as they did, he looked at Marcus and told him to pick up some rocks that were close by. As soon as the two had as many rocks as they could carry, he told Marcus, "Now comes the fun part." Smiling, he edged around the room until they were past where Emiril and Breanne lay. As soon as he located Edlin, Gilund threw the first rock. It soared high into the tree and landed with a thud about four feet from Edlin's lumpy form. Marcus quickly followed with a well thrown rock of his own. It too landed near Edlin. The cave which had been noisy before, suddenly became unbearable; even Gilund and Marcus had to cover their ears. Birds by the hundreds suddenly took flight, started to circle the room, flying faster and faster, their voices raised in utter terror at the intrusion of the rocks into their safe haven. They flew so low that if Emiril and Breanne had not lain down, they surely would have been hurt by the small rocket like creatures.

Gilund threw a few more stones into the tree to dissuade any of the birds from resettling on the branches. Marcus, having way too much fun, threw his remaining rocks as well. The question of whether he needed to remained unanswered. Eventually realizing that they were not going to find peace in the tree again today, the birds started to fly in a spiraling pattern up toward the opening. They flew as water going down a drain flows, around and around, filtering out of the cave and into the sky above until they were lost to sight.

The cave was deathly quiet. Emiril and Breanne sat up slowly. They had not been able to witness the spectacle, but they had heard it. Emiril was glad now that they had reacted cautiously when they awoke to find the birds. If they had startled them, they most surely would have been hurt. It just goes to show that even the tiniest creature can be a force to reckon with.

"Edlin," Breanne hollered at him. "Edlin, you can get up now." She waited a moment longer, and then walked closer to him. As she approached the figure of Edlin, she could hear him snoring. She couldn't believe her ears; he had slept through the whole thing. She turned to the others. "He's asleep," she told them. They started to laugh.

"Well, wake him up, Breanne, that lazy boy," Marcus chided.

Breanne shook Edlin's shoulder. "Edlin, wake up." He groaned and stirred but then went back to snoring. She shook him more violently. "Edlin, wake up." This time he lifted his head and pulled the cloak back.

"What?" he said groggily.

"Edlin, it's time to get up," Breanne scolded.

"What, oh, Breanne." His eyes flew open and he sat up blinking back the sunlight. "I am sorry," he said quickly, "I was dreaming. How long have you been up?"

"Long enough, you sleepy head, you missed everything."

He looked at her, shocked, stifling a yawn. "What did I miss?" he asked, sounding disappointed.

She told him what had happened. "Oh, I heard the birds," he said, "but I just ignored them and went back to sleep. I did not know there were that many. They were rather loud though."

She laughed. "Edlin, you are so funny. I don't know how you slept through all of that, but I admire the ability."

"Ok, now that the excitement is over," Marcus said. "Gilund and I brought back some breakfast." He scanned the floor of the cave for the eggs and greens he had been carrying when he and Gilund had returned.

He saw them over by the doorway. One of the eggs had broken, but the rest were fine, and the greens would be fine after they were washed off.

Breakfast was good, the first hot meal the small group had had in days, excluding Gilund of course. They sat back and let it sink in for a few minutes. No one was eager to leave this beautiful place but they all knew they would have to very soon.

Chapter 38
The Long Night

His eyes slowly opened, his heart pounded, sweat dripped from his forehead. It was but a mere flutter in the farthest reaches of his mind, but it was a flutter, he had felt it. He was not entirely sure who had sent it, or to whom, but he knew it was a thought transfer, and now he knew they had left the glen.

He rose on unsteady legs. He would need to rest first; he had been in the spirit world far too long this time. It had taken its toll on him, draining him of his energy, making him weak and sickly. He needed to eat; he couldn't remember the last time he had eaten. He summoned his servant and demanded food and drink. He sat at the table waiting, relishing his good fortune. She would be pleased, it had been far too long since he had anything to tell her. She grew impatient and that was not good.

Quietly the servants entered and presented food and wine. He ate lavishly, rewarding his body for the sacrifice it had made for his mind.

The creature too was restless, with nothing to do it had become unpredictable, lashing out at anyone that came near it. The servants were too afraid to even feed it. They would stand on the precipice above and hurl the meat down to it, what landed out of reach, stayed out of reach.

Now the creature would be set free, free to hunt, free to kill. Maybe all this idle time was a good thing after all, with the pent-up energy the creature had, it would not take long to find its prey and once it did, nothing would stop it.

The Dark Mage felt satiated, both in body and mind. He rubbed his extended stomach. It had been too long since he had felt it so full, and now his mind was free to enjoy this moment. Tomorrow he would release the creature, he would have to lock minds with it, he would have to be one with it. Only through their union could the creature find its prey, but until then, he was free to enjoy his good fortune and enjoy it is what he intended to do. He called for more wine and dancing girls.

As the music played and the girls danced, their rhythmic swaying bodies silhouetted by the firelight, his mind wandered and he quickly fell into a deep sleep.

He was standing in front of his mother's cottage. He could hear her voice singing to the birds, a habit she had had from the time he was a small boy. His knees trembled, he felt ill, he could not face her, this loving woman who had raised and nurtured him. He was ashamed of who he had become, of the things he had done. The singing grew louder, closer, he turned and ran. He ran into the darkness, trees whipped at his face, grabbed his clothes, as he stumbled, regained his footing and pressed on. He had to get away from this feeling of shame, had to hide from her. He didn't want her to see him, afraid she would know, afraid all the things he had done would somehow present themselves to her. He couldn't let that happen, he wouldn't let that happen, so he continued to run, sweat now pouring from his brow. He had been running for what seemed an eternity and yet he could still hear her singing. He ran farther, still the singing, he didn't know how long he could hold this pace. The singing continued to haunt him as he stumbled, lost his footing and fell.

He hit the floor with a thud. His eyes came open to find worried onlookers They seemed hesitant, unsure whether to come to his aid, or pretend nothing had happened. The girls continued to dance, only their eyes betraying them as they kept shooting fearful glances his way. The singers kept on singing, only other singers could have noticed their voices had risen and octave or two. That song, that song from his dream, he had to make it stop. He got to his knees and motioned the servants to come to his aid. He was immediately surrounded and, in a few seconds, seated again in the chair he had so recently vacated. As he regained his composer, he sent the dancers and singers away. He had enjoyed himself far too much this night and wanted to be alone now; soon he had sent everyone away. He sat alone in the empty hall to contemplate his dream, to figure out why it had contained in it, the one person in his life who he did not want to see. Oh, he loved his mother, but when he had taken up with Ogolel, he had accepted the fact that he would never be allowed to have contact with her again. Never that is, unless he changed his ways and repented from his evil doings. Something which he had not done, nor did he intend to do any time in the near future. So why, of all the things he could have dreamed about, did it have to be her? Was his mind trying to tell him something?

Chapter 39
Breanne's Resolve

With renewed energy from their pleasant stay in the cave, pleasant that is, except for the bird incident, and a hearty breakfast that Marcus and Gilund had provided, the small group reluctantly left their sanctuary. Their destination was a small town on the shore of the Sea of Storms called Estova, from there, they would travel to The Island of the Ancient Ancestors and to a fate as yet unknown.

Single file, they wound their way down the mountain. Now that it was daylight, Breanne saw for the first time the sheer drop offs beside the trail. The drop was hundreds of feet, and big boulders awaited any unlucky soul who lost their footing. She was so scared she almost told Emiril she would stay at the cave and never leave it. (A little dramatic, yes, but she was terrified of heights.) Instead, with her heart beating a million miles an hour, dizziness overtaking her at times and the constant urge to vomit, she rode behind Marcus, her eyes closed tightly. A few times, she would look to her left, surveying their progress, yet making sure not to even glance to her right. She rode like this the rest of the way down the mountain. Once, Edlin, who was riding behind her, tried to talk to her, she hissed him to silence, and did so with such ferocity, that he didn't try to talk to her again that day.

After the harrowing ride down the mountain, Breanne was exhausted. She realized then that being stressed out mentally was far worse than being stressed out physically, it drained a person's mind and body. She hoped they would rest soon, and was elated when the group stopped just inside the forest beside a small stream to have lunch.

"We should reach Estova by tomorrow mid-day," Gilund told them. "We will have the cover of the forest most of the way, but for a while we will be out in the open, so we will need to be very careful then. We must watch the skies and be vigilant. I don't know if the Dark Mage knows where we are. Emiril, that would be your area of expertise," he said nodding to the elf. "But I for one don't want to meet that creature of his."

"Nor do I," Marcus added, looking at Breanne in that way two people who have shared an experience look at one another.

"Yes," Breanne agreed, then she looked at Edlin and hoped he would not have to go through the same experience she and Marcus had.

"Well, I do not think he knows where we are yet," Emiril told them. "But it is just a matter of time until he does. Whether we make it to the island without incident remains to be seen." She looked at the others, hoping they would make it without the Dark Mage finding them, but secretly doubting they would.

"Edlin," Breanne said softly.

Edlin turned at the sound of his name. He looked at Breanne and thought, even after all they had been through, she still looked beautiful. He felt his heart start to beat a little faster. "Yes?" he asked.

"I am sorry I snapped at you back there on the trail. It's just that I am afraid of heights, and I was really scared. I didn't mean to."

He smiled his brilliant smile at her. "It's ok," he said, elated that she had not snapped at him for any other reason. "I understand, I have done that myself."

Breanne smiled back at him, and his heart fluttered for a second time. Even though he did not know it could be possible, he had come to grow more fond of her since they had started their journey together, and he was not sure yet, but he thought he might be falling in love with this young girl from another world. "Thank you for understanding. I know it's no excuse, but I couldn't help myself. You can talk to me anytime you want to."

"Ok …so, how is it going?"

Breanne laughed at his playful joke. "You're funny, Edlin," she said.

"Funny in a good way?" he asked, his eyes sparkling.

"Funny in a good way," she said mesmerized by his beautiful eyes. She wondered if the way she felt right now was how you felt when you fell in love with someone.

Emiril watched the two young people and wondered if they were ever going to get past the awkward stage of this whole falling in love thing. She was happy for them, yet she was also worried about them. When Breanne went home, what would they do?

"Time to go," Gilund said, suddenly standing up and packing up his things. "We've got a long way to go."

Everyone packed up and they were soon on the trail again. The forest was a pleasant change for Breanne. She could actually ride with her eyes open, and that was nice, but also it was cool, it smelled good, and it made her feel good. With so many people here now, the events that took place the last time she was near a forest did not plague her mind.

Marcus rode about ten horse lengths ahead of the group, watching the skies for any signs of danger. He felt odd. There was no reason he could put his finger on, he just felt it. He wished he could mind link with Emiril, but even the slightest link, even one in passing, could alert the Dark Mage to their presence, and he did not want to endanger the group. He knew eventually she would ride up to where he was and he would be able to talk to her about the way he was feeling. Until then, he would be on guard and use all his skills as a fighter to protect them, if need be.

Emiril was thinking about the caves under the mountain and how lucky she was that there was one that went deep enough to be able to train Breanne in. She knew it was a risk to attempt taking her into the spirit world. Ogolel could sense their presence, and if she did and she could not protect her, Breanne would not stand a chance. Ogolel would surely try to kill her if she could. But there was no other way to prepare her for the upcoming encounter with Ogolel. She had no idea how to enter, or more importantly how to return from, the spirit world. She had almost died that time she got dragged into it by accident. She did not want to see her die now. She could think of no other way, but she would keep trying.

Breanne could not shake the feeling that something was not right. She had been feeling this way for about an hour now. She didn't want to worry anyone so she kept it to herself, but the feeling was becoming so overwhelming, she was starting to think maybe she should tell Emiril. She hurried JC so she could catch up to the elf who was riding slightly ahead of her.

As she approached, Emiril glanced up, startled, apparently lost in thought. "Breanne, how are you doing?" She noticed the odd look on Breanne's face and immediately became concerned. "What is it?" she asked, concern now evident in her voice.

Breanne looked at her a little embarrassed, now that she was here, she had second thoughts on whether to say something or not.

Emiril could see the confusion on Breanne's face, "Breanne, it is ok, whatever it is, you can tell me." She smiled to reassure the girl.

Breanne smiled back, she was so glad that she had come here and gotten to know Emiril; she was such a great friend. "Well," she began hesitantly, "I don't really know how to say this, and I don't know whether it is anything or not, but…" Emiril looked at her, waiting not as patiently as she was trying. "Well, I just feel like something isn't right.

I don't know how else to say it, but I feel that something is like, going to happen or something."

Emiril's eyes grew wide; she began to search with her mind, trying to be careful not to let anyone detect her presence. She searched as far as she could but did not detect anything. She looked at the girl, her face was flushed, her eyes held a deep concern. She was definitely worried about something. She could not detect anything though, not even the hint of trouble. "What does your feeling tell you?" she asked.

Breanne looked a little confused. "Well, it tells me we are in great danger, all of us, and that we are not safe, like something is about to happen and we don't have much time to get away from it." She was starting to tear up.

Emiril searched again, and again, nothing. Was it possible that Breanne could foresee what she could not? She pondered the question a moment. Then at last she made a decision. "Stay here, Breanne," she said decisively. "Tell the others to stay here as well." Then she rode ahead at a fast gait to where Marcus was.

Breanne waited for Edlin and Gilund to catch up and then told them to wait with her until Emiril got back.

"What's wrong, Breanne?" Edlin asked nervously.

"I am not sure yet," she replied. She tried to smile, but she could tell it came out all wrong. Edlin started to say something else, and then decided not to. The horses stood pawing the dirt uneasily, the tension seemed to radiate from rider to beast. Breanne stroked JC's neck to calm him.

"Well, let's move over here under the thicker canopy of trees," Gilund said suddenly. "We might as well take precautions if we aren't sure what's going on."

Breanne and Edlin agreed and joined the dwarf in the more densely wooded area. Now more protected from prying eyes, they sat in silence, waiting for Emiril's return.

"Marcus," Emiril called out.

Marcus turned to see Emiril coming up quickly behind him. He pulled his horse up and waited for her.

"What's up?" he asked as she drew nearer.

"I am not sure, but I think we might have a problem."

He looked at her eyebrows raised, not sure whether to be amused or worried. "What's going on then?" he asked.

"Breanne told me she feels as if we are in danger," she said, a look of concern on her face.

"Well, are we?" he asked questioningly.

She looked blankly at him, not knowing what to say. "I don't know," she said finally.

Marcus' eyebrows lowered. Now he too was confused. "Do you think she is overreacting?"

"I do not think so," Emiril said quietly, "but Marcus," she continued ardently, "I searched and I could not detect anything."

Marcus was surprised. "That is strange," he said thoughtfully. Then he looked at Emiril. He didn't want to say this but he had to. "Emiril, do you think she might be," he hesitated, "well, you know, more perceptive than you are?" He watched as Emiril's face turned a pale color. He felt bad for asking, but if their safety depended on it, he would ask again.

"I have thought about that," she said, sounding a bit put out.

"What do you think we should do?"

Emiril sighed. She looked at Marcus and for the first time in her life, she felt helpless. She couldn't talk to her grandmother or her father, she couldn't sense what Breanne was feeling, and she literally had no idea of what they should do. "Maybe you should decide that Marcus," she told him, her voice sounding hollow. "I think I am out of my realm right now."

Marcus looked back at the others; they had gotten off the main path and taken cover under the thicker canopy of trees. Good thinking, Gilund, he thought. He looked back at Emiril. He felt sorry for her, he knew this had to be hard for her, he had never seen the elf at a loss for ideas before. "Well, I think we should start by joining our fellow travelers under the trees," he said gently.

Emiril nodded and they turned and walked back to where the others were waiting.

Gilund watched Marcus and Emiril approach. He noticed that Emiril was looking out of sorts and gave Marcus a look as if to ask what was going on. Marcus followed with an 'I'll tell you later' look and he let it go.

"So, here we are," Marcus began as he and Emiril joined the others. "I guess some of you are wondering what is going on." He looked at Edlin and then pointedly at Gilund. "The reason we are here, under cover, is because Breanne has a feeling that we might be in danger." He waited for Edlin and Gilund to register what they just heard; when they had, he continued, "Emiril and I have discussed it and have decided the best thing to do is to go deeper into the forest, into the thickest part and make our way to the coast under the forest's thicker canopy. It is a natural defensive shield, so to speak, and we will be better hidden there. It may take longer to get there, but it will be safer going." He waited a few minutes, letting anyone who had an objection or a better plan have an opportunity to voice it, and when no one spoke up he then said, "Let's get going, shall we?" He turned to Breanne and gave her a wink. Breanne felt better instantly. If Emiril and Marcus believed in her, then she felt vindicated, not that she needed to be vindicated, but still it made her feel less stupid and less afraid of being wrong.

One by one, they rode into the heavy thicket of trees, riding the only way they could, single file, and no one spoke.

Twenty minutes after they had left the main trail, a shadow was seen flying overhead. The shadow moved slowly, purposefully, sometimes circling an area a few times before moving on. When it approached the spot the travelers had branched off at, it circled six times before moving on. The animals in that area fled and did not return for several months.

At dusk, Marcus called a halt to their procession. He had stopped in the biggest clearing he had seen since leaving the main trail, and it was not very big. They would be lucky to be able to fit all of them in it to sleep tonight. Of course, they would be one less person as he, Emiril and Gilund would each take a turn at watch tonight, a precaution up until now, he had not felt compelled to do. The day's turn of events had changed his thinking a whole three hundred and sixty degrees, however, and he was now in warrior mode, and he would run the group as if they were his army, and they were fighting to stay alive, because now, he felt it to be true.

With no fire once again, the weary travelers ate a cold dinner and settled in for a dark night. Breanne decided to sleep close to Edlin so they could talk before sleep took them. She felt safe around him, granted, not as safe as she felt around Marcus, but Edlin was special to her. She had finally decided that she may perhaps be falling in love with him, and she wanted to be close to him as often as she could.

Emiril lay awake for most of the night, wondering what Breanne could have felt, and why she had not felt it. Perhaps it was because Breanne was the chosen one, or perhaps Emiril was losing her powers, she didn't know the answer and it was driving her crazy. If she couldn't detect a threat, how was she supposed to protect them? She needed answers and she had no one to ask.

Gilund's snores could be heard several yards away. Marcus thought several times about waking him, and decided it would be better to have him fresh for a fight than weary from exhaustion. It was a difficult decision to make though.

Nothing moved in the night, no frogs croaked, no owls hooted. Marcus sat listening in the stillness, a growing fear welling up inside him. When it was time to wake Emiril, she suddenly appeared beside him.

"You didn't sleep?" he asked her softly.

"I could not," she replied bleakly.

"Worried about not sensing whatever it was she felt?"

"Yes."

He thought about it for a moment. "Emiril, wasn't it you who said she was the chosen one?"

She looked at him in the dark, only a shadow, his features obscured by the blackness. "Yes, I was," she said hesitantly, "Why?"

"Because, the way I see it is this, if she is the chosen one, she is bigger than you and I, than all of us really. It stands to reason she would have powers far greater than mine obviously, and yours as well. Otherwise, why would we have needed a chosen one at all, we could have done away with Ogolel ourselves a long time ago."

Emiril sat quietly for a moment. Marcus was such a good friend, and this was one of the reasons why; he was absolutely right. Breanne should have powers greater than hers; she was the one who would save their world, she had to have strong powers or what use would she be. "You know," she said softly, "this is one of the reasons I keep you around."

Marcus stifled a laugh. "I'm only glad that I can be of service to you, my lady," he said jokingly.

"That is good, keep it up and you will be around for a long time." She too was trying to keep from laughing loudly. "Seriously though, you have made me feel much better, and from this point on, I think that you should take the lead in protecting us. If I sense anything, I will tell you, but we need your expertise now, not mine."

"Alright then," he said, "but what about Breanne? Should we tell her to let us know each time she has a feeling?"

"Yes, I think it would be in our best interest," Emiril agreed.

Chapter 40
The Dragon Above

Morning was dark and somber under the thick canopy of trees. The travelers packed quickly and quietly while eating the Elven bread made especially for traveling.

Gilund was irritated and told Marcus so. "You should have woken me," he grumbled.

"I would have, friend," Marcus told him. "Honest, but Emiril and I couldn't sleep anyway, and we were talking all night, so it seemed pointless to wake you for no reason."

"Well, yah, I guess, but you still should have woken me, and then I could have seen that for myself." He stared at Marcus, trying to stay angry.

Marcus smiled brightly at his friend. "Gilund," he said gently, putting a hand on the dwarf's shoulder. "I know you would have taken your turn at watch, I don't doubt that for a moment, but honestly, I would rather have you fresh for a fight, than sitting up for no reason. You are after all, my right-hand man."

That last comment did it. Gilund couldn't help but smile back at his friend. "Sat up all night, did ya?" he asked warily.

"All night," Marcus said raising his right hand, "warrior's honor."

"All right then," Gilund conceded, then quickly added, "but mind it don't happen again, Marcus, or I don't know what I'll do to ya." With that said, he turned and walked away, head held high.

Marcus chuckled to himself, that dwarf was a proud one, that was for sure. He was going to have to remember his friends' feelings next time it was his turn to take the watch and wake him no matter what. It was better to let a man show his valor, even if it is not needed, than to let him think he has been underestimated. A point, he thought quickly, that should have been proven to him in Edlin's case, yet he had overlooked that lesson. Well, now he would always remember, it took two good friends to make sure of it.

"Let us not make that same mistake again," Emiril whispered in Marcus' ear.

Startled, Marcus jumped a little. "Stop sneaking up on people, woman," Marcus said sternly, but playfully. "And yes, let's not make that mistake again," he agreed.

Breanne and Edlin mounted their horses and sat waiting for the others. "How did you sleep last night?" Edlin asked her.

"Not well, unfortunately," she replied. "I kept dreaming of that evil creature the Dark Mage had. Emiril said she is certain he has a new one, I don't want to meet it."

"I do not blame you," Edlin agreed. "I have never seen it, but just the thought of it frightens me."

"And I can tell you, that in real life, they are way more scary than you can imagine (no exaggeration)" she said eerily.

Edlin was anxious to get going. It wasn't often they were ready before the adults, and now he was getting a feel for what it was like to wait on someone. He thought to himself, from now on he would try harder to get ready faster.

After a few last-minute things were packed, they were once again on their way. The trees filtered out all but a sliver of sunlight, making the travelers feel as if they were traveling at night. The forest was silent as they rode single file through the densely packed trees.

They had ridden for about fifteen minutes when Marcus called a halt to their procession. Emiril caught up to him to ask what was wrong. "Do you hear that?" Marcus asked her in a hushed tone.

Emiril strained to hear whatever it was Marcus heard —— nothing, she cocked her head, still nothing. "I am sorry, Marcus, I do not hear what you are hearing," she said quietly.

"Exactly," he said, looking worried.

"What?" she asked confused.

"You don't hear anything, right?"

"Right."

"Well, that's not right," he said matter-of-factly. "We should hear something, anything, a bird, a squirrel; it shouldn't be this quiet." He looked her straight in the eyes. "Something's wrong."

Now Emiril looked worried. She understood instantly what he meant. How long had it been this quiet? She looked back at the others; they had to do something, but what?

"We need to move deeper into the forest," Marcus said.

Emiril looked around them. The trees were so close together already, if they got any more dense, they wouldn't be able to move around at all, at least not with the horses. "Are you sure that is the only way?" she asked him.

As if reading her mind, he too looked at the closely packed trees. They couldn't very well leave the horses behind. Oh, think, Marcus, he told himself. "Emiril, if we run into the creature, are you going to be able to kill it like you did last time?"

Emiril looked a little scared. "I do not know, Marcus, I feel this creature is far more powerful than the last one." She looked away as if she were ashamed of herself.

"Hey, you," Marcus said. She looked back at him, sorrow in her eyes. "You have absolutely no reason to feel that way. After all, these demons are brought up from the netherworld and there are only a handful of people who could kill one in the first place, and you are one of them. If this one is too strong, it is not your fault, so don't you dare feel bad." He gave her a big smile.

She smiled back. "I think we should ask Breanne if she can sense any danger."

Marcus knew what it had taken for her to say that. She was used to being the one who knew these things. It was painfully obvious that she was having a hard time with it.

"Why do you think she can sense things now when she couldn't before?" he asked her.

Emiril thought about it for a moment. "I think it has to do with how long she has been here, the longer she stays the more her powers grow."

"That makes sense," Marcus said, adding, "I wonder just how powerful she will become."

Emiril thought about it. She too wondered how powerful the girl would be, especially after she took all of Ogolel's powers as well. "Well, we will not know until it happens," she said a little more shortly than she intended. "Let us get her up here and see what she knows, if anything."

Marcus waved to Breanne to come up. She was a little hesitant, but she did.

"Breanne," Emiril started, "remember when you told me you felt something was wrong?"

"Yes," Breanne said looking wide eyed.

"Well, we need to know if you feel that way still." She looked at the girl and noticed her hands were shaking a bit. Her heart melted. She had been feeling a little put out by the sudden realization that Breanne was more powerful than she; after all, she had been the third most powerful elf in Ibacion. It was a little hard to find yourself suddenly replaced, but looking at this young girl before her made her feel foolish. How could she begrudge someone as sweet and innocent as Breanne? She moved her horse closer to Breanne's and gave the girl a hug. "It is alright Breanne, you do not have to be afraid, we are here with you and we will take care of you."

Breanne melted in Emiril's embrace. She had been so uptight and worried, she now felt all that leave in a moment's time. Tears welled up in her eyes, and she was afraid she would start to sob. Emiril just held her, letting her take her time to regain her composer. When she felt better, she sat up and wiped her eyes with the back of her hand. She smiled timidly at Marcus, who had been watching the scene play out before him and thinking of his own daughter and how much he loved and missed her. "I was not sure if I should tell you every time I felt something," she said slowly, "I could be wrong, you know," she added hastily.

"Breanne," Marcus said gently, "we understand how feelings work. We know that sometimes you just feel weird for no reason, and nothing happens, but we also know that sometimes feelings are there to warn you about something, something that really is going to happen, and that is why we always listen to our feelings, because you never know what kind of feeling it is. Do you understand?"

Breanne nodded.

"And," Emiril added, "we will never be upset with you if nothing happens. We always want you to tell us when you feel something, and we will take it from there. Ok?" She smiled at Breanne and squeezed her hands gently.

Breanne felt better, knowing that her friends would support her no matter what.

"So," Marcus said, eyebrows raised, "anything?"

"Yah," Breanne said softly, "I have still been feeling like something is…well, like something is following us, but is not quite sure where we are." She thought for a moment. "I think yesterday it came very close to finding us. I am glad we left the main trail." She gave Emiril and Marcus a look that made their skin crawl.

"Do you have any idea what this thing is?" Marcus asked, afraid he already knew the answer.

Breanne looked him in the eyes and instantly he knew. They had shared an experience together that could be passed between them with just a look, this look. "Only worse," Breanne added to her look. Marcus shivered involuntarily.

"Breanne," Emiril asked, "you said it does not know where we are, do you think it will find us if we keep going the way we are?"

Breanne closed her eyes and concentrated on the feelings she was having. She felt the threat, but it felt as if it were parallel to them, not on the same path with them. She tried to see further into the future. She could just make out the faintest feeling that the threat would indeed cross their path, but not for a while yet. She opened her eyes and told them what she had seen.

"Thank you, Breanne," Marcus told her. "And Breanne, we musn't tell the others what we know. They would only worry needlessly. When the time is right, I will tell them, Ok?" Breanne nodded, although she didn't understand why the others couldn't know now. She figured Marcus knew what he was talking about though, and she wouldn't say anything.

Emiril noticed Breanne thinking about what Marcus had told her., 'She doesn't understand,' she thought, 'she has a right to know, in fact, she needs to learn this stuff.' "Breanne, the reason the others do not need to know right now, is the fact that they will be afraid. You see, fear is a sense that is very easy to pick up on; all animals can sense fear, it is built into them. A good example is when you are afraid, JC becomes agitated, does he not?" Breanne nodded. "Well, it is the same with any animal, and if the creature is near enough, and there is enough fear in the air, he will be able to pick up on that, even without us using thought transfers, he will be able to find us."

"I see now," Breanne said, "JC does become afraid when I am nervous. When he does I just sooth him by sending him calming thoughts."

Emiril froze, her eyes widened.

Breanne saw her reaction and was suddenly more scared than she had been. "What's wrong?" she asked.

"Breanne, you send thoughts to JC?" Emiril asked quickly.

Suddenly Breanne felt extremely guilty, "Yes, sometimes," she said softly.

"When was the last time you did that?" Emiril pressed.

Breanne thought about it for a moment. "At the entrance to the dwarf cave." Tears were rolling down her cheeks now. "I did something wrong, didn't I?" she asked, looking from Emiril to Marcus and back to Emiril.

Emiril looked at Marcus. They both knew now why the creature was summoned and why it was looking for them in this area.

"Breanne," Marcus began, "you did not do anything wrong per se. What happened was, we did not fully explain about the thought transfers. We told you not to send thoughts to people, but it seems we left out the part about not sending them to animals as well."

"Breanne, do not cry," Emiril said gently, "you did not know. We should have explained it to you better. I did not think about your love for your horse and how you might communicate with him. I also send thoughts to Tanja. I do not blame you at all, in fact, I blame myself for not telling you." She put her arm around the girl and held her. This day was proving to be a bad one for poor Breanne.

After a few moments, Breanne sat up and once again dried her eyes. "So, when I sent the calming thoughts to JC, I gave away our location to the Dark Mage," she said matter-of-factly.

Marcus looked at Emiril. She knew more about how that worked than he did.

"Yes and no," she said. "You did alert him to the fact that we have left the glen, but you did not give away our position. Thought transfers to animals are not as strong as thought transfers to people. Animals are more sensitive and pick up on more subtle thoughts. So, if the Dark Mage felt anything, it would have been very faint and fleeting. He would not have been able to pinpoint where we were, he would only have gotten a general idea, which is why the creature has not found us yet. But I do not think I need to say we should not send thought transfers to anyone or anything from this time forward," she added.

Breanne sniffed and rubbed her now red and puffy eyes. "I am never sending another thought in my life," she said (Not exaggerating she thought).

"Don't be hard on yourself," Marcus said quickly, "and don't presume to think you are the only person who feels bad about this."

Breanne looked at him, clearly stunned. "You feel bad?" she asked.

"Well, sure I do," he said, "and so does Emiril. Don't you think we feel guilty about forgetting to tell you? We don't want you to accidently do anything that could harm you, and we messed up by not telling you something that could have been really bad. That makes us feel bad."

"I don't want you to feel bad," Breanne said quickly.

"And we don't want you to feel bad," Marcus replied back. "Especially because it wasn't your fault; you didn't know any better." He smiled at her.

"I see what you are getting at," Breanne said finally. "I guess I should only feel responsible for some of it, and not all of it, because like you said, I didn't know it was wrong."

"Yes and no," Marcus said. "You shouldn't feel bad at all because you didn't know. What you should feel is educated, now you know, and now if you do it again, then you can feel bad. Understand?"

Breanne smiled, feeling better. "Yes, I understand."

"Good," Marcus said happily, "because what matters now, is what comes next." He looked at Emiril.

Chapter 41
The Last Spell

The creature circled high above the trees, its shadow swirling rhythmically below. The sun shone brightly on its scales, reflecting back the brilliant rays. The Dark Mage was growing impatient. He knew the girl had left the glen, he had been searching for her from the moment he knew, but he still had not caught her. He knew too that Ogolel grew impatient as well. He could feel her ever growing presence. If he did not find her soon, she would surely take it out on him. And now that she was aware of his growing hatred of her, she may well kill him this time.

The blue sky echoed a false sense of serenity. The birds were not fooled however, from their vantage point high in the tree canopies, they could see the evil that glided silently above, and fled the forest for safer roosting sites. Other animals too sensed the evil presence bearing down on them from above and they also fled the now ominous forest.

Marcus and Emiril looked at one another, their keen senses picking up on all of this. Breanne had given them a hint of what was to come and they needed to decide if it was preventable or if they needed to find a place to make a stand.

"If we are caught here in these trees, we will be unable to offer much of a defense," Marcus said ominously.

Emiril nodded in agreement. The horses barely had room to turn around and they would not be able to stand as a group amid the dense thicket. "We should find a more open area that is easier to defend," she agreed. "But not too open," she added.

"Then it's agreed," Marcus said resolutely. He glanced around them and once again noticed the now silent forest and the ever growing feeling of doom. "We best hurry," he told Emiril, and she knew not to take what he said lightly.

As the group hurried, as best they could in the dense forest, to a more suitable staging area, the Dark Mage felt a presence. He had felt the presence before, yet it was somehow different. It was her, he had found her. He tried in vain to peer through the thick canopy of trees below. She was somewhere under that thick blanket of green, he knew that now. He had the creature circle lower over the tree tops; it was no use, he could see nothing. They were moving, however, he could now sense the direction in which they were traveling. He sent the creature ahead of the group until he found a clearing that would be directly in their path. It was here that he would finally catch them, catch them, and kill her. He grew hopeful for the first time in a long time. He felt his quest was nearly done, but then he became afraid. A fear gripped him like none he had felt before. It was a deeper fear even then he had felt while fighting the creature by the pond. It was also a realization, one he had refused to let himself consider before this moment, once the girl was dead, she would not need him anymore. As this realization sunk into his mind, nothing else seemed to exist, the trees vanished, the blue sky faded from view, all was centered on just one thought: she will surely kill me then. What was he going to do? What could he do? There was nowhere to hide, nowhere to run to, nowhere that she couldn't find him.

Marcus could see a splash of light up ahead, he knew must be a clearing, and his heart began to beat faster. He could feel the creature's presence. He knew it had been following them, from when exactly he did not know, but at some point, he had been able to sense it. He was sure Emiril could sense it as well, what he didn't know however, was if Breanne could. This was it then, this was where it would happen. They would face the creature once more in a life or death struggle, the outcome of which he did not know. He thought once more of Iola and his daughter. He pictured them as he had last seen them, waving

302

goodbye, smiles on their faces. He silently prayed that he would see them again.

Emiril interrupted his thoughts. "Well, this is the place then." Her voice sounded cold and distant, a voice that most warriors seemed to use when preparing for battle. He looked into her eyes and was surprised to see fear in them. It was reasonable though, that she would be afraid, she had fought the last creature and won, but this creature was far more powerful and she may not be able to defeat it. He wasn't sure how much help he was going to be either. Last time the creature had come, it had proven to be much more than he could handle. The odds were not looking good for their little group.

"How do you think we should play this?" Emiril asked him. She had decided to let him plan the battle and she would follow his lead.

"I had thought that you and I would go into the opening and draw the creature in. You could use your magic to distract it while I try to kill it. Gilund will stay just inside the tree line and use his bow to try and wound it. I thought if he could blind it, it would give us the advantage."

Emiril was impressed with his plan. Her spirits lifted somewhat, but what about Breanne and Edlin? She didn't need to ask out loud, he anticipated the question.

"Breanne and Edlin will stay in the trees, far enough back to not be seen, and if things go badly," he paused, swallowing hard, "they are to run away as fast as they can, and try to make it back to the glen, or to Mindoneth, whichever is easier for them."

Emiril nodded. It was a good plan. She wished now however that they had brought more people with them. They had been found and the element of surprise was gone. Now would be a good time to have some troops with them. She pushed that thought out of her head; the situation was what it was and could not be changed. They would fight till the death if need be. They would protect Breanne the best they could. She did wish she could send one last thought to her father though, just to tell him that she loved him. It was still too dangerous though, with the Dark Mage's presence so near, he could easily slip into her mind once it was unlocked, and if he didn't already know all their plans, he would then.

The group got together and Marcus went over the plan with all of them, making sure each one knew their role and making absolutely sure that Edlin and Breanne would follow orders and flee if things turned bad. "If things go badly, don't let our deaths be in vain by staying here and letting yourselves be killed as well," he had told them. Shivers coursed down Breanne's spine at the thought of her friends' deaths. She prayed earnestly that all would go well. She could not stand the thought of losing any of them. They had become as close to her as her family back home, and she would be devastated to lose them.

Marcus held his sword in hand, the few rays of sunlight that filtered through the trees, seemed to find their way to the blade, causing it to shine brightly in the dark forest. It appeared to radiate fire as it moved back and forth with the movement of the horse. Breanne was suddenly struck with the thought that this could be the last time she would see Marcus alive. Tears streamed down her face as she looked at Emiril, and once again felt the ominous feeling of death. She could not let this happen; how could she allow her friends to die for her? Maybe the feelings she had would not come true, like the ones she had had about the creature finding them, but deep inside she knew they would. At least they would if they followed the path they were on right now. There was something about the decisions they had made that was wrong, but she couldn't put her finger on it. She only knew that the battle would not go well if they fought it the way they intended. She wanted to say something, but it was too late. Marcus spurred his horse and they rushed out of the trees and into the waiting arms of death, Emiril following closely behind.

The Dark Mage waited, slowly circling the clearing. He knew that his prey would come to him, and he could sense victory on the heels of the battle to come. He allowed himself to feel happy even though he knew that with victory there might also come defeat, his defeat. His happiness wavered and he tried to push the unwelcome thought aside. Surely, she would not kill him, he tried to convince himself, but he knew, just as surely as he knew his own intentions concerning the girl, that she would kill him as soon as he had finished the job. The creature could feel something was amiss and it turned its mind toward the Dark Mage, searching for the comfort it had come to rely on from the man. The two had become close, closer than any creature had ever been to a man. They functioned now as if they were one, each one relied on the other, a bond that had been formed in the ever-lurking shadow of Ogolel. Her presence had unwittingly created this bond between man and creature, a bond that had, unbeknownst to the Dark Mage, become too close. He reassured the creature that all was well, and turned their focus to the meadow below.

Breanne watched in horror as first Marcus and then Emiril galloped off to their death. Just as surely as she had known the creature was near, she knew they would die. She turned to Edlin.

"Edlin, we have to help them" she screamed.

Edlin jumped in his saddle, surprised by her sudden outburst. "What?" he asked confused and scared. "What do you mean help them, we are supposed to stay here," he told her authoritatively.

"Edlin, we can't stay here, we have to save them." She gave him a look that chilled him to the bone.

"Breanne, you are not making sense."

Breanne realized she wasn't making sense, only she knew what was about to happen. "Edlin, listen to me because there is no time to explain,

Marcus and Emiril are going to die." He looked at her with both surprise and skepticism. She shook her head. "There is no time to explain, Edlin, you have to believe me. They are going to die and we need to save them. There is no other way, and not much time left." Her voice was near hysterical and tears were coursing down her cheeks.

Edlin looked at the terrified girl and calmly stated, "What do you want me to do?"

"Follow me," she said quickly, relief evident in her voice.

The two started to circle around the clearing. She did not know why they needed to be on the other side, she just knew. Gilund did not notice the two shadowy figures as he was watching in horror as the biggest, most evil looking creature he had ever seen came swooping down into the clearing. All present and those miles away heard the terrible cry it made when it came in for the kill.

Emiril shivered as she saw the creature, huge wings beating rapidly, slowing itself as it came hurtling into the clearing. With feet outstretched, claws gleaming in the sun, red eyes fixated on Marcus, it resembled and eagle going after a mouse. Marcus' horse screamed in terror and Emiril froze. She saw the horse turn on its haunches and jump in the opposite direction it had been traveling, with Marcus holding on for dear life. It happened in a mere second or two, but to the terrified elf, it felt as if many minutes had passed. She suddenly regained her composure and reached out, palm outward and began to recite the spell of light. The creature was taken by surprise as the hot, white light seared its body. It screamed anew and turned its attention to the new antagonist, momentarily forgetting its intended target. That momentary lack of attention gave Marcus the time he needed to skirt around the creature and get ready to counterattack.

The creature flew straight towards Emiril, its sole intent to kill the elf. She recited the spell again, again the white light flashed from the palm of her hand. The creature did not slow, Emiril turned pale. She quickly began to recite the spell yet again, putting as much of her power into it as she could. This time the light was brighter, more intense, as the creature was hit square on. It reeled backward, claws grasping the air as it tumbled back the way it had come. Emiril was shaking, sweat dripped from her forehead. She watched now as Marcus ran under the tumbling creature, sword swinging, trying to slice the creature's vulnerable places, places that were not covered by protective scales, places that were too few.

After tumbling for many seconds, the creature righted itself, shook with rage; it could feel the places where the sword had found tender skin, and they throbbed with pain. The light was new to it, never having encountered such magic, it didn't know how to fight magic, but its alter ego did. The Dark Mage took control of the battle, sending the creature skyward. He had to regroup and reassess the attack, it being clear now that brute force would only result in the creature's demise, just as it had the last time.

Breanne and Edlin hurried through the tangle of trees that surrounded the meadow, which was now for all intents and purposes a battlefield. The going was slow and Breanne knew their time was running short; she had to get to the other side before it was too late. Edlin followed her blindly, not knowing what he was supposed to do to help her, but willing to follow her direction, to the death if need be. He was certain now of his love for this girl. Why else would he follow her without knowing why, if he did not love her?

Marcus watched the creature fly skyward. He cursed this move as he knew what was happening and he knew that it was not good for them. If the Dark Mage took control of this battle, they would be fighting a far more dangerous creature, they would be fighting a creature that could think like a man. He rushed to where Emiril stood. She too was watching the creature; she too knew the tables were about to turn against them.

"We are no longer fighting a mindless creature."

The words were ones she was about to speak as well. She looked at Marcus, he had blood on his face and hands. "How much of that blood is yours?" she asked, sounding concerned.

He looked himself over, and smiling, stated cheerfully, "A little less than half."

Emiril couldn't help herself, she too broke into a smile. "Well, I guess that means you have won just over half the battle then?" With that they both began to laugh.

Then Marcus looked deep into her eyes and without saying another word — they didn't need to express out loud what each was thinking — turned and crossed the meadow. They waited. Gilund stood resolute beside the clearing, bow in hand, arrow knocked, waiting for the shot that would take out an eye. He too cursed when he saw the creature spiral up into the sky. If he couldn't get the shot, he would be of no use to his friends. He prayed that chance would come.

The Dark Mage took note of where Marcus and Emiril were. He did not know where the girl was, or who else was there, so he concentrated on what he did know. He chose Marcus, and sent the creature after him.

Marcus prepared himself, watching as the creature came shooting towards him. At the last second, he spurred his horse and ran across the meadow, the creature right behind him. Emiril shot white light towards them, the creature dodged the stream. She was too far away. She tried again and again, the creature dodging each attempt. Marcus would have to lure the creature closer.

Marcus could see the light looked behind him, and saw the creature dodge first one spell, then the other. They were too far away from Emiril for her spells to be effective. They would have to get the creature closer, but it was gaining on them. If they did not turn and circle, it would get them before they were in range. He turned the horse sharply, mud flying in all directions, turned up by the horses' hooves digging deeply into the damp ground. The horse was having a hard time gaining its footing, slipped and almost went down. Marcus was caught by surprise when the horse faltered, he was thrown violently sideways and lost his stirrup. He held tightly to his sword as he flew through the air, his head hitting the ground before the rest of his body. He heard a sickening thud, things began to go dim, and just before he lost consciousness, he heard the creature scream in victory as it turned to finish him off.

Emiril watched in horror as Marcus was thrown from his horse. She saw the creature turn and she began to run. She cast spell after spell as she raced to Marcus' side, but none of the light hit the creature; she was still too far away. Tears blurred her vision as she ran faster, she ran to save the man who had so many times before saved her. As she grew closer, she saw the creature land where it stood at Marcus's feet, its white teeth gleaming in the sunlight, saliva dripping from its mouth. Emiril tried one last time to use the spell, praying she was close enough this time.

Gilund pulled the bow string back as far as he could, steadied his breathing, closed one eye and exhaled as he sent the arrow flying. He watched, silently praying it would find its mark. He saw it head straight and true toward the creature's eye, but just before it hit its mark there was a blinding flash of light and Gilund lost track of it. When he could see again, the events that took place horrified him. The arrow had found its mark, the light was from Emiril, but things had gone terribly wrong.

Emiril ran towards the creature not caring for her own safety. She cast the spell and saw the creature's attention divert to herself; Marcus forgotten for the moment. Through the light she saw an arrow pierce the creature's eye and silently thanked Gilund, but then things went terribly wrong.

"Here, Edlin," Breanne yelled as she sprang from her horse, hitting the ground at a dead run. Edlin grabbed his sword and he too jumped to the ground, finding himself struggling to keep up with the frantic girl.

"Wait," he called to her; she did not slow. He chased after her until they reached the edge of the clearing.

She stopped short, turned to him, and between gasps for air told him what he had to do. His eyes grew wide. Was she kidding? He had never done anything like that in his life. He had not really planned on having to be on this quest, had figured Marcus and Emiril would have things well in hand. He was not sure he was ready. He had been trained, yes, but never had he used his training. He looked into Breanne's eyes and what he saw comforted him. She did not look scared or hesitant, she looked determined and confident. He drew on her strength and began to believe in himself. He could do this, he now felt like he could do this. She smiled.

His attention was diverted from Breanne to the meadow as a brilliant light suddenly lit up the clearing. He saw the creature rear up, saw it begin to writhe in pain, its body swaying back and forth. Then he saw it turn and as it did, he saw its enormous tail hit Emiril and send her flying into the air, somersaulting many times before she came crashing down on the hard ground. She lay motionless forty feet from where she had stood.

"Now," Breanne yelled, and the two young people ran into the clearing together. Breanne summoned all of her strength, the full force of which she herself was about to discover, and with both hands, she sent a light towards the creature, a light so brilliant that even she could not look directly at it. Edlin ran under the light's rays directly toward the creature. He did not feel afraid, he could still see Breanne smiling at him and he knew this would work. He did not know how he knew, he just did. He could see the creature's belly as it reared up against the light. He could see the spot, although he did not know how he knew, he knew the spot to strike. Twenty feet, ten, he kept running until he was directly under the creature. He raised his father's sword above his head, holding onto it with both hands. Any second now, and then, just as he knew it would happen, the creature came down on all four legs. He felt the blade slide between the creature's scales, felt it travel through muscle and tissue, felt it push through soft flesh, the flesh which was its beating heart. Blood rained down on Edlin as he heard the creature scream in pain and rage and saw its legs begin to tremble, He let go of the sword and ran out from under the now dying creature just before it collapsed. The dying creature turned its head and caught a glimpse of its killer just before it was pulled back into the spirit world, the blinding white light helping to hasten its journey from this world back to its birth world. But it was not alone on this return trip, as it had been when it was born into this world, someone travelled with it, someone familiar, he was with it, he was being pushed/shoved into the spirit world as well.

The Dark Mage watched in horror as the girl standing in front of the creature cast the spell. He could feel the pain the light caused, but it was more intense than any he had ever felt before. She was indeed far more powerful than Emiril, and then he felt a new sensation, a feeling of being pushed, pushed from this world into the spirit world. He panicked, struggled to return to his body, but she blocked his way. He clawed at the fabric of this world, trying desperately to get a handhold as she pushed harder, he could feel himself slipping. The creature shuddered as the blade was driven deep into its heart. The Dark Mage felt the pain. How can this be? He was so close to winning, how could it all fall apart so quickly? He slipped again and a terrified scream escaped his body's lips, a body waiting for its mind to return. The servants were too scared to go near the limp body of their master, too many times they had seen him appear dead and then rise again, full of life. This time however, something was different. He had never made a noise before, not until he had awakened, and he was not awake. They watched as blood started to ooze from his pores, as his body began to convulse, then, just as suddenly as it had begun, it ended. His body was gone, only a bloody outline remained where once flesh and blood had been. The servants all fled from the castle, never to return again. His mind screamed and clawed and fought, trying to regain its hold in this world, to no avail. He could see the light fading, he could feel the darkness taking hold. In the darkness he felt himself reunite with his body; he did not understand what magic could do this. He reached out for the creature and found it, clung to it, and together they passed through the doorway into the spirit world. He saw many other creatures as his eyes adjusted to the near darkness of this new world he found himself in. But more frightening was the fact that they saw him too. They began to advance as he scrambled onto the creature's back, then the creature took flight. He did not know where they were going. He did not care, he was alive and he intended to stay that way.

Chapter 42
Battle at Daedhrog

Edlin sat up from where he had dived for cover when the creature went down. He was shaking, but not from fear. He was elated, he had done what was asked of him. He had killed the creature, no doubt with help from Breanne, but he had been an intrical part of the creature's demise and he was overwhelmed with pride. A noise drew his thoughts outward again, moaning. He got up quickly and hurried toward the sound where he found Marcus lying on the ground, blood trickled from his mouth and nose. "Marcus," Edlin screamed as he knelt beside the moaning man. "Can you hear me?" Marcus groaned louder. "Hang on, Marcus, you are going to be alright." He heard running feet behind him, turned to see Gilund hurrying toward them, and sighed with relief. He quickly scanned the area and found Breanne kneeling beside Emiril, who was sitting up and appeared to be dazed.

"How is he?" Gilund asked breathlessly.

"I do not know yet," Edlin said quickly, a hint of fear in his voice. "He is moaning but not really awake."

"Let me look," Gilund said kneeling beside his old friend. He wiped the blood away from Marcus' face and found that it was coming from a cut on his lip. He was relieved that he could probably rule out internal bleeding, and the blood from his nose appeared to be simply a bloody nose. "Marcus, it's Gilund, wake up you old dog, wake up."

Marcus groaned again. He could feel his head pounding and he felt sick. He tried to open his eyes but found it very difficult. What was wrong with him? He heard voices but could not place them. They seemed to be talking to him, but were too muffled to hear what they were saying. He drifted away from the noise, drifting toward the light, a brilliant, beautiful light that beckoned him and which he followed.

"Edlin, go get Emiril. Tell her she has to come, even if she has to crawl here, she has to come." Gilund's voice was full of fear as he visibly shook.

Edlin did not hesitate, sensing things were bad for Marcus, he ran as fast as he could to where Emiril and Breanne were sitting.

Breanne saw Edlin racing toward them, sensed something was wrong, very wrong. She jumped up and met him part way. "What is it?" she asked, her voice raised in fear.

"It is Marcus," Edlin gasped, "something's terribly wrong, Breanne, I think he is dying." Breanne saw tears in Edlin's eyes and her heart sank. "Gilund wants Emiril and he said she has to come, no matter what." Edlin's voice broke and he had to choke back a sob.

Breanne hugged him briefly, and then pushed passed him. "I know what to do," she hollered as she raced to where her friend lay dying. She hoped she would get there in time.

How she knew what do was a mystery to Breanne, just like how she had known Marcus and Emiril would die if she and Edlin did not intervene. But she did know what to do, knew he was following the light. She knew if he did, he would die, so she had to reach him before he passed into the light, or he would be gone forever. She knelt by his side and looked into his face. She loved him like a father and could not stand the thought of losing him.

"Where's Emiril?" Gilund asked, his voice betraying the fact that he was crying.

"She's over there," Breanne said, indicating where she had just come from.

"We need her here," Gilund shouted, "didn't Edlin tell you?" His voice clearly showed his fear and frustration over Marcus' condition.

Breanne looked into Gilund's eyes. He froze, his fear and anxiety vanished in an instant. He saw something in those eyes of hers, didn't know what it was, but it made him feel calm and relaxed, and he welcomed the feeling.

Now that Gilund was calm, Breanne turned her attention to Marcus. She placed her hands on the sides of his head and closed her eyes. She entered a dark place, a place that had once been a very active mind, but was now shutting down. She saw a few memories here and there, remnants of a life that was passing, a life she was determined to save. She called out to the man, but heard only silence. She began to search every corner, every dark place, until she saw the faintest glow off in the distance. She hurried towards it. She felt as if she had been running forever and the light was still fading. She began to worry she would not catch it in time. "Marcus!" she called frantically, "Marcus, wait, don't go." The light flickered. Did it slow down? She seemed to be catching up. She ran faster. "Marcus, it's me, Breanne, come back, Marcus. I am here, come back." This time she was sure the light flickered, she saw movement. Something or someone was between her and the light, moving back and forth, seemingly confused which way to go. Her heart leapt; she was sure it was Marcus, it had to be him.

"Marcus!" she screamed. The shape was now a figure, and the figure turned towards her, starting to move towards her. She ran faster, the figure took a familiar shape — it was Marcus. He stared at her, a look of confusion on his face. "Marcus," she cried out, "it's me, Breanne." He simply stared at her, not recognizing her. She walked up to him and stared into his eyes. "Marcus, you need to come with me," she said softly. "Your friends are waiting, Iola and your daughter are waiting for you." She could see a slight flicker of recognition in his eyes. She

315

continued more earnestly. "Marcus, Emiril is hurt, she is waiting for you to help her."

His eyes widened; she could tell he was struggling to comprehend what she was telling him. "Edlin and Gilund are waiting for you too. Poor Gilund is beside himself with worry." Marcus shuddered and his eyes rolled back in his head. He stood motionless for several minutes. Breanne thought he looked like one of the zombies she had seen in some horror show one time. She touched his cheek, it was cold, she grabbed his hand, it was rigid. "Marcus," she started, then stopped as he suddenly looked her in the eyes. She could see he recognized her, and her spirit soared. "Hi," she said softly.

"Hi," he replied back, even softer.

"You ready to go home?" she asked him gently.

"Ya."

They turned and started to walk toward home, toward friends and family, but most importantly, they walked toward life. Marcus began to cry, Breanne squeezed his hand, her own tears blurring her vision.

Gilund watched calmly as Breanne sat in a trance over Marcus' body. He barely noticed as Edlin, helping a limping Emiril approach. No one spoke, everyone knew the seriousness of the situation. Emiril wondered if Breanne really knew what to do. Emiril herself had never brought someone back from the walk of death, although she had seen it done many times, though only by the most powerful elves in the kingdom. Anyone else would surely get lured into the light as well, so it was forbidden for them to try it. Bringing someone back from the walk was dangerous because you were no longer dealing with only good spirits and good magic, you were dealing with evil spirits and dark magic, for it was dark magic that was the driving force behind death. After a person died, they could go to the good place, but the journey was taken hand and hand with the darkest spirits and they did not like anyone interfering with the souls in their charge, a fact Breanne was about to find out.

Breanne could feel the others surrounding Marcus as she looked at him and smiled; they were almost out. Then suddenly she felt a presence, an evil presence. She turned quickly to see red eyes glaring at her. A body began to take shape around the eyes with long dangling arms, hands and feet tipped with razor sharp claws. A grey wrinkled body sporadically covered with coarse hair. Ears like bat ears. It was naked except for a ragged loin cloth. But mostly she noticed its mouth, snout-like with sharp shark-like teeth. Her blood ran cold. "Run," she whispered to Marcus, "Run!" He looked at her with guilty eyes. She shook her head and let go of his hand. "Run!" He did.

Marcus opened his eyes, blinked back the sunlight and slowly his friends came into focus. Breanne still knelt beside him, her hands on his head. Gilund sat close beside him, his face covered in white streaks where tears had coursed through layers of dirt. Edlin and Emiril were standing over him, they too were crying. "What's going on?" he croaked. "You'd think someone was dead." The clearing suddenly burst forth with noise as three voices in unison cried out, "Marcus, you are alive!"

It took him a minute for all the memories to repopulate his mind: the quest, the fight, the light, then suddenly he remembered the demon and Breanne telling him to run. He looked into the face above him, eyes closed, brows furrowed. She was still in there, in there with that creature. He told Emiril about the demon and she turned pale. "What can we do?" he asked weakly.

Emiril knew there was nothing they could do, that neither one was powerful enough to fight what she knew to be a demon of death. She only knew of one other person who had encountered one while saving

317

someone from the walk of death, and they had succumbed to the demon, although the person they were saving had been saved. No one could help Breanne now. She only prayed Breanne was as powerful as they all thought she might be, and maybe she would be the first and only person to overcome the demon. "We can wait for her," she said, her voice cracking, "wait and pray."

Once she was sure Marcus was ok, Breanne turned and faced the demon. She could see the hatred in its eyes, hatred for her because she had robbed it of its prize, Marcus. She saw saliva dripping from its long fangs, smelled its foul stench. All of these things confronted her senses, yet she was not afraid. Why wasn't she afraid? She didn't know the answer to that question, but she somehow knew she was more powerful than this creature, just as she had known that Marcus and Emiril were going to need her and Edlin's help if they were going to survive the fight with the creature. The demon took a step towards her. She did not hesitate, took two steps towards it, and felt a power welling up within her. She did not need to summon it, it was just there, reacting to every action. She looked anew at the demon, her eyes boring into his and suddenly he knew, more than she did, who she was and what would happen to him if he did not flee. He did not know how she got here, but here she was. He wasted no time, he turned and ran for his life. Breanne felt the surge of power continue to well up inside her. She stood rooted to her spot and with head tilted back, arms stretched out to her sides, she let it come. It was a good feeling, a warm feeling, the feeling you get when you swallow hot chocolate on a cold winter day, only this feeling wasn't confined to her chest, it coursed throughout her entire body. She closed her eyes and relished the feeling. Then without warning, she found herself standing on a narrow ledge on the side of a very tall mountain. The air was crisp and she could see her breath. She could see several valleys below her and other mountain ranges in the distance, rivers coursing through the valleys, the sunlight glittering on the water

318

as if it were studded with diamonds. It was as if she could see the whole world laid out before her. She marveled at its beauty, her fear of heights momentarily forgotten.

She heard a noise behind her and turned to see a big, black opening in the mountain side. She peered in, but could not see what had made the noise. She took a few cautious steps into the opening and strained to see into the inky blackness, heard movement and hurried back out onto the ledge. The cold air that emanated from the blackness smelled musky and rank and a sense of foreboding overtook her. She took another step away from the cave's opening, then could take no more. The rustling sound inside the cave intensified. She felt fear grip her very soul, her heart began to pound. Yellow eyes peered out at her from within the darkness, puffs of steam billowing from below the eyes. She stood frozen, too afraid to scream, nowhere to run. The thing within the cave took another step towards her, revealing a long snout, sharp teeth protruding from within it, a serpentine neck, tree stump legs ending in feet accented with sharp claws and still more of this creature was hidden from view. She could feel her heart beating against her rib cage, her breathing rapid, and her body trembled. The creature stared at her with unblinking lizard-like eyes that bore into her mind, filling every crevice with its presence. She felt violated as even her most guarded secrets were revealed to this trespasser.

She tried to shut her mind off, to push the creature out; she could not. She was an open book, and he was reading her cover to cover. Many minutes passed before she could feel it start to retreat from her mind. Slowly, purposefully it retreated, vacating first one section of her mind, then another. No place was left untouched, nothing was left private. When she was sure it had gone, she searched her violated mind, checking for damages, closing doors it had left open, hiding secrets that were no longer secret. As she was closing the last door, she stopped. There was something lying on the floor in the middle of the room. She looked at it hesitantly; she hadn't seen it before; it didn't belong in here; where had it come from? Had he left it behind? She walked slowly, hesitantly, toward it; it moved; she froze. She watched as the thing began to rock slowly back and forth, then the rocking became faster and still faster. She heard a sound as if something was being ripped. She watched unbelievingly as the object on the floor broke open, then lay still. She took a cautious step closer, trying to see what was inside, took another and stopped, horrified by what she saw.

Lying inside this mystery object was a baby. It looked at her and she immediately felt that she should know this child, but she did not, could not. She felt torn, part of her wanting to go to the child and part of her wanting to turn and run. Run from a truth about this child she was sure to find out if she went any closer, a truth she was not prepared to know. She turned and ran from the room, ran from the truth, shutting the door behind her, refusing to acknowledge that she had seen anything. Once outside her mind, she looked into the cave, but the thing with the yellow gazing eyes was gone. She felt herself falling off the ledge, as if someone had pushed her. She tumbled downward, the sound of her terrified screams filling her ears, things rushing past her in a blur. Then, without knowing how it had happened, she was once more in Marcus' mind, and then just as quickly as she had found herself in Marcus' mind, she was in the clearing, her voice coming to her loudly as the last of her screams died away. She opened her eyes and found herself staring into Marcus' eyes, her hands still on his head, and then she collapsed beside him. When she woke again, she didn't know where she was, it was dark and she could see firelight, she heard her friends' voices and she smelt food. She sat up and saw Edlin sitting near her feet smiling broadly, clearly happy to see her awake.

Chapter 43
The Breaking of Chains

Edlin got up and came to her side. "How are you feeling?" he asked her, obvious concern in his eyes and voice.

She smiled. How much she had come to love this boy who she was now sure, loved her too. "I'm alright," she said hoping it was the truth. She actually had no idea if she was alright or not, she needed to talk to Emiril. Her heart quickened. "How are they?" she asked, almost afraid to hear the answer.

Edlin put his arms around her, a move which both shocked and pleased her. "They are all just fine. They owe their lives to you," he added as he pulled her close.

She hesitated for the briefest of seconds, then allowed herself to be pulled close to him. His body was warm and he smelled good; she melted into him; he held her tightly. After several minutes, she looked into his face, his eyes soft and gentle. She loved him, she knew beyond a doubt, she loved this boy and she hoped he loved her too. He leaned closer and as she closed her eyes, his lips, warm and moist found hers. They kissed that first kiss, the one that everyone tries to recapture for the rest of their lives, yet always eludes them. He leaned back and looked into her eyes. He saw tears and became concerned. "What is the matter?" He was afraid he had upset her by kissing her.

She smiled, "Nothing, nothing is wrong, everything is right." She hesitated, then decided to tell him, "I love you." She waited nervously for his response.

His eyes grew bigger, his body trembled. Had she really said it? Had she really told him she loved him? He was elated, he loved her so much, yet he had been afraid she did not love him back, could not love him back, he was an elf and she was a human after all. "I love you too," he managed finally, then leaned down and kissed her again. She kissed him back, more fervently than before.

Emiril watched from a distance this love scene unfolding before her. She was both happy and concerned for the two participants. How fickle love was, even in the midst of death and destruction, its roots could take hold and thrive. Sometimes it seemed that love thrived even more so amid these types of situations. She did not understand the ways of life sometimes, and was glad she did not have to. She walked back to the fire as silently as she had come where she would wait for them to come to her.

"Can you get up?" Edlin asked, offering her his hand.

"Yes," she replied, gratefully accepting his help.

"Everyone will be glad to see you up, they have been so worried," he told her. It had been apparent he too had been worried when she found him by her bedside.

Hand in hand they walked to where the others sat around a relatively large fire, talking softly. As they approached, they all stood up smiling.

"It's good to see you up," Gilund told her. He stuck out his hand, hesitated, then pulled his hand back and gave her a big hug, after which he sat back down feeling awkward. Dwarves did not typically show affection openly.

"As always, we have been worrying about you," Emiril said cheekily. She gave Breanne a big hug and kiss on the forehead.

Next, Breanne looked at Marcus. His face was swollen and bruised, but it was his eyes that told the real story. They were sunk in and looked as if they belonged to a man ten times his age. She smiled at him and detected a slight glimmer in those eyes. She felt then, that he would recover from his ordeal, an ordeal that no one should have to go through. He took one step and had her wrapped in a big bear hug; she hugged him back just as hard. Tears streamed down both their faces and no one spoke. After many minutes, the two released each other and they all sat down to eat. Breanne studied each of their faces in the flickering light of the fire. She felt as if she had known these people her whole life, yet it had only been a very short time since she had found herself here in this world, a world that was so different from her own. How was she ever going to be able to leave now that she had grown to love them each so much? But when she thought about her parents and her siblings, she knew she would have to leave when the time came. She missed them just as much as she would miss her new friends, except perhaps Edlin, with his big blue eyes and soft-spoken way, he had captured a part of her soul that no one else could, a part that she was sure had always belonged to him, she just hadn't known that until now. She would miss him more than she dared admit.

"Hey, Breanne," Emiril said in a playful tone, "guess what we are having for dinner?"

Breanne looked at the huge smile on Emiril's face and chuckled. "I don't know, but I'm sure you're going to tell me," she replied, happy to be here playing this game.

"Romon," Emiril said and started to laugh. They all began to laugh then, remembering Breanne's reaction the first time she had seen one of the creatures. All that is, except Gilund, Edlin filled him in and he too laughed at the joke. It was not a great joke, but it made some of the tension go away and they all needed that right now.

"Well, I'm hungry enough to eat a Romon," Breanne stated (No exaggeration, she thought as her stomach growled loudly) and proceeded to dig in. Everyone laughed even harder as they too helped themselves to the much needed hot meal.

Gilund rubbed his extended stomach as he lay back against a log, smoking his pipe. Now that the creature was dead, they could enjoy a few of the pleasantries they had been foregoing these past days. Emiril did not think they were in immediate danger as they had moved quite some distance from where the battle had taken place and as long as they still refrained from sending thoughts, she did not think the Dark Mage could find them, unless he had already gotten a new creature. She doubted he could summon one so quickly, so they relaxed and prepared to discuss the events that had recently taken place.

"Breanne, I want to start by thanking you for saving mine and Marcus' lives." Emiril smiled at the girl. She had to be patient and struggled to hold back the flow of questions that were waiting to spill forth.

"Ah yes, and I as well," Marcus said quietly. He didn't have to say more, everyone there knew how grateful the man was, and just how close to losing him they had been.

"I want to know how you knew they needed saving," Gilund interjected, stealing the question from everyone's minds and they were all grateful to him for doing so. They all wanted to know the answer.

Breanne smiled, a bit embarrassed, still not used to being the center of attention, but she knew on a deeper level that she would have to get used to it. Her life had just changed dramatically and she still wasn't really sure what had happened.

"I don't really know how to explain how I knew," she began slowly, "I just got this overwhelming feeling and images began to enter my mind, images of Marcus and Emiril." She stopped, unsure whether to go on. She glanced at Emiril, who nodded, so she continued. "I saw them, you know….dead." She looked at the ground and held back the tears she felt would come if she was not careful. "I somehow knew that Edlin," she smiled at him, "and I, had to help them. So, we did." She made it sound as if it were not as abnormal as it was, but everyone knew that this was far from normal.

"Breanne," Emiril said, feeling she needed to be careful in forming her questions. "Edlin said you knew exactly where to go in the clearing. Is that right?"

Breanne nodded her head. "I don't know how I knew, I just saw the clearing, and I saw you and Marcus get killed. I saw it just like I was there." Tears filled her eyes. "I knew that if we didn't get over there and help, that what I was seeing would come true."

"Did you see the alternative outcome as well?" Emiril asked quietly? "The one where Edlin killed the creature?"

Breanne nodded, "I knew he would do it and I knew we would save you guys."

Emiril wrestled with this information for several minutes. The fire was burning low and Marcus threw more wood on it, causing sparks to fly into the air. She watched as they floated just so high and then disappeared.

"I feel like I have changed." Breanne's words interrupted her thoughts.

"How?" she asked.

"I feel almost as if something has woken up inside me." Breanne struggled for words. "I know things that I didn't know before, I can do things that I didn't know I could do." Emiril knew she was talking about casting the spell. Which spell she did not know, it was not a typical light spell, that much she knew. "I cast that spell, Emiril," she looked scared now, "the light spell you used on the first creature. But it wasn't just a light spell. I don't know how to explain it, and Emiril," she looked the elf directly in the eye, a haunted look on her face, "I sent the Dark Mage to the nether world."

Emiril sat up straight. She was in shock. Her eyes were big and her heart was beating fast. "How do you know that?" she asked quickly.

"I don't know," Breanne said, sounding frustrated. "I just know that when the spell hit the creature, it hit him too, and it sent him out of the creature and into the nether world, his spirit and his body, he can't come back." She let those words linger a moment as the fire crackled and popped. She continued, "I also know that I was in the spirit world when I helped Marcus. There was a demon and, Emiril, he was afraid of me."

Emiril told her about the demon and how no one had ever faced one before and lived. She also told Breanne that she was right, she had been in the spirit world and Emiril was surprised she had been able to travel within it without assistance.

Breanne didn't want to tell Emiril about the other place she had visited while in the spirit world; she didn't know if the king would want her to. There was so much happening so fast that she really didn't know what to say and what not to say.

Emiril looked at Marcus and then at Breanne, at a loss for what to do. If the Dark Mage really was in the nether world, what did that mean for them? How would they find the book without him to show them where it was? If he was no longer on the island, they might meet Ogolel there now instead. They were not ready for that, at least she did not think they were ready. There were so many changes happening with Breanne that she honestly did not know if they were ready or not, in fact, she did not know if they should even go to the island now; it might be too dangerous. She found it hard to believe, but she found herself in way over her head. They had to get help, and she knew there was only one person who could help them now.

"We need to revise our plans," Emiril stated flatly. To her surprise, no one voiced opposition to her statement. She studied their faces, no one looked surprised. "I think we should turn back and go see Mindoneth, all of us this time," she continued with still no opposition. Apparently, she was not the only one who felt that things had taken a dramatic turn and that they needed help. "Ok then, first thing in the morning we will head to Malarcis."

The fire burned low and no one spoke, each lost in their own thoughts, thoughts that they could not share with the others.

Marcus took first watch; morning would come all too soon.

Chapter 44
Edlin's Sacrifice

Ogolel felt something odd. She couldn't tell what it was exactly and that bothered her. She sensed a presence that was both familiar and unfamiliar to her. The presence set her nerves on edge, a feeling she was not used to. She was the one who set other peoples' nerves on edge, not vice versa. She closed her eyes and called to him — nothing. Her brows furrowed as she tried again — still nothing. Where was he, why was he not answering her? Suddenly, she realized what that odd feeling had been. The creature, its presence, was gone. She had pushed it so far back in her mind that she had all but forgotten it, and now, it was gone. There was only one way the creature's presence could simply be gone, it was dead. She tried to call it again, and once again, she heard nothing. She became enraged, and then she became fearful. Was the Dark Mage dead too? She felt her heart rate quicken and she began to sweat.

Slowly, with the help of her cane, she crawled out of bed. With bent back and shaky legs, she crossed the room, sitting with difficulty in a chair beside the fire. Her mind raced. What if he too were dead? He was the only one who knew her secret, the only one she trusted. Who would take care of her in this world? She could not manage on her own. No one knew this, no one except the Dark Mage. And that was not the only secret of hers he knew. Did he take that secret with him, or did he reveal it? If he told them, the girl would discover her true powers and then there would be no stopping her. All her planning, all these years of waiting for the right moment, how had it all gone so wrong? She knew how the girl had accidently crossed over. This in itself would not have been so bad, but she had to run into Emiril and that loathsome family of hers. They had ruined everything. The girl's powers grew stronger every day, powers that were rightfully hers, powers she had planned on taking when the moment was right. Now she feared the girl would be too powerful, fearing she would not be able to take her powers from her as she had planned. All these years wasted. Unless of course, the girl could be lured into the spirit world. There she was all powerful, not this wretched hag that she inhabited in this world. In the spirit world everyone and everything feared her, and rightfully so.

She had to know if it were true; she had to know if he was dead. She leaned back in the chair and closed her eyes. Even before they were all the way shut, she was there. She felt the burden of her old body lifted from her, she felt strong and powerful. She saw something scurrying away from her sudden presence and she killed it. It felt good, it lifted her spirits. She began to search for him.

Chapter 45
The Sorceress Defeated

First light found the small party packed and heading back the way they had come. What an interesting trip this is turning out to be, thought Emiril. She wondered if Mindoneth would somehow know of their arrival just as she seemed to always know when she was coming. She hoped they could catch her off guard just this once, it would be a first. She smiled broadly imagining the look on her grandmother's face.

"What's so funny?" Marcus asked.

She turned to him and smiled. "I was just imagining the look of surprise on Mindoneth's face when we come riding up," she said still chuckling.

Marcus smiled, "yah, that would be a first, wouldn't it?"

"What do you think about this plan, Marcus. I mean really, do you think I made the right call?" she asked him, her voice giving evidence to her concerns.

"I know you made the right call," he told her confidently. "No one could have seen this coming, and I really believe that Ogolel is going to be much more dangerous now that the Dark Mage has been removed from the picture. I, for one, don't want to meet up with her on that island."

"I am glad you feel that way because, Marcus…" she glanced around to make sure no one would overhear her, and when she was sure no one was listening, she said in a low tone, "I am a little scared." She studied Marcus' reaction to her revelation.

He looked deep into her eyes. "Don't you feel bad, Emiril, because to tell you the truth, so am I. We are dealing with stuff that neither of us has ever dealt with before. I don't know what to do, and you apparently don't either. It's best to leave this to the only ones who may have an idea of what is really happening here."

Emiril sighed with relief. She felt better knowing that Marcus also felt they should be consulting Mindoneth on this matter. Now she only hoped their trip there would be uneventful.

Much to her relief, it was.

They rode up to the house and dismounted before Adwin emerged from the barn to take their horses. "My lady," he stuttered, "I was not expecting you."

Emiril smiled. She had done it; she had surprised her grandmother. "It is ok, Adwin," she said still smiling, "I had not sent word that I was coming." She turned quickly toward the house, perhaps too quickly, or she would have seen a small glimmer in Adwin's eyes. "Let me go in and inform her of our visit first," she said to Marcus.

He knew how much this pleased her, knowing that she had finally gotten one step ahead of the wise old elf. "Alright," Marcus said holding back a chuckle, "we'll help Adwin with the horses."

Emiril smiled at him and hurried toward the door. She was in the process of knocking when the door suddenly swung inward. "Come in," her grandmother called from across the room, "come, sit."

Emiril was stunned and confused. She stepped through the open door to see her grandmother sitting at the table, which was laden with a tea pot, six cups and many types of pastries as well as other food.

Emiril walked slowly toward the table, her spirits dampened. "How did you know?" she asked.

"Child," her grandmother chided, "I know everything, have you not figured that out yet?" She smiled and winked at Emiril. "Where are the others?"

"They are outside, I will get them." She started for the door and her grandmother called her back.

"Let us talk for a moment first," she said quietly.

Emiril sat down, unsure of what her grandmother wanted to talk about.

After pouring them both some tea, and much to Emiril's utter shock, without waiting until it was drunk, her grandmother started to talk. "I was waiting for you... after the battle with the creature, I knew you would come." Emiril started to ask her how she knew about the battle, then decided it did not matter, the truth would probably only confuse her more. "I also know a lot more about Breanne than I did before." She looked out the window and could see the girl standing by the barn stroking her horse and chatting with Edlin. "They are a fine match," she said approvingly.

"Who," Emiril asked?

"Edlin and Breanne," her grandmother said, "they were meant to be."

Emiril followed her grandmother's gaze and saw the two standing close beside one another. "Yes, they are a good match, a much better match than I thought they would be in the beginning," she agreed. She wanted to ask her grandmother a million questions, but knew better, instead just sipped her tea and waited for her to continue.

"Emiril," she began, "there is something you do not know about Breanne. When we discussed that she must have been here before, we were right, she has. Her mother is from here." She put up a hand to

Emiril's question. "Not the mother she knows, but her real mother. Emiril, Ogolel is Breanne's mother."

Emiril's eyes grew wide and she started to say something.

"Wait," her grandmother said. "There is more."

What more could there be, Emiril thought. Why had they not told her?

"Breanne knows who her mother is; we did not think it was wise that other people knew," her grandmother continued as if reading her thoughts, but Emiril knew she had not, or at least she thought she knew. "But has she spoken to you of her father, does she know who he is?"

Emiril was confused; she studied her grandmother's face. "She has not said anything, do you know who he is?" she asked finally. The old elf's eyes turned dark as she took a sip of tea and Emiril could see that her hand was shaking. Emiril grew concerned. "Do you know?" she asked again.

"Yes," her grandmother said finally, "Yes I do." She took another sip of tea with her shaking hand. "Emiril, what I am about to tell you, you can tell no one. We will discuss it with Breanne, and Marcus, but no one else can know." She looked deep into Emiril's eyes. "I mean it," she said firmly.

Emiril grew frightened by the way her grandmother was acting. "Alright," she said, her voice barely audible.

"I want to start by telling you I do not know how it's possible, so do not ask." She looked sternly at Emiril. Emiril nodded her head, she would not ask, but she knew she would want to. "Alright then," the old elf continued, "as I said, Ogolel is her mother, but Breanne does not have a father." She stopped, thought for a moment, then continued, "Well, not a human father."

"He is an elf too?" Emiril asked.

"No," her grandmother shook her head, "no. He is not…. he is a… a … oh!" She took a deep breath, "Emiril, Breanne's father is a dragon!" she stated, exasperatedly.

Emiril stared at her grandmother, opened her mouth to say something and then shut it, only to open it again and shut it just as quickly.

"I know," her grandmother said. She understood Emiril's shock, she had felt it too.

"But," Emiril started, and then remembered there was no answer to how.

"Emiril, we are talking about Ogolel here, the spirits only know how she did this. I have never heard of such a thing. I do not think she could have done this without the help of evil spirits."

"I think you are right," Emiril said, and she told her grandmother about the demon Breanne had faced and how Breanne had told her it had been afraid of her.

"That would make sense then," her grandmother said. "The demon would know what she was and would know she was powerful, very powerful. Have you noticed anything different about her?"

Emiril told her all about the fight with the creature and how Breanne had foreseen hers and Marcus' deaths. She then told her about how Breanne had saved Marcus from taking the walk of death. "And to tell you the truth," she added, "I have felt the power growing in her for quite some time now. That is part of the reason we are here now, I do not know what to do anymore. I need your help."

"Well, you are here now, we will figure this out together. Now go get the others, we will have tea and then we will talk to her."

Marcus took one look at Emiril's face and coupled together with the length of time she had spent in the house, he knew something was going on. "Was she surprised?" he asked, but he was sure he knew the answer.

Emiril smiled, "Not even close," she said, shaking her head.

"Better luck next time," he chuckled, then looked at her with that what's up look of his.

"We are going to have tea and then you, Breanne, Grandmother and I are going to talk. I hope Edlin and Gilund will understand," she said, concerned they would feel left out.

"Oh, they'll be fine," Marcus said reassuringly. He noticed Gilund nearby and knew he had heard her. "We'll just give them extra food to eat." He laughed heartedly.

"I heard that, you oaf," Gilund said gruffly.

Marcus turned and smiled at his friend. "Well, would that ease your hurt feelings or not?" Marcus asked playfully.

"Only if I get more food than Edlin," Gilund said, eyeing Edlin who had also been listening to the banter.

"Oh, what the heck," Edlin shot back. "Now how is that fair?"

Now they were all laughing. Marcus patted Edlin on the back. "Don't you worry, lad, I'll make sure you get your fair share. I won't let this greedy dwarf eat it all."

Gilund laughed even harder. "Don't you go making promises you can't keep, Marcus. I wouldn't listen to him, Edlin," he said rubbing his belly. "You don't know how much a dwarf can eat compared to a twig of an elf such as yourself."

Edlin looked at Gilund's big, round stomach. "Perhaps you are right, Gilund, I think you could eat yours, all of mine and then some."

Now everyone was laughing hysterically and they had to shush one another before they could enter the house. After the last chuckle faded, they went in and had tea, after which, Gilund and Edlin excused themselves and they went out to the barn to play cards with Adwin, who was more than happy to have the company, as he told them, no one ever visited him.

Chapter 46
Who She Truly Is

Breanne was not sure why Emiril had sent Gilund and Edlin out and she was a bit nervous. She was pretty sure it had something to do with her new powers and her saving Marcus in the spirit world, but she didn't understand why they couldn't be here, they knew all of that. Perhaps, she thought, it was because they were going to talk about what was happening to her. She hoped that was the case because she wanted to know what was going on and she knew Mindoneth was the only one who could tell her. She looked at Marcus who winked at her and smiled that comforting smile of his.

Emiril, done helping Gilund and Edlin carry the food her grandmother had insisted they take out to the barn, sat down beside Breanne, putting a hand on hers. Breanne smiled and was immediately comforted by the gesture.

"Would anyone like more tea?" Mindoneth asked.

"Yes, please," Marcus said holding his cup out. Breanne and Emiril also took more and Mindoneth poured herself some, then the four of them sat for several minutes sipping tea, each one lost in their own thoughts.

After a bit, Emiril started to wonder what her grandmother was waiting for. She started to ask her, when the door suddenly opened. She turned to see her father standing there. Surprised, but pleased, she rushed over to him, all ceremonious greetings forgotten, she threw her arms around him and hugged him tight. He smiled and hugged her back, overjoyed by the idea that his daughter still showed him such unabashed love from time to time. How he would miss that if it ever went away.

"Father, why are you here?" she asked, looking up into his smiling face.

"To see you of course," he replied. "Why else would I be here?"

She narrowed her eyes skeptically. "Are you sure that is the only reason you are here?" she asked.

"Well," he said looking slyly at Mindoneth, "there might be another reason, but it is not more important than seeing you." He looked over at the table, "and you Marcus, and you too Breanne," he said winking at her.

"Oh, and what about your old mother," Mindoneth asked him feigning hurt feelings.

"Well you, my dear mother, are the person I wanted to see most," he told her eloquently, crossing the room and bending down on one knee to kiss her cheek.

"That is better," she mumbled.

Breanne, Marcus and Emiril laughed at this display and Marcus retrieved another chair for the king to sit in.

"Tea, father?" Emiril asked.

"Thank you."

When the newcomer was settled and they had all exchanged pleasantries, Mindoneth began. "Emiril, would you please tell us everything that has happened on your trip thus far?"

"Yes," she said quickly and eagerly. She had been waiting to unload on someone and now both her grandmother and her father were here. She told them everything, with Marcus and Breanne filling in the pieces she was not witness to. "And now here we are," she finished.

King Badhor and Mindoneth looked at one another, they did not need to send thoughts to each other to know what the other was thinking. Everything they had suspected about Breanne had been true, and there was so much more that neither of them could have dreamed, not to mention the fact there was a lot that none of them knew yet.

"Thank you Emiril," her father said gently. "I know how much of a burden this has been on all of you. I know also how strange this turn of events has been. Things are happening now, that no one could have foreseen, not even Mindoneth or myself. What matters now is how we deal with these changes and revelations. Breanne, I want you to know that no matter what you experience or learn about yourself, you are no different today than you were yesterday."

Breanne swallowed hard. She felt the ominous tone of his words. She wanted to read his mind and get it over with, but she knew they were still not allowed to, so she waited for him to tell her what she knew would be something huge. Some revelation that he was afraid would shake her to the core. Well, she would surprise him, she would surprise them all, because what they were afraid to tell her, she thought she already knew. She smiled at him and he continued.

"Breanne, Mindoneth and I have been doing some research so to speak, about you and who you are. You already know and I'm sure all of us here, except maybe Marcus, know who your mother is." He glanced at Marcus and saw that he indeed did not know. "Her mother is Ogolel," he told him. Marcus' eyes grew wide, but he did not say anything, he simply gave Breanne a sympathetic look, which was not wasted on anyone.

"Yes, well, to continue," he said, feeling his heart ache for what she already knew and what she was about to find out. "Mindoneth and I have discovered wha...., uh, who...., we know who your father is." He looked to Mindoneth for help. She merely smiled at him. He rolled his eyes and continued. This was proving to be much harder than he imagined it would be. "Breanne, we think, well, we know that you were sort of created by Ogolel." He looked at Mindoneth, she nodded and he kept going. "She is your mother, but your father is not what you would consider normal, in fact we do not really know how this can be, we have never heard of this before, but your father is, well, a dragon." He looked into the girl's face to see her reaction. She simply stared at him, appearing unmoved by what he had just told her. How can that be, he thought, I am a wreck. Maybe the news had not sunk in yet. That must be it, he thought.

"Breanne, you ok?" Emiril asked her. She didn't answer.

Marcus was more shocked than Breanne, apparently. His face went white and his eyes got huge. "How do you know this?" he asked the king.

"We have been given this information by the spirits. They knew that Ogolel had done this and they were not happy about it so they came to us, hoping we could stop her."

"Stop her from what," Marcus asked, "she has already succeeded in doing it.

"There is more to her plan than just creating Breanne," the king said.

"Yes, there is," Breanne said hauntingly. They all looked at her as she still sat unmoving, staring blankly ahead. "She did create me, using her essence and that of a dragon. I was hatched from an egg. She didn't want me, she wanted my powers, the dragon's powers. Mixed together, the power of an elf and the power of a dragon would be unmatched, she would be unstoppable. I was only brought to life to be drained of my powers and then killed." The silence when she stopped talking was numbing. She went on, "I was sent out of this world so that no one would know about me or her plan. I wasn't supposed to come here yet, my powers weren't ready to harvest. I think the Dark Mage was supposed to be watching over me, which would explain why there were two books, so that he could leave here and go to my world and then use the book over there to get back. But they didn't know I would find it." Suddenly her eyes got bright. "I just thought of something," she said, her eyes wide, her voice trembling. "When I found the book, it was hidden. If the Dark Mage used the book to return here, he would not have been able to hide it." She looked around the table. "Someone else knows about me, someone in my world — they were the one that hid the book."

"Breanne," Emiril asked in astonishment, "how do you know all of this?"

"I had a dream, well, not a dream, I don't know what it was really." She told them about being on the mountain and what she had learned there.

"Breanne, I think the spirits spoke to you," Mindoneth said.

"Yes, so do I," the king agreed.

"Who would be helping the Dark Mage and Ogolel?" Marcus asked.

"I do not know," Mindoneth said thoughtfully. "I cannot think of anyone who would help her. No one would dare."

"Well, someone is helping her and we need to find out who it is. They may be spying on us right now," Emiril said nervously.

"We will figure it out," the king said, "but we need to stay calm and focused. It will not do us any good to get excited right now." They all agreed he was right.

"What matters now," Mindoneth said with authority, "is that until we figure this out, and until you learn to use your powers, Breanne, you are not safe. And apparently, you may be in danger in your world as well. I think there is little question that you need to stay here for now."

Breanne was stunned by her revelation that someone in her world could be in on Ogolel's plans. Who could it be, her mother and father, her grandparents, all of them? She had never before in her life felt the way she felt right now, unloved, unsafe, with nowhere to turn. But she did have somewhere to turn, she had Emiril and Mindoneth, the king, Marcus, Gilund and most of all, Edlin. She knew her friends would be there for her. She knew beyond any doubt that they loved her and would give their lives for her, they had proven that. What was hurting deeply though, was the fact that now she didn't know if her parents felt the same way. What if it was all a lie with them as well? What if they knew they were raising her, just to hand her over like a lamb to slaughter? But then again, it could be her grandparents who were working with Ogolel, or it could be a stranger, of course a stranger would not have access to her grandparents' attic, would they. She was so confused and heartbroken, she started to cry. Emiril held her close, not knowing what to say to the girl, so she just held her and let her cry.

It was decided that Breanne would go back to Daedhrog with Emiril and King Badhor, there, with the help of Emiril and Mindoneth, she would learn to use her powers. In the meantime, they would try to contact the spirits again and see if they could learn who was in Breanne's world working for Ogolel. Until they knew who it was, it was unsafe for Breanne to return home. They decided they would leave the following morning. They all needed some sleep, especially Breanne who was worn out both physically and mentally from the day's events. She didn't want to be alone, however, so she sought the company of Edlin and lay next to him, wrapped in his arms. He held her all night, stroking her hair when she moaned in her sleep, wishing he could drive the demons from her dreams. She slept from pure exhaustion, her body unable to stay awake any longer, or she would not have slept at all. Her dreams were

342

of dragons and loved ones trying to kill her. She ran from everyone, not knowing who she could trust. She ran until she saw Edlin; he held out his arms and she melted into them; it was only then she slept peacefully.

When they returned to Daedhrog, Breanne began to accept all that was happening to her. She focused on going home; she needed to find out if her parents were the ones who were working with Ogolel. She needed to see them again regardless, she loved them and missed them, and until she knew for sure if they were the ones, she would continue to love them, a love that ran deep within her, giving her strength to go on every day. Of course, she had people she loved here in this world too, and they loved her as well. Together they would learn what they needed to know.

The End